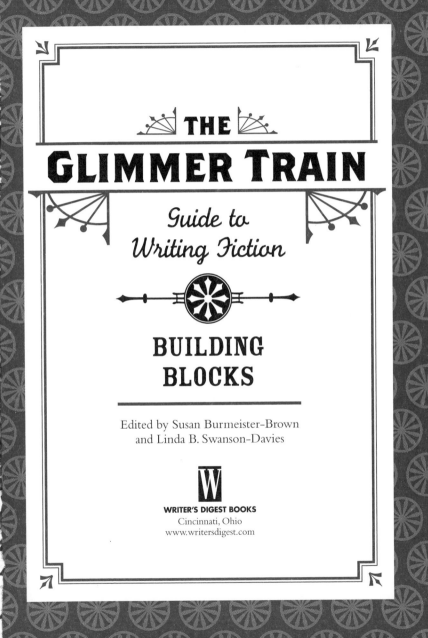

THE GLIMMER TRAIN

Guide to Writing Fiction

BUILDING BLOCKS

Edited by Susan Burmeister-Brown
and Linda B. Swanson-Davies

WRITER'S DIGEST BOOKS
Cincinnati, Ohio
www.writersdigest.com

The Glimmer Train Guide to Writing Fiction: Building Blocks © 2006 by Glimmer Train Press, Inc. Manufactured in China. All rights reserved. No part of this book may be reproduced in any form or by any electronic or mechanical means including information storage and retrieval systems without permission in writing from the publisher, except by a reviewer, who may quote brief passages in a review. Published by Writer's Digest Books, an imprint of F+W Publications, Inc., 4700 East Galbraith Road, Cincinnati, OH 45236. (800) 289-0963. First edition.

Distributed in Canada by Fraser Direct, 100 Armstrong Avenue, Georgetown, ON, Canada L7G 5S4, Tel: (905) 877-4411. Distributed in the U.K. and Europe by David & Charles, Brunel House, Newton Abbot, Devon, TQ12 4PU, England, Tel: (+44) 1626 323200, Fax: (+44) 1626 323319, E-mail: postmaster@davidandcharles. co.uk. Distributed in Australia by Capricorn Link, P.O. Box 704, Windsor, NSW 2756 Australia, Tel: (02) 4577-3555.

Visit our Web site at www.writersdigest.com for information on more resources for writers. To receive a free weekly e-mail newsletter delivering tips and updates about writing and about Writer's Digest products, register directly at our Web site at http://newsletters.fwpublications.com.

10 09 08 07 06   5 4 3 2 1

Library of Congress Cataloging-in-Publication Data

The Glimmer Train guide to writing fiction : building blocks / edited by Susan Burmeister-Brown and Linda B. Swanson-Davies. -- 1st ed.
p. cm.
"Knowledge and opinions of over one hundred accomplished literary writers interviewed over a sixteen-year period"--Foreword.
Includes bibliographical references and index.
ISBN-13 : 978-1-58297-446-0 (hardcover : alk. paper)
ISBN-10 : 1-58297-446-2
1. Fiction--Authorship. 1. Authors--Interviews. I. Burmeister-Brown, Susan. II. Swanson-Davies, Linda B.
PN3355.G55 2006   2006020558
808.3--dc22

Edited by Lauren Mosko
Designed by Grace Ring
Production coordinated by Mark Griffin

ABOUT THE EDITORS

Susan Burmeister-Brown and Linda B. Swanson-Davies are sisters and the co-editors of the literary short story quarterly *Glimmer Train Stories*, founded in 1990, and *Writers Ask*—the quarterly from which *The Glimmer Train Guide to Writing Fiction* evolved—founded in 1998. They live in Portland, Oregon.

ACKNOWLEDGMENTS

We must first thank the interviewees, accomplished writers who so openly shared themselves, and the interviewers, who, because of their love of reading and their respect for the writing process, thought to ask all the right questions.

We gratefully acknowledge the tremendous contributions of Scott Allie and Paul Morris, without whose intelligence and dedication this book would never have been possible; our wonderful editors, Jane Friedman and Lauren Mosko; and our longtime friend and advocate, Sheila Levine.

And, finally, as in all things, we thank our husbands and our children, whose joyous love and optimism keep us thinking, caring, and looking forward.

TABLE OF CONTENTS

FOREWORD

In these pages you'll find the gathered knowledge and opinions of over one hundred accomplished literary writers interviewed over a sixteen-year period. Some of them are in the early upswing of their careers, many are in their publishing peak, and three of them have passed on since their interviews. Thanks to the joint focused efforts of the authors and their interviewers, their insights are preserved here.

The result? Perspective. You'll find that authors for whom you have great respect can differ entirely on nearly every aspect of the writing process. And, interviewed at different moments in their own lives and under different historical circumstances, one writer may very well disagree with himself.

> A writer's job is to observe and record the human experience.
> How can a writer not use her/his words to try to make the world more humane?

> Write no less than 250 words every single day.
> Write only when you can no longer hold back.

> A strong sense of place is essential to the root of a story.
> A writer's toolbox contains many things; place is only one tool and may not be required in every story.

You must know where your story will end so that you can write to it.
If you are not surprised by your own ending, the material is dead before the words are on the page.

Description provides the anchoring details for a story.
Don't underestimate your reader's imagination by providing unnecessary details.

Third person is generally considered the most flexible, appropriate point of view—except when it's not.

This much is clear: Literary writers are not of one mind.

We're offering all these voices and perspectives to help writers find their own unique way in a wonderfully wide world.

—Linda

Eight years ago, this project was born. Recovering from surgery, given a bright bill of health, I counted all the blessings that lay before me: my husband and two-year-old son, my family and friends, my work. I was forty and felt absolutely new. While taking stock of what remained ahead, I began to wonder what else *Glimmer Train* could do. We had published scores of interviews with writers over the years, and I spread them out all over my bed. Clearly, writing fiction is a way of finding the truth.

I wanted these words to live again. In my refreshed mind I began to see links in the material: dialogue, point of view, place and setting, characterization, description and detail, naming and titles, theme.... The building blocks of writing fiction.

This much is true: Reading and writing are important. Choosing a life of reading and writing is choosing to live consciously. It's a brilliant road. And now you have company.

—Susan

CHAPTER

1

POINT
OF VIEW

Erin Grace, 1998

GIVING THE STORY TO THE RIGHT PERSON

Antonya Nelson, interviewed by Susan McInnis

The central questions for me are, Who should be telling the story, and Why at this particular moment? Once I've established those details—which sound like simple decisions, but are not at all simple—the stories tend to have their own tone and setting and sense of movement.

Point of view and timing present different sets of freedoms and restrictions. If I were to choose a small child to tell the story in the first person, I'd be putting myself under some pretty severe limits from the outset, and I'm not really willing to do that. Typically, if it's a child's point of view, I will step back and put the story in third person so I can retain the right as narrator to use language the child is incapable of using.

Do you ever start out in one perspective and discover it isn't working for the story?

Yes, but usually well before I get to the writing, during the pre-writing mulling and thinking phase. I try to get through those stumbling blocks before I get to the page. It's not always possible. I have written fifteen or twenty pages only to realize, This is not this guy's story. I have to stop and tell it from his wife's point of view.

Once I give the story to the right person, though, it takes off. I know where I am, and I know that I should have been in this place all along. Sometimes you don't know where you ought to be until you try writing from the wrong place.

Melissa Pritchard: I generally decide how a story is going to be told before I begin writing. I run the story through different filters—first person, second person, third, listening to how each voice sounds, waiting until my body responds viscerally. When that happens, it's like a thrill of recognition, Oh, that's it, and it's almost always the voice I stay with. After listening and waiting, I heard "Port de Bras" in first person. Eleanor stepped onstage and began talking.

as interviewed by Leslie A. Wootten

LANGUAGE AND VOICE

Carolyn Chute, interviewed by Barbara Stevens

How do you decide whether to write in first person or third person? This is something I really struggle with sometimes.

I struggle with that, too. I think I've given up on first person.

Why?

You can do almost all the same stuff with third-person subjective that you can do with first person, but the thing is you can get a little bit fancier with the language with third person. First person really limits you in that anything a character wouldn't see you can't talk about, or it will sound too contrived. You're really limited. With the first person you have to enjoy using voice, but you have to have each voice different. I don't think I can work with first person anymore. Somehow I've lost it. And sometimes I like to pull back and not see what's in characters' heads, because sometimes it's even more powerful to just see what they're doing.

....

VIKRAM CHANDRA

interviewed by Jennifer Levasseur and Kevin Rabalais

Your fiction places a strong emphasis on oral storytelling. Do you think you will continue to use this narrative style in your work?

This must be because the first stories I experienced were told to me, and because this experience was profoundly moving, so rich, and so heartbreaking and sustaining. All the old Indian epics use this structure of concentric storytellers, of having characters say, "I must tell you a story," and then slipping you down another level of narrative. This form is unimaginably rich to me, full of opportunity and pleasure and complexity and irony, and it feels familiar and venerable and a part of me.

When I started to write *Red Earth and Pouring Rain*, this form came easily and naturally to me. In the book I'm working on now, I've moved away from this kind of structure, but there is still some of this delight in telling a story, in having a story move from one person to the other. This is an old pleasure, and an eternal one.

THE AMERICAN IMAGINATION
Patricia Hampl, interviewed by Susan McInnis

⟹◆⟸

The first-person voice doesn't seem attention seeking in *Virgin Time*. It permits the writer to examine interior and, as you say, exterior realities: Someone strolls through Prague, climbs the hills outside Assisi, and reflects on the place of prayer and of culture in her life and the lives of those around her, taking the reader along from place to place and thought to thought.

I also think the American consciousness is most congenial in the presence of the first-person voice. Not because we're egotistical, but because, for good or for ill, we did predicate this nation on individuality. We're not communal at our base. We're individual. "Life, liberty, and the pursuit of happiness"—what a strange concept on which to base a nation! But that's us. You only need to listen to our greatest poet and our greatest poem, Walt Whitman in his "Song of Myself," to hear this self echoing through the American spirit.

We speak in the first person not because we're especially self-absorbed, but because it is the way American imagination works. *The Great Gatsby*, even *Moby Dick*—both naturally gravitate to the first-person voice, and both are recognized as our most American novels. Not personal, not autobiographical, but national at base, and necessarily written in the first person.

THINK LIKE A NARRATOR

Elizabeth McCracken, interviewed by Sarah Anne Johnson

You said in an interview: "I believe that most people are extraordinary… to me that is one of the pleasures of writing fiction, getting to know characters in a complex way, in a way that you sometimes don't get to know mere acquaintances." How do you get to know your characters?

Largely through the writing, and through extra writing assignments. When I was first working on the book I'm working on now [*Niagara Falls All Over Again*], the narrative was third-person multiple point of view, and now it's a first-person book.

I feel like the key to writing a first-person book is to train yourself to think like the narrator; everything else takes care of itself. The deeper you delve into the book, the easier you slip into it when you sit down to write, because you've probably been living in it for hours anyhow. It's not a matter of saying, "What would Peggy do now?" You're thinking like Peggy, so accessing her brain is easy. That's how it felt when I was writing *The Giant's House*, and that's how it feels on this new book, too.

When I was working on *The Giant's House*, I thought it was a tremendously autobiographical book. Then when I read it, I realized that it was in no way at all autobiographical. The narrator and I have certain characteristics in common, but she's a completely different person. I guess I had to believe that it was autobiographical in order to write the book, because I was thinking like her. When it's working well, it feels like channeling. You have your characters say all kinds of unbelievable things. They're better people than you are, and they're worse people than you are. Their strengths are not your strengths, and their weaknesses are not your weaknesses, but you may not even have thought about your own strengths and weaknesses until you began to write this character.

One of the reasons I wrote things in the voices of other characters outside of the text was that it was hard for me to shape the characters with Peggy narrating, partially because of her personality. If I have one major dissatisfaction with *The Giant's House* as it is now, that's it. Peggy obscures the other characters, which makes some logical sense, since that's intrinsic to her character. But the next level of characters, like James, Caroline, and Oscar, are not as vivid as Peggy. Part of that is just Peggy; her general clumsiness with other human beings means that she couldn't quite fathom them. That's something that I'm working on in the new book. Once I am able to think like the narrator, then I can develop the other characters beyond them.

Siri Hustvedt: I wanted to write a third-person narrative after I finished *The Blindfold*. It was hard for me. The tone wasn't easy to get, and I struggled with it for a long time. It's a narration that's close to Lily [in *The Enchantment of Lily Dahl*], but the story is not told in her voice. I remember that in early drafts I toyed with entering the point of view of different characters, but dropped the idea. For Lily, a nineteen-year-old girl, I needed the freedom of the third person, because the narrative voice required a greater flexibility and range of language than Lily has access to.

as interviewed by Jennifer Levasseur and Kevin Rabalais

FINDING VOICE AND TONE

David Malouf, interviewed by Kevin Rabalais

Your first two novels are first-person narratives, but they are extremely different in voice and tone. How do you find the voice and tone of a novel? Do they grow out of the landscape of the story?

I wrote the scene with Ovid and the poppy in *An Imaginary Life* without knowing if it was a scene in a novel or a short dramatic monologue. The voice established itself strongly from the start, and it was enormously easy to let that voice develop over the rest of the material.

In the first paragraph of *Johnno*, for instance, the kind of irony we get, or comic view, is part of the novel's tone and of the narrator's character. His voice tends to be innocent and transparent, but it also throws up all sorts of contradictions and comic reversals. *Johnno* begins, "My father was one of the fittest men I have ever known." In the first paragraph, we are told how he is examined for a new insurance policy, and the letter that declares him A1 in health turns up two days after his death. That's very much the tone of the book, and so much like the kind of reversals on which the book is based, because it plays with one of the problems of first-person narratives. What he knows then is everything that comes after and that went before. The narrator is often aware, at that point, that what he told us earlier was wrong, because he didn't know enough then or didn't see things in their proper light.

At almost every point in *Johnno*, what the narrator thinks is happening and what is actually happening are completely different. The novel is about the way people change, and what changes they are capable of. It's not only what happens that changes, but the difference between what they see now and were able to see then and what they once felt and feel now.

....

RELIABILITY AND CONSCIOUSNESS
Sue Miller, interviewed by Sarah Anne Johnson

In *While I Was Gone*, you return to using the first-person point of view, as you did in *The Good Mother*. Why did you decide to return to the first person? What did you gain from it in the telling of this particular story?

I've always felt that the first person is more propulsive, and more immediately seductive to a reader, so that was part of it. I was also interested in and wanted to play with the notion of unreliability in that particular narrator. That wasn't the focus for me in *The Good Mother*. In that book there was no real question about what the narrator saw or didn't see or didn't understand. She had blindnesses, but they were not problems in her personality that caused her to be blind to certain things.

That's not true for Jo in *While I Was Gone*. Jo is trying very hard to explain to you, the reader, at all times what is truly going on, but she's not fully conscious of all that's going on. I hoped the reader would see things in spite of the fact that Jo didn't sometimes. That was the pleasure of the book, playing with that only partially conscious narrator, but still a narrator trying hard to be conscious and take everything into account.

THE DISTANCE BETWEEN YOU AND "YOU"

Jim Grimsley, interviewed by Jim Schumock

—◆—

What about the voice you use in *Winter Birds*? It's almost like a long soliloquy in second person.

The book is written in the second person, speaking about Danny as "you," and I made the choice when I eliminated the other two main points of view. I tried the book writing about Danny as "I," and I couldn't make it work, and then I tried it again, writing about Danny as "he," and I couldn't make that work either. Both of those points of view tended to put the wrong kind of distance between me and Danny, the point-of-view character.

When I hit on using the second person, which is a very common point of view for poetry but isn't used very often in prose, it worked for me in a very clear way—and I think eventually what I understood was that it is a long monologue. It is the older Danny telling the story to himself, but with some kind of strange separation between himself as the older person and himself as the remembered eight-year-old. So I think the point of view actually gives you exactly the right distance and connection between the narrator and the point-of-view character.

It's infrequently that we read a confessional novel written in second person. It's so much easier to write in first person, don't you think?

It is terribly easy to write in first person; in fact, I think it's so easy that unless you're *really* gifted, like Kaye Gibbons, you're going to use it in a cheap way. The first-person point of view is incredibly plastic—it'll take you anywhere you want to go. And the tendency that *I* had, at least when I was writing *Winter Birds*, was to meander with that point of view, whereas when I hit on the second person, it focused me very much on the moment I was trying to write about.

First person is really good for retrospective novels, but that wasn't what I was after. What I wanted was to take adult readers and, as much as possible, place them inside that child's mind, almost to the point that they *become* the child. The reader is accused by this very subtle voice of being "you," and that tends to place him or her in the book, and that's what I wanted.

THE REASONABLE PERSON

John McNally, interviewed by Stephanie Kuehnert

How do you decide what point of view a story will be in? Do you experiment a lot or just get a sense right away? Has there ever been a story you had to completely rewrite in a different point of view?

"Smoke," which is the first Hank and Ralph story, was originally written in third person from the mother's point of view. Plus, Kelly, the sister in "Smoke," was an older son in the first draft, and there was no Hank or Ralph. Tex, the dog, may have been the only character who survived intact, and he's, well, a dog.

I like writing in first person, and I'm probably more naturally drawn to it, but sometimes I have to ask myself, Is there a reason for writing in first person? I mean, a book like *Catcher in the Rye* had to be a first-person novel. So, these days, I like to think that there's some necessity for it, either in terms of voice or in terms of narrative strategy.

ANDREA BARRETT
interviewed by Sarah Anne Johnson

The story "The Behavior of the Hawkweeds" in *Ship Fever* interweaves the historic story about Gregor Mendel and his scientific quest with a contemporary love story. How did this interplay occur for you?

I initially wanted to write just about Mendel and the behavior of the hawkweeds, which is a true story. Insofar as I was able, I tried to tell this story factually, but at that stage in my writing life, I wasn't able to tell it only about him. I didn't know how to manage the material.

That was the first story where I used historical material to that extent, and the contemporary strand was like having water wings on when somebody throws you into the pool. I could tell the historical parts about Mendel and I could try to bring him and his life to the page, but I didn't have to commit myself fully because it was framed by the contemporary story, through Antonia's voice.

There's a sense in which, as a writer, I can hide behind a first-person voice. If she makes a mistake in telling the story of Mendel, *she* did it. So there's a level of security there; at least there was for me. I learned a lot writing that story. It was after that, where I had the blending of the contemporary and the historical and felt a little more secure, that I was able to write "The English Pupil," which is my first wholly historical story. I felt able to forgo the contemporary frame and the first-person, contemporary narrator.

WRITING FROM A CHILD'S-EYE VIEW

Susan Richards Shreve, interviewed by Katherine Perry Harris

=====>·◦·=====

You have written books for children as well as for adults. Is there a significant difference in the way you approach one or the other? Or are you essentially interested in the same things in both?

In writing for children and adults—and this is a technical answer—the approach, which is to say imagining the character and what happens and why it matters, is the same. The bare bones of structuring a book are identical for adults and children. In the books I write for children, the structure seems simple (though the prose is often described as elliptical). In the books I write for adults, I am more concerned with the metaphoric implications of structure. For children, the story is nearly always linear, usually told from limited third-person or first-person point of view, mostly past tense, very occasionally present.

But the defining difference between my work for adults and children is point of view. I look at a children's story from the point of view of the protagonist, who is a child, usually between six and twelve years old, and that determines the range of the story. What is known in the book is only what a child that age is capable of knowing—which is a lot, and pure in instinct, but not adult.

....

Richard Bausch: I once made a student rewrite the beginning of *The Great Gatsby* in the third person because she glibly said it was in the wrong point of view. I said, "By next week I want you to have the opening chapter rewritten in the third person."

as interviewed by Jennifer Levasseur and Kevin Rabalais

MARY YUKARI WATERS
interviewed by Sherry Ellis

"The Way Love Works" is one of two stories in *The Laws of Evening* told from the first person. It describes a Japanese-American teenager's return to Japan with her mother. I'm wondering why you chose first person point of view for this particular story, and if this story is in any way autobiographical.

It's partly autobiographical, actually—more so than many of my other stories. You can see clear similarities, like the fact that the main character is half-Japanese, just like me. But it also follows the pattern of the other stories in the collection, where a lot of real-life details are used within a fictional framework.

As for first person, there was no compelling reason to use first person in this story. It could just as easily have been third person, I suppose. Most of my other stories are. But then again, I didn't write this story with the idea of a collection in mind, and that's been the case with most of these stories.

The most likely answer is that I was tired of third person at the time, and needed a change. Isn't that mundane? But sometimes we do make artistic choices for mundane reasons.

THE (OVERLY) PRECOCIOUS NARRATOR

Dan Chaon, interviewed by Misha Angrist

The narrator in "Prodigal" is such a dichotomy: an astute observer, sharp, bitter, but with a big heart. He says: "When I was young, I used to identify with those precociously perceptive child narrators one finds in books…. Now that I have children of my own, this bothers me…. I think of that gentle, dewy-eyed first-person narrator and it makes my skin crawl." I'm wondering if you really feel this way about those types of child narrators, and do you often see that in your students' stories?

It's funny, because that piece actually began as an essay about this particular type of first-person story, which I was seeing a lot of at the time—not only in students' work, but also in *The Atlantic Monthly*, *Best American Short Stories*, and everywhere else, it seemed. I began to feel that there was this certain type of ubiquitous first-person narrative voice that was lyrical, poetic, puffed up, and…

Annoying?

Yeah. Ultimately, I think it's condescending—it's because the "I" is the only feeling entity in the story. So there's a kind of creepy narcissism there; as a reader I became very bothered by it. I suppose that part of it had to do with becoming a parent and seeing all of these child's-eye-view stories from the other side.

Patricia Henley: I started *Hummingbird House* in 1989 during a summer in Guatemala. At first, for years, really, I was just taking notes, interviewing people, doing library research, and writing scenes. The novelist Charlie Smith said to me around that time, "Just write the islands," meaning, Just write the scenes you can see, and it will all come together eventually. I wrote around two hundred pages in Kate Banner's first-person voice. But gradually I began to want to include a strong storyteller's voice, which would range beyond Kate's point of view. I had to start over. That starting over was about voice. Once I got in the groove—once I found the voice the story required—the writing unfolded.

as interviewed by Andrew Scott

THE COLLECTIVE CONSCIOUSNESS
by George Makana Clark

After I wrote "The Pit-Bull Drill," I felt I developed as a writer, and so I rewrote it into the novel as the voice of the squad. In the novel, there's not a first-person, but rather a limited-omniscient narrator that jumps from character to character with a gesture or a look, a glance. I stole it from Flaubert in *Madame Bovary*. They pass the narrative baton on to the next person; and then there's also a first-person plural which is the collective consciousness. I stole that from Conrad in *The Nigger of the "Narcissus."*

I don't want to be confused with my narrators, but they are all a part of me in a sense. In the novel there are thirteen people in the squad. I think that each one of them is a different aspect of myself, which is why I think the collective-conscious voice fits so well. None of them are very attractive characters, but hopefully the reader will sympathize with them.

WRITING ADVICE from David Long

Most of my stories are in a third person that's so intensely focused on one character that it's almost like being in the first person. There's a line from "Blue Spruce," for instance, just to give you an example: "[Laurel] had no intention of staying on in Montana, much less with Eva. Good Lord, what an arrangement." So, you've got two sentences. The first is a general exposition sort of sentence, and the next one is down inside Laurel's thoughts. I *could* have written: "Good Lord, she thought, what an arrangement." But it was quicker and more supple to just dip down inside. So, what happens is, you become the narrator part of the time and you become the character other times. You're kind of moving in and out. Hopefully, it's done with enough grace that the reader doesn't find a great discrepancy.

as interviewed by Linda B. Swanson-Davies

Siri Hustvedt: I am always eager to write a completely different book from the one I wrote before. I knew that it was time to write as a man. Both of the other books were from a female perspective. For this particular book, I wanted a voice from the center. It had to be a male voice. Nevertheless, he's a Jew and an intellectual, which puts him outside the heart of the culture. He is me, too. He was just waiting to come out, I suppose. That's one of the mysteries of making art—all the people we carry around inside us.

as interviewed by Jennifer Levasseur and Kevin Rabalai

AMY BLOOM
interviewed by Sarah Anne Johnson

In *Come to Me*, you have a section called "Three Stories" that deals with the lives of David, Galen, Violet, and Rose from three different perspectives. "Hyacinths" is told from David's point of view, "The Sight of You" from Galen's point of view, and "Silver Water" from Violet's point of view. Each story is told during a different time in the family's life. What interests you about going into each different character's point of view, and what does the overall narrative gain from this?

One of the great pleasures of writing for me is to be God, to look at everybody as they stand there cupped in your hand. You actually can understand and be this person, and this person, and this person.

And life is entirely different depending on who is seeing it. Even if you are empathetic, even if you are kind and observant, it is still unexpectedly different.

I have a friend who has twins and one older single child. One of the things I love about this family is that what it's like for the two twins is a completely different family than what it's like for the older single child, and that's completely different than what it's like for the mother, who's on one hand the mother of a single child with whom she forms a pair, and on the other hand the mother of twins who have already formed a pair. I love the fact that you can hold up anybody's family to the light and turn it around and see it differently.

Each story, though intertwined, stands on its own. Was this difficult to achieve?

No. To me it's exactly like family life. Of course you're interconnected, but you don't walk around with the other four people attached at the hip at all times. It's exactly like that.

You do this again with Henry and Marie in the stories "Faultlines" and "Only You," so that readers are drawn deeper into the lives of these characters who were introduced through their dealings with Galen and David. How do these stories come about? Do you meet the characters and then want to explore their lives more deeply?

Yes, I think so. The last story in that entire bunch of five stories was "Hyacinths," which is David's story. That's because I thought I would like to try to tell David's story, which wasn't clear to me until I had done everything else. I thought, What about David? He's not just a nice guy and a psychiatrist. I mean, how do you get to be a psychiatrist who's married to a lunatic? Not to mention, what's it like to be a psychiatrist with a schizophrenic daughter?

THE GREAT AUTHOR/CHARACTER DIVIDE

Frederick Reiken, interviewed by Eric Wasserman

⟫⟪

Roth has become a master of portraying the character as writer. Both of your own novels possess characters who have blatant writer personalities: Philip finds a bit of a writer in himself, Anthony sees everything around him as a legend, and his cousin Timmy expresses a desire to write books someday. However, you are fairly rigid in drawing boundaries between author, character, and narrator. Are there lines that shouldn't be crossed without good reason?

I think it all depends on your sensibility, your aesthetic, and what it is you're trying to do. Philip Roth, for instance, has invented Nathan Zuckerman as an alter ego, and at times is so merged with Zuckerman's identity that there's an odd flatness to his prose, in which it does not feel imaginatively projected, and hence doesn't feel like fiction at all. The first hundred pages of *American Pastoral* are like that, but Roth is such a good storyteller that it doesn't matter. Even if Zuckerman gets self-indulgent at times, Roth is always looking outward, at the big story. That's his secret and it generally works.

Many other writers who play with the boundary between author and character are doing so simply out of authorial narcissism, and I have read many books in which the subtext is simply: Here's how I see it and I'm right, so please adore me. Most young writers simply don't know any better, which is why as a teacher of writing I'm always stressing the need to see your protagonist as an "other," even if the protagonist is in fact based on yourself. Some people have the capacity to do this naturally; others don't.

Another strategy, and one that Roth makes use of all the time, is to focus the story on some larger-than-life character who is rendered through the point of view of the authorial stand-in. For instance, the place where *American Pastoral* starts to come alive is precisely the place where Zuckerman stops talking about himself and begins to project instead the story of Swede Levov. This is more or less the same strategy used by F. Scott Fitzgerald in *The Great Gatsby.* As a narrator, Nick Carraway is a cipher because he's basically a stand-in for Fitzgerald, and hence Fitzgerald never really envisions him. But the book works because its focus becomes the larger-than-life, if enigmatic, Gatsby. I'd say the same thing about Conrad's *Heart of Darkness.* Marlowe is a cipher, but the book works because Marlowe mostly stays focused on Kurtz.

One of the problems, as I see it, is that in crossing the line and having a protagonist act essentially as a stand-in for the author, the reader often winds up being asked to become complicit with whatever the character is involved in. Occasionally this approach works—for example I would point to the racial issues raised by Roth's technique in *The Human Stain.* In not knowing for the first eighty-eight pages or so that Coleman Silk is really an African-American, Roth essentially tricks us into becoming complicit with the same racial stereotyping that becomes the thematic focus of the book.

But Roth is so acutely aware of what he's doing and hence maintains such a balanced perspective on the matter—placing us alternately on either side of the argument—that it never feels as if he is asking us to share his own beliefs, but rather is asking us to explore various perceptions by looking at the situation through the eyes of various characters.

More often—and usually due to a lack of conscious intention— an approach that asks the reader to become complicit fails because the writer starts to use his characters as mouthpieces for his or her own myopic arguments or beliefs.

JAYNE ANNE PHILLIPS

interviewed by Sarah Anne Johnson

In *Machine Dreams*, why did you choose to write from each character's point of view rather than a third-person, or omniscient narrator? What does the narrative gain from this?

In all my books I use time in a particular way. In *Machine Dreams*, the family in the book becomes familial to the reader because you encounter the same characters after lapses of time, where suddenly you see them at a different point. I wanted readers to inhabit the minds of each of the people in this family. I wanted them to have a sense of recognition each time they encountered one of these characters, or saw these characters operating in a section of the book in which they weren't the point of view.

Was it difficult to differentiate each voice in these chapters?

No. But it depends on what you're trying to do. In both *Shelter* and *Machine Dreams*, I wanted readers to circle through the world of the book, whereas in *MotherKind*, I wanted readers to remain inside the mind of Kate, because that is, in fact, where she stands in the book: in this isolated yet very intensely sensory space.

Julia Alvarez: *¡Yo!* is the story of the making of a writer. It's Yolanda's story, but Yolanda's never allowed to open her mouth. It's the story of the making of a writer told to us by the people who have known her, people who have had to endure this trajectory. So we hear from her mother and father. We hear from her sisters. We hear from her teacher. We hear from her students. It's sort of a portrait of the artist via the people. In a way, I was trying to answer the challenge that the writer's always the one who gets to tell the story.

as interviewed by Mike Chasar and Constance Pierce

READ MORE, WRITE BETTER
Chitra Banerjee Divakaruni
interviewed by Sarah Anne Johnson

In your article for the *New York Times*, "New Insights into the Novel? Try Reading 300," you explain how reading three hundred novels in five months as a judge for the National Book Award gave you new insight into what makes a successful novel and what does not. After that experience you returned to your novel-in-progress, threw out two hundred pages, and started again. What did you discover that made you want to throw out those two hundred pages?

That was a painful experience. I was very happy, actually, as I restarted the novel, because I knew it was going to be so much better. What I learned from reading so many novels is that the novel, as it goes on, has to expand. It has to give you a sense of a larger life, not just the story you're dealing with, no matter how well it's told. There must be a sense of resonance, a sense that in that story is the knowledge of a whole larger story whose presence is felt. I realized that my novel wasn't doing that.

How did you undertake the work of re-visioning and re-beginning that novel?

I had to change the narrative structure. I had the novel in a multiple-narrator perspective, some who saw the story up close, but I had to add the omniscient narrative voice. I'd used this voice sporadically, but it hadn't been a big part of the narration. It's like changing the lens on a camera. Sometimes you're seeing it up close and sometimes from afar. I hope this gives the novel a sense of opening up and expanding. I think it does.

CHANG-RAE LEE

interviewed by Sarah Anne Johnson

[You] employ a similar technique for creating a subtle sense of suspense, and this is to reveal a bit of information without the surrounding details. For example, in *Native Speaker*, we know Henry and Lelia had a child who died, but we don't learn what happened until well into the book. What reasons are there for waiting to reveal key information beyond the fact of creating a narrative drive?

It's very true to a first-person story. People will tell you things that have happened in their lives without going into the real story. You get the fact before you get the real story. The deeper revelation comes later. That seems like a natural rhythm to me. It's not meant to be dramatic in real life, but it feels that way. The teller isn't telling a story, but a story is that kind of advance of real detail. That's true to who those characters are. They're all very different, and they do all have in common that they're not dealing with what they need to deal with right then and there. But that's true of most people. It's a natural rhythm we have, to survive the moment. We marshal our forces and then later on we're able to talk about it, tell the tale.

....

TOBIAS WOLFF

interviewed by Jim Schumock

Several stories in *The Night in Question* have a serial point of view.

There are a couple stories in there in which the point of view does shift. It is an unusual move to make in a short story, and one that you had better have a good reason for doing, because it can feel like a cute device. It can feel like fancy footwork. You have to have good reasons for doing it.

I did it in the story "Casualty," where there's a change of point of view at the end of the story to that of a nurse. I was even thinking of calling the story "The Nurse's Story," to alert the reader that this change was coming. The point is that our way of thinking about war is almost incurably romantic, because we get seduced by the figure of the young soldier who tragically loses his life or his character and becomes someone other than the decent person he started out to be. There is something romantic even about anti-war novels like *All Quiet on the Western Front*. It's our love affair with the young man, really. I wanted to break the hold of that vision and show another perspective, show the terrible damage that radiates out into the human community through an event like that. In this case, it's a nurse.

At the end, you break away from the story's concentration on the soldier. You are in another mentality altogether, a feminine mentality that has been shaken to its roots by the things she has had to witness and attend to. And it's had terrible consequences for her. I wanted to widen the perspective and give a sense of how this event, the detonation of these events, reaches far, far beyond the tight focus in which we're accustomed to seeing war.

THE FORBIDDEN SHIFT

by Thomas E. Kennedy

When I was studying the craft of fiction in an MFA program, some of the instructors held tight to what had become a traditional approach: one story, one point of view; shift the point of view, and you puncture the story's bladder. That was enough to make me want to split point of view, to find examples of successful point-of-view splits in famous stories. Joyce did it in *Dubliners*! And I was delighted when a story in one of our workshops, which had been built in neat symmetry on a double viewpoint, and which had been "view bashed" by the instructor, ended up winning a national prize!

Nonetheless, point-of-view shifts, when carelessly done, can threaten the integrity of a short fiction—or "the singleness of effect" which Edgar Allan Poe referred to in his definition of the "short prose narrative." Wayne C. Booth in *The Rhetoric of Fiction* suggests that the contemporary reader is troubled by a shift in point of view because it reminds us of the author's presence. He also notes that there can be no illusion of life when there is no bewilderment, and the omniscient narrator clearly is not bewildered: He looks down upon the fictional universe as if he were some god.

In *The Art of Fiction*, John Gardner suggests that growing doubt of the existence of God or objective truth was accompanied by mistrust of the author-omniscient technique, which led writers like Dickens, Conrad, James, and Crane to employ various points of view, a series of unreliable narrators.

An unyielding and dogmatic position on the point-of-view shift in fiction would seem to me as ill-advised as a lack of concern. With growing awareness of the technical aspects of fiction, an aspiring writer reaches a place where he or she is incapable of summarily dismissing the question of point-of-view shift.

When viewpoint shifts, we see it and ask ourselves, "Why did he do that?" We are aware of "he," the author, authorial intrusion, and the illusion is threatened. Booth points out that we no longer dwell in that garden of innocence in which people read the Bible, the Gospels—ostensibly objective histories—never wondering how the author could so freely make "illicit entries into private minds." Since the disciples were all asleep, who heard Christ ask his Father to "let this cup pass"?

It seems to me there is only one single rule that has to be followed regarding point-of-view shift: The writer must be aware of what she or he is doing and must do it with care. It is a little bit like shifting lanes when driving. You must signal your intention to change, then signal your intention to change back; you must execute the move smoothly and crisply, making certain that those around you are aware of what you are doing. If you begin to swing all over the place without warning or care, you begin to resemble a drunk driver on New Year's Eve, reeling all over the highway, confusing the drivers around you.

So if shift you must, then shift, yes, but do so with care and consideration for the integrity of your fiction, as well as for the possibility of your reader to follow the change.

THE PROBLEM OF INCONSISTENCY
by Monica Wood

The point-of-view mistake I see most often is inconsistency in the third person. Many beginning writers find it hard to differentiate between third-person omniscient and third-person limited. The difference is too complicated to fully explore in this space, but I can try to explain it briefly. When working in third person, remember this:

Omniscience works from the outside in: Felix looked like a run-over squirrel.

Third-person limited works from the inside out: Felix felt like a run-over squirrel.

The "limited" in third-person limited POV refers to the fact that everything in the story is filtered through one, and only one, character. In other words, the writer must make sure that the reader can't see, hear, feel, or know anything that the POV character can't see, hear, feel, or know. POV seems "off" when the writer unwittingly goes from limited to omniscient and back again by inserting things that the character can't see, hear, feel, etc., or by switching briefly to another character's POV just for the convenience of the story. You'd need a long example to see how violating POV can sabotage a good story, but I hope you can get the idea from this short example:

> Billy felt nervous as he took the stage. He could pick out his mother's beaded dress from the dimness of the front row. His only choice now was to open his mouth and hope that God might belatedly bestow mercy on his tuneless throat. Doris, sitting in back, realized something was wrong when the boy missed the first cue. Billy took another breath, praying like a Trappist and hoping all those fanatics predicting the world's impending demise would turn out to be right.

By letting Doris stick her nose into this paragraph, you have violated what was gearing up to be a nice third-person limited narration, with Billy as the POV character. By focusing on Doris, however briefly, you force the reader to move from the inside (third-person limited) view—i.e., Billy's perspective—to the outside (omniscient) view. Most readers won't be able to identify why they feel distracted or annoyed, but they will feel that way nonetheless.

Third-person limited, by the way, is usually a wiser choice for a short story than omniscience. Omniscience, which allows the reader access to the perceptions of more than one character, is often too wide-ranging for the circumscribed world of a short story.

Andre Dubus: The book [*The Lieutenant*] was based on a story that actually happened. I changed the events a little to make the novel. I told the story so many times, and somebody said I should write it. That started in first person, too. I gave a chapter to my wife, and then realized I was writing everything that happened as I remembered it, every detail from the ship. I started over in third person. First person feels like talking to me.

as interviewed by Jennifer Levasseur and Kevin Rabalais

MARGOT LIVESEY

interviewed by Ellen Kanner

How did the idea for *Eva Moves the Furniture* come to you?

With enormous difficulty. It's loosely based on the life of my mother, of whom I know enough to fit on a postcard. She died when I was two and a half. One of the few things I knew or had been told about her was she had what we call in Scotland the sixth sense. She was regularly visited by poltergeists. She saw people not visible to others. You can imagine that was immensely intriguing.

I began the novel in 1987, thinking I'd write a novel about my mother and the supernatural. As I wrote, it wasn't enough to make a novel. I had to be prepared to make things up to a far greater extent; there was something painful about that because it meant acknowledging just how little I knew about her. At first, it never occurred to me to write the novel in first person; it seemed heretical to take on the voice of my mother, wildly presumptuous. I tried writing the novel from every other possible point of view.

OMNISCIENCE

Ann Patchett, interviewed by Sarah Anne Johnson

This is your first omnisciently narrated novel, and it has the fullness and breadth of a vision realized. Do you feel that it was a leap for you in terms of craft?

Huge. It's what I've always wanted to do. It is exactly the thing that I have not been able to pull off in my last three books. In my last three books, every time, I was trying to do this, and I couldn't. With *The Magician's Assistant,* I finally moved into the third person, but it's a very first-person–ish kind of third person. In *The Patron Saint of Liars*, I have those different first-person narrators because I couldn't figure out any other way to do it. I didn't know how to do third person, and I didn't know how to do omniscient, but I did know that these characters didn't communicate with one another. The only way I could structure it was to have three first-person narrations, because they're all feeling things they can't say to the other ones.

Then in *Taft*, I have those little Taft scenes that are in third person, which was like a little running jump at something. In *The Magician's Assistant*, I have the limited third person. So you can see the trajectory of where I'm going with this.

What were the challenges in writing it from the omniscient point of view?

The challenge of balance, especially when you have sixty characters, to feel like you're seeing everybody in a sweep. It's not just that you have this scene and you're in their head, and you have the next scene and you're in this other character's head. There has to be an easy flow between point of view. You also don't want to create a situation where the reader is more interested in one character than another. It's the responsibility of the narration to keep the story even in its interest.

You were saying earlier that when you're writing from the omniscient point of view, you don't have that voice in your head that you can latch onto. It's not a voice-driven enterprise. What does drive it forward?

Nothing! That's what makes it so hard. *Bel Canto* was like a piece of knitting. I'd work on it fiercely for two weeks, and then I'd put it in a drawer for three months. Every time I finished a chapter, I felt like it was over—I didn't know where to go next. I didn't have anything that compelled me from point to point. It was just sheer will. So it took me a lot longer.

. . . .

Annie Proulx: I'm very happy with third person. I find writing in first person enormously constraining. It's like having a bloody straitjacket on, and who needs it? I love being able to back up as far as possible and literally look at the landscape from a vantage point above or to get directly close to the characters and even, in some sense, get inside them.

as interviewed by Michael Upchurch

RUSSELL BANKS
interviewed by Rob Trucks

There's almost no way for me to discuss point of view with you since, throughout your fiction, it's never as simple as first, second, and third person, but you have, in a sense, an outside narrator in *Trailerpark*. Even though he lives on the grounds, the reader knows nothing about him.

That's right. In fact, if you count the stories and go against the number of trailers that are identified in the park, you know where he lives. He's a member of the community.

But the outside narrator is a point-of-view technique that you've used several times. Is there anything particularly telling about your use of first person? Outside of *Rule of the Bone*, its use is not what most would term as standard.

In *Trailerpark*, because that was published before *Continental Drift*, that kind of narrator made it possible for me to imagine the narrator of *Continental Drift*. I got to imagine, in a fairly literal way, the narrator of that story by inventing a character who wasn't there, and that let me understand the narrator as a character. Even when it's third-person omniscient, it's still a character in the story. It's a part of the story and has a responsibility then as one of the actors, and it was sort of overt there, and then it became a little more subtle, though it's a *loa* speaking, in *Continental Drift*. Or at least it's a narrator who's inspired by a *loa*, who invokes a *loa*, and is taken over by a *loa*, in order to tell the story, so it's maybe a long, ongoing process of inventing myself as storyteller. And creating a role for myself in the work as a storyteller.

I never want to write about myself in any pointed or obvious way. I mine myself. I pillage myself as much as I pillage the newspapers.

And that gives you distance?

Sure. And it also gives me a kind of freedom, too. I just use myself as raw material, the same way I use history or dreams or literature. It's just raw material.

. . . .

HEEDING THE VOICE

Elizabeth McCracken, interviewed by Sarah Anne Johnson

I was finishing library-science school and I decided to wait to start writing, which is not unusual for me—I don't write every day. I went to the Work Center, sat down for my first day of work—I thought the book [*The Giant's House*] was going to be narrated by James's cousin, Alice.

I wrote an opening, a third-person opening, and I thought the book was going to be third person. This opening included the line, "Everybody said the librarian was in love with him." I thought, maybe this librarian could be an important character, because she'll be the person who establishes the museum and then leaves it to Alice, and Alice always feels the shadow of this great librarian looking over her shoulder. Peggy Cort was scarcely going to be in the book. She was dead before the book began, but I decided to write a little bit in her voice, to get a handle on her, find out what she was like. Well, she just wouldn't stop talking.

PAM DURBAN

interviewed by Cheryl Reid

I did have a great time writing "Soon." It was the first story I wrote when I finished my novel *The Laughing Place*. I was like, oh boy, I can really have fun with it. It has the kind of language I would like to write in, clear and immediate language.

There isn't much interpretation of emotion in the story. There is a voice, as in "Gravity," almost omniscient—close to one character, but grand in its compass of time and perspective. Is it a voice that you've recently developed?

Yes. I love that voice because it gives you such range.

It's a real storytelling voice, and that has a relationship to time, like Chekhov's voice.

It's a storytelling voice and it's the voice of the novel I'm working on now. It's the voice of time. It enables me to say, "In 1740 this happened…," as part of the narrative. The voice or the perspective can then take in that span of time. I'll never write another long piece in first person again. It can be so self-conscious and so limited. It's like living with somebody who talks about himself all the time.

Especially if you're writing the novel for seven years?

Yes. You get tired of that consciousness after a while. The voice that I am working with now is so interesting to me because it can range, it can go so many places.

Again, it seems to me related to a larger scope in time. That voice can take in much more than first person or a close third-person narrator.

This voice allows all kinds of layers and levels that are coming to the novel. There is a whole layer of the narrator being able to say, "Imagine this…," and, "Imagine that…," and, "Imagine this is what this is…." It's not anybody's voice. It's the voice of the narrator, and the voice of time and history. That's how I first imagined it, as the voice of time, which is bigger and more encompassing than all the events.

INVENTING COMPLEX VIEWPOINTS
Robert Olen Butler, interviewed by Jim Schumock

You give some real comic relief to a woman spying on her unfaithful husband in "Woman Uses Glass Eye to Spy on Philandering Husband." It seems to me that in less adept hands this story could have gotten out of control.

Well, all of the stories had that sort of challenge to them. This one is about a woman who's with a pretty bad guy. He's verbally abusive to her. At some point, her glass eye accidentally pops out and she suddenly realizes that she can see through it independent of her other one. She's a court stenographer, in a divorce court. So when she begins to suspect that her husband is cheating on her, she leaves the glass eye in a glass of water on the bed stand one day to spy on her husband when she goes off to court. Indeed, he is cheating on her. All this takes place while she's in the midst of a court stenography session with a woman who is getting a divorce. Things get very complex. It was a very interesting, challenging point of view.

ANN PATCHETT
interviewed by Sarah Anne Johnson

Do you conceive of a story in the voice of a narrator, or in key images or characters, or in events?

Not in terms of a narrator. That changes a hundred times. More in terms of character and plot. I'm a very plot-driven, story-driven writer. But who tells it, how it's told, is the thing that I have a really hard time with. That's the thing that I write over and over again at the beginning.

At what point do you decide upon a narrator?

Before I start writing it, because it's hard to write a book without a narrator. The last two things I do before I start writing a book are decide on a narrator and decide on the characters' names, and I think that because they're the last two things I do, they're the two things that inevitably really stump me, because I never want to start.

What is your process like for developing the narrator's voice; for instance, someone like John Nickel, who is so different from you?

I develop it off stage, before the book is started. I don't develop it as I go along. All I do is think about it. I don't think, Hey, I'm going to go hang out with black men in blues bars. You just figure it out. That's the lovely thing about writing first person. You get that voice in your head, and the voice is then compelling. It's the thing that takes you along. Whereas with the third person, the voice in your head is always you, and so I'm not as compelled.

Edwidge Danticat: You don't have to tell a story in just one way. When I started writing "Children of the Sea," I wanted to write about the experience of being a refugee from the perspective of both the person who leaves and the one who remains behind. This form allowed me in essence to tell two stories in one, which was great.

as interviewed by Sarah Anne Johnson

IMAGING THE CHARACTER

Sue Miller, interviewed by Sarah Anne Johnson

You have four different points of view in *Family Pictures*. You use third-person personal with David, Lainey, and Mack, and the first person with Nina. How did you decide whose point of view to use to narrate different parts of the story?

Each time I started a new chapter, I spent a lot of time looking at what I had, and then trying to decide with whom I should be for this chapter. It seemed a matter of balance in each case: Now I needed to move over here so that we'd have a sense of how this character was growing and changing and feeling. There was also the matter of dynamism. With whom were changes occurring at this point in time? Who was being most affected at this point in time by the family's situation, and therefore whom should I be tracing? Whose reactions were important; whose life was in flux in responding to what was going on in the family most at any given time? I sought in each case to imagine the character very deeply.

Sometimes I've fretted, moved back and forth—tried passages in the first person, then in the third person. For instance, the whole of *For Love* is very close to Lottie's point of view, almost a first-person narration, but not quite, and that's partly because I also tried it in the first person. But I ended up feeling that I liked the third-person ability to step back and say what she was thinking, even things she might not have been entirely aware that she was thinking: to note slightly subconscious responses that she was having to things.

I also think that the first person is very confining, finally. It was wonderful to work with it in *Family Pictures*, where I combined it with the third person, because I got away with a lot, but more typically you only have one person's perspective, and only one person's experience of the story. You don't have the possibility of looking at the way the person she's interacting with felt about the same events. Unless there's a compelling reason for a story to be in the first person, I wouldn't choose it. You can lose a lot more than you gain. It seems easier, and in many ways it is easier, but you slowly become aware of what you cannot do as you work through a first-person novel. You may want to give the history or the feelings of someone else and you can only do it as the first person perceives it or doesn't perceive it. It's a complicated decision, and one I've not always been certain of when I undertook a book at the start.

More of my books are in the third person. I love the third person because you can use it in so many ways. You can move in so close to a character, and then pull way back and be very God-like and comment on the whole thing. That's great freedom, and I really enjoy that. It can be hard to work it well, but I love it.

CHAPTER

2

VOICE

Hermann Burmeister, ca. 1955

Susan Richards Shreve: The importance of observation for the writer—isn't it everything, in a way? This is something I have said to students. A story may be told a million times, but only you can tell it. A writer brings what he or she sees to a reader, and in that translation is empathy and originality and the humanity implicit in recognition.

as interviewed by Katherine Perry Harris

MAKING THE LEAP

Robert Olen Butler, interviewed by Linda B. Swanson-Davies

You seem to be comfortable writing things that people tend to steer clear of—a lot of first person and a lot of inhabiting people who are way outside yourself.

I didn't actually start writing in the first person until my sixth novel, and I didn't start writing the voices of women until my seventh book, which was *A Good Scent from a Strange Mountain*. The thing about the artistic unconscious is that, well, first of all, it's scary as hell there, and that's why to be an artist means never to avert your eyes, because your impulse, your deepest impulse, is to flinch, to look away. That's why so many writers are very comfortable in their heads—it's safe there.

And a little dull.

Yeah. So if you go into your unconscious and you don't avert your eyes and you do that day after day, story after story, book after book, eventually you will break through to a place where you are neither male nor female, neither black, white, red, nor brown, neither Christian, Muslim, Sikh, Hindu, nor Jew, neither Vietnamese, American, Albanian, Serbian. You are human. And if the authenticity comes from that deep place, and if your life experiences are eclectic and broad and intensely observed on the surface levels as well—because that's important—then you can draw that universal human authenticity up through the vessels of characters who might be, on the surface, quite different from you.

Part of the reason artists are who they are is so they can reassure the world that the things that seem to divide us—race, gender, culture, ethnicity, religion—are not nearly as important as the things that unite us. And we never question the artists' ability to do that in realms that I would suggest require a greater leap of imagination than leaping over matters of gender and race and so forth. For example, I am a middle-aged white male, born in the Midwest; I am an only child. A year ago last December, my parents celebrated their sixty-eighth wedding anniversary. And not a day has gone by when we have not been in contact with each other, and most days the word *love* is freely and sincerely exchanged.

It is a greater leap of imagination for me, I would suggest, to write in the voice of a middle-aged white male from the Midwest who came from a large family which suffered an early divorce and where the word *love* was never used, than the voice of a ninety-year-old Vietnamese woman who is an only child whose parents stayed together forever and was in a family where love was overtly expressed. We never question the artist's ability to leap over all those other kinds of issues, the deeper issues.

Siri Hustvedt: You discover over time what you can do and what you can't. Not everything is a matter of choice. As a young person, it became clear to me that no matter how much I admired Wallace Stevens or Henry James, I could never write like them.

as interviewed by Jennifer Levasseur and Kevin Rabalais

VALERIE MARTIN
interviewed by Janet Benton

I once heard you say something like, "If people are questioning the details in your story, if they're saying something doesn't seem plausible, the real issue is that the voice isn't doing its job, because if the voice is strong enough, people will believe anything." I mean, look at the first line of Kafka's "Metamorphosis."

Right. I don't *believe* he turned into a cockroach.

So is that what takes a while when you're working on a book in the beginning, finding the voice?

It does. Once I find the voice, then I feel quite free and happy. I mean, in that hundred pages of this New England book, *Property*, I had a lot of trouble getting started. I often start too early in the action of the novel, and I wind up writing, say, forty pages before I get to the beginning, throw those away, and go on. At first I can't hear the voice: It's not coming in very clearly, it's uneven, or I don't know who this person is.

And what's the feeling when you get the voice?

You just have this sense of ease. I mean, it's a hard thing to describe. It's not mystical, but then it is kind of mystical. It's like meeting somebody. Presumably all these are voices that I somehow know. A lot of them are combinations of voices, I think. Some characters speak in the manner of people I know. Paul's diction in *The Great Divorce* is very much a combination of some Kingsley Amis characters and John. So it's a voice that I'm familiar with, certain turnings of phrase, certain ways of putting things. I guess Mary Reilly's voice was the strangest to come by, because it really is so completely different from anybody I know.

WRITING ADVICE from Chang-rae Lee

Don't listen to anyone else. It's great to get opinions and advice, but you need to follow the particular private passion or obsession that you have for a story, giving no quarter to anything else. In the end, that's where writers come up with something unique. That's why novels still mean something even in this age—they're distinctive performances, utterly singular and surprising. Follow your passion. Feed your obsessions and in the end that will work best.

as interviewed by Sarah Anne Johnson

RECLAIMING THE POETIC FEMALE VOICE

Julia Alvarez

interviewed by Mike Chasar and Constance Pierce

Certainly in *Homecoming*, and less, perhaps, in *El Otro Lado*, you use various traditional forms in your poems—in Annie's anthology, for example. Do you feel any tensions between working in these forms and claiming and cultivating your own voice at the same time?

Well, I move back and forth. I want every room of our mother's mansion—or our father's mansion, as the Bible calls it—I want to claim them all. Why can't we women write our own sonnets and sound like ourselves and not just be in sonnets as romantic decoration? Why can't I want that?

I want a sonnet to be a place where a woman can have a cup of coffee and talk to a woman friend about something. And I want the sestina to be a form in which a woman who is Latina can put in Spanish words, then English words, since words and the repetition of words is so much what a sestina is about, and to have that weaving of the two languages. I want to be able to move into all these spaces and to populate them with voices that are human and humane, that sound to me like the people whom I know.

It's not like, "Throw the white men out, here we come!" Their voices can be wonderful, too. It's just that I shouldn't be trying to write like a William Butler Yeats.

THE MIND OF THE STORY

David Long, interviewed by Linda B. Swanson-Davies

You've said that the mind of the story has an attitude, or a personality. Do you have a particular attitude that you find yourself writing?

I think it's different in every story. Every story has an intelligence behind it. I'm on shaky ground here, theoretically, because I'm not sure I've worked this idea all the way out, but I know when I read any writer I've read a lot of, there's something that transcends the individual work.

But every individual work has its own voice, as opposed to the writer's. If the story's in the first person, then the voice of the story is the voice of the person telling it to you, and sometimes these are clearly invented voices. Other first-person voices you can almost assume sound like the writer, but even so, there's something that makes each individual work different. In some larger way there is an intelligence that transcends it, that is uniquely that writer's.

I don't know if I'm capable of talking about my own work that way. It's a lot easier for somebody to look from the outside. I can see that the voices of a number of the stories are related somehow. I notice that there are words I reuse and that there are sentence rhythms I find myself falling back on, and habits of composition.

Stephen Dixon: My style didn't drive anyone crazy at first because I didn't have a style till my thirties. My early style was readable and functional and forgettable and inimitable because nobody would want to imitate it since it was the style of other writers, Hemingway and Saroyan, mostly.

as interviewed by Linda B. Swanson-Davies

RELINQUISHING CONTROL
Lynne Sharon Schwartz, interviewed by Nancy Middleton

At one point in *Ruined by Reading* you say that what you love to read isn't necessarily what you end up writing. That the subject chooses you—and even the style.

It's true that the subject of the story chooses you. But it's the style even more. I wrote about this in connection with Natalia Ginzburg, who wanted to write very lush prose, yet writes extremely spare prose. Bruno Schulz, a Polish writer who died in World War II, is a very fantastical and wonderful writer. His work is rooted in the banal, as my writing is, but he lifts his subject up out of the banal until it becomes very surreal—an act of levitation. And I think, why can't I do that?

But you sit down to write and what comes out comes out. I don't mean you don't have any control—there's a lot of revision. I'm an obsessive rewriter. I love the rewriting process. Still, the result is not totally under the writer's control.

Toi Derricotte: I was thinking about what attracts an artist to—not even to the material—but to that certain kind of energy that stays consistent. Over and above the content of the work, or even the themes of the work, there's a kind of a passion that artists have that is recognizably the mind inside the poem, or an energy inside a poem, inside the work of art. I think that's really what we like or dislike about artists.

as interviewed by Susan McInnis

LEARNING THROUGH MIMICRY
Beverly Lowry, interviewed by Stephanie Gordon

———❖———

I do a lot of discussion with my students about line editing and the creation of a personal writing style, or voice. My hope is that they will develop their own writing style, backed up with their own research and materials. So I suppose I am teaching a general merging of all those different elements. I also try to impress on them the need to write the book *they* have to write. However, the development of a personal voice is very important for a beginning writer.

Phillip Lopate came last year, and I suddenly had all these students writing what I called [laughs] "Lopatian" essays, which means that they were complicated, against the conventional grain, and sardonic. I emailed these students and told them that they didn't have to write in his style—it had taken Phillip a while to develop his way of writing, his voice and attitude, you know, and they shouldn't just go in there and try to please him by trying to sound like him. Or not necessarily. But in the end, some of them did it anyway and did it pretty well. So in that case maybe it helped.

CONSTRUCTING VOICE

Chang-rae Lee, interviewed by Sarah Anne Johnson

I can't understand a story without understanding its sound. That, for me, is the glory of writing. That's where I find excitement and heartbreak and sadness and melancholy. That's where I find it all. Unless I find that language, it's hard for me to understand the story at all.

Jerry Battle comes to life in *Aloft* because of how he expresses himself. His particular American vernacular is something that I found, and if I hadn't found that I couldn't have written his story. He could have been a side character, but not the hero. That's what sustains a first-person novel. Holden Caulfield is an interesting young man, but what we remember about him and delight in is the smartness and edge of his language.

Do these books come to you with that voice?

Yes, Jerry did and Hata did. In *Native Speaker*, Henry Park is trying on a lot of different voices. That's something I was consciously working on. An exploration of language as a costume. The next book, which is in third person, I had to find a voice for as well; more of an overriding voice, but a voice.

WRITING ADVICE from Lynn Freed

I wrote some very bad, sentimental, predictable short stories while I was a girl. And then a few stories that were better. And then two novels. And only then did I find a voice with which I was comfortable, with which I was at home. This voice came first with a story, "Foreign Student," and then, more strongly, with *Home Ground*.

I have no rules for this process of finding one's voice, but I do know that, for me, it took time. Years. A decade or more. In other words, it took a lot of false writing to come upon a voice in which I could tell the truth as I saw and felt it—to know the truth as it was revealed through the writing.

This, I suppose, is what authenticity on the page is all about. It is an aspect of ear. So much of training in writing lies in the training of the ear, which is what I emphasize in workshops. What is more difficult to get across in this age of instant gratification is the time it takes, the lifetime it takes, to come to this. If ever.

as interviewed by Sarah Anne Johnson

THE WRITER'S PERSONAL LANDSCAPE

Susan Richards Shreve
interviewed by Katherine Perry Harris

You have said before that for some writers, there is only one story. Why do you think this is so?

It depends on what fires the imagination. For the writer with one story, the story is often his own. But one story also pertains, I think, to the territory a writer takes on—returning again and again to the same actual, spiritual, personal landscape. The writer is recognized not only by voice, but also by a kind of repetition of character, place, subject, metaphor, or all of these things.

BALANCING ACT

Susan Richards Shreve
interviewed by Katherine Perry Harris

What do you think is the hardest thing for writing students to learn?

Voice and character. Fiction—at least narrative fiction, which is my particular interest—is character, and character is difficult to create. To invent a credible and sympathetic character with the abstract tools of language is a tall order. The reader must know from the start with whom he is keeping company. I like to draw whimsical stick figures but have tried and failed in three-dimensional drawing, finding it too difficult to give shape to the image on the page.

And voice. I think of voice as some mysterious combination of one individual's true language and language itself, akin to riding a bicycle. Remember? Holding onto the handlebars, swinging your legs over the bar, feet on the pedals, pedaling, tumbling. Then magically, one day, you balance the bicycle. And away! You may get old and rusty and tired, but you will never forget how to balance. It's in your bones.

TAPPING INTO YOUR OWN FEELINGS
Carolyn Chute, interviewed by Barbara Stevens

Did you always have your own style?

I have learning disabilities. I have a lot of learning disabilities. I have a real problem with memory. I have a real bad problem with … word recall. And as I work, I can't even hang on to a thought. It's just gone. Some people say, Oh, that's because you're a Gemini, but I just have a real struggle when I work, and I think I've had to work around those disabilities somehow and develop what I could do, and what I could do was work with dramatic situations, because I did have a lot of mess in my life, dramatic kinds of things.

I am a dramatic person. I have very strong feelings about things. When I get mad I bust up the house. When I'm happy I'm dancing around the house, and everybody's got to hear about how happy I am. So when I work, I work around that drama, around that sense of drama, around that sense of everything being very deeply felt.

DANIEL WALLACE

interviewed by Linda B. Swanson-Davies

A lot of writers tend to use very similar voices from story to story, similar characters moving through different circumstances. The voices in your three pieces are quite different from one another. How do you manage that?

I like to do different voices because what intrigues me about a story is the voice. So much of the stuff that I do is in first person. Not all of it. With *Big Fish*, you're not really sure what person it's in.

It feels first person.

But it's really first person about somebody else. The death scenes are in first person. He's saying, My dad did this, my dad did that. It is first person but he's never saying "I." In "The Main Thing," I had to rewrite the first paragraph or two, the first couple of pages maybe, fifteen or twenty times before I got the exact rhythm of the voice. And once I got that, I was able to get the character. Without knowing how he talks, I can't understand who he is. I can know all this stuff—you should be able to know when your character was born, what kind of childhood he had, what kind of socks he has in his drawer, but that information is not what catapults me into the story. I don't know that it's necessary to know all that information to write a believable character.

You draw a picture with the words that you use and the sound of the words that you use, the rhythm. It's like hearing somebody doing a great impersonation of a famous person. It makes no difference if you don't look at the person. You believe it is that person. So if you have the voice down, then I think that you've got the character down. Then you have to have a situation for the character to live in and something to happen. With this story, once I got the situation of the basic compulsion, the friction that made the engine of the story go—which was his being overly admired by somebody he admired—all I had to do was to refine my idea of who the character is supposed to be. Once I get into that, then the story really moves quickly. But the beginning moves very slowly until I get the voice. And every story's different in that way. The voice defines the story for me. The last novel I wrote was very voice-centered as well. The character's a little unstable. That was all inspired by the way he was talking to me.

AMY BLOOM

interviewed by Sarah Anne Johnson

How did you develop your own way of writing a short story?

Ignorance is a wonderful thing. I read a lot of short stories. I didn't know any other writers. I didn't talk to any other writers. I didn't read any books on how to write a story. I guess the stories were taking shape inside of me, and I do read quite a bit. The voice was there. I don't understand it any better now than I did ten years ago. I'm grateful, but I have no idea.

WRITING ADVICE from Joyce Thompson

Not everyone would agree with me, but I think that every story has a unique voice. Every writer has a unique aesthetic. These are complementary but not exactly the same thing. The right voice for a story seems to know the story and tell it easily and well. The wrong voice stutters and stalls out.

It's not uncommon for writers to feel as if they've "channeled" a story, as if a voice found and used them to bring a story into the world. These tend to be the times we transcend our limitations and do our best work. Needless to say, if this happens to you, be available. Get to your keyboard and let her rip. Also note that it won't happen every time you sit down to write. It seems to be a reward for faithful practice, kind of like a karmic dog biscuit. Sometimes it's how one gets seduced into being a writer in the first place.

How do we stay open to new voices over a span of decades? Be at pains to stay open in every way possible, in mind, body, heart, and spirit. Avoid numbing routine. Refuse to think shopworn thoughts. Periodically learn new skills. Put yourself in uncomfortable situations. Exercise regularly. Read poetry. Listen hard.

JAYNE ANNE PHILLIPS

interviewed by Sarah Anne Johnson

What's your process like when you're working on a novel?

It's the same process no matter what I'm working on. I work according to language. I work starting with language, so that my process is simply to work my way into the next sentence. Sustaining the voice of a book is level one, where I have to stay to move forward. I work very slowly, until I find my way into the middle of the book and I know what to write next by reading what I've already written until I know where to go next.

SHOWING YOUR TRUE SELF

by Sigrid Nunez

You have a relationship to the world and to people and there is so much that you don't let people see. Of course, that's true of everyone. There's something about writing passionately or intensely that enables you to expose yourself, in a way, and show your mind at work and your imagination at play and what kind of sensibility you truly have. This doesn't have to be in an autobiographical work; this can be in any kind of writing.

I don't think that much of all that comes out in your daily life, so I think that you're showing *so* much of who you are and how you feel about things, and your view of the world, through your writing. Absolutely.

CHAPTER

3

THEME

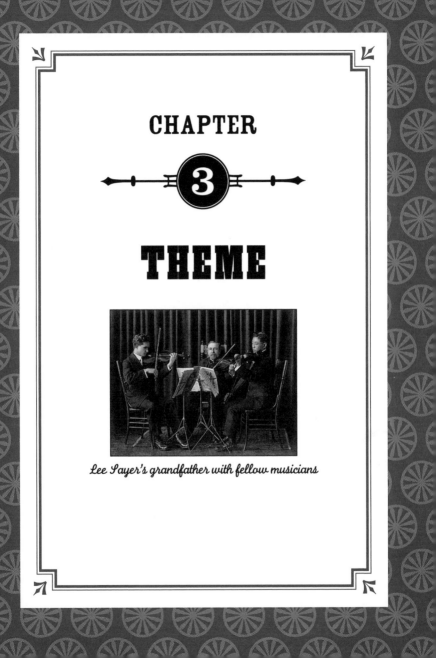

Lee Sayer's grandfather with fellow musicians

Mary Morrissy: It'll be interesting when I'm started on another novel and also writing stories. I think a debut collection of stories from a first-time writer inevitably concentrates on childhood. The stories I'm writing now are less concerned with childhood, although there's always at the center the nugget of something that has happened a long time ago. Writers are recycling their childhoods all the time.

as interviewed by Ana Callan

MARY YUKARI WATERS
interviewed by Sherry Ellis

The world is packed with people who can write well, but the only way a writer is going to stand out is to be completely emotionally honest in a way that resonates deep down in a reader's mind. You can call it soul, or outlook on life, but whatever it is, it's a certain aura about your writing that's a result of every experience you've ever had, every emotion you've ever felt. And that aura, that insight, is the most important thing you have to offer.

In that sense, a work of fiction can be, and should be, every bit as emotionally "real" as a memoir. I think that's partly what Virginia Woolf was talking about. If you ask ten different writers to look at a tree, they'll all see it differently, as if each one was wearing different colored glasses. And that's because each writer sees it through his or her emotional context. I think it goes back to the themes we were talking about earlier. Writing is a way to get these themes out so you can see your own self in a clear light. And in the process of being honest with yourself, you might reach another reader who has similar issues buried deep inside. When that connection happens, it's magical.

ON LOVE AND LOSS

Lorrie Moore, interviewed by Jim Schumock

[In Who Will Run the Frog Hospital?] you're dealing with the loss of friendship over time, and the recognition that usually the friends we make early in our lives won't be with us in our later lives.

That's very true. There are ways of being with people that can only happen at certain times in your life. There are ways of being with people when you're children and there are ways of being with people when you're adults. And you do find many adults pining for these lost chapters, missing them in some way, and puzzled as to why these kinds of relationships can't be brought about in their adult life.

On the other hand, a real grown-up marriage can't be brought about in childhood either. There's a way in which the relationship between these two girls is very much a child's relationship. It's extremely self-absorbed. They're the stars of their own show, and they're not looking around very much. As a result, the narrator even acknowledges at the end of the book that she failed to pay attention to some other real and complicated things in her life that she should have been paying attention to.

But it is a novel about all the various kinds of loss in your life and how difficult it is to even think about them. Because every life, even the luckiest life, has so much loss in it, and it's very hard to get through all that and endure it, yet one must. To that extent, this is an anthem to adolescence, and is about the things that can be retrieved in memory, but obviously in memory only. You lose a lot as you proceed through life toward other things, accumulating other things, but losing the things you leave.

COMMON THEMES, UNIQUE PERSPECTIVES
by Melanie Bishop

I would say that there are many story *lines*, but perhaps a somewhat limited set of themes or topics. If you look at themes broadly, you can say most stories are about love or loss or longing or sex or death or fear or family…even this list could go on for a ways. But this is because these are the things the human experience is made up of.

Where originality comes in is in the uniqueness of each of our lives. Sure, we've all lost in love, but my loss is different from yours, and so on. We all have a first sexual experience, but the specific details of my loss of virginity and the details of yours are what allow us to write two very separate and very fresh stories.

I try to hammer into my students how absolutely unique their lives have been, how no one has seen inside their families the way they've been able to, no one had been inside their heads, thinking their thoughts, dealing with their fears, their confusions, their quests. Anyone can write a wealth of fresh tales; otherwise, the short-story form wouldn't have survived as long as it has. Just look at how many stories are being published by small journals each year. And no one is the same as the other, even though probably many of them take on a similar theme.

Only you have access to the specific details of your life and memory, and the specifics of what you observe about others on any given day. Use these, and I doubt you'll ever run dry on fresh ideas.

THE STORY QUESTION

Patricia Hampl, interviewed by Susan McInnis

You've mentioned that Isaac Bashevis Singer, when he got an idea for a story, said he first had to ask whose story it was. You've said you look first at which questions are yours. For example, in *Virgin Time* your question was not Is there a God? but What is the place of prayer in life, what is contemplation? How did you find your question? How did you know Is there a God? was not your question?

You know something when you write it. You make a statement on paper and you think, Yes, that's it. At that point you have constellated it. It may be that the constellation in just a few words is the result of a good deal of conflicted thinking, and non-thinking, for a long time. Sometimes you write the thought and cross it out. Whatever it was, it doesn't belong. It's not there. It's not yet constellated.

THE REASONS FOR RECURRENCE

Andre Dubus
interviewed by Jennifer Levasseur and Kevin Rabalais

⟫◇⟪

Themes run throughout your work, where the same idea repeats itself. Do you revisit scenes or sections of dialogue because you feel you've reached a new understanding of the matter?

It's not intentional. I knew I had written about abortion, for instance, in "Finding a Girl in America," and I didn't look at it again. I didn't want to go back in that direction in "Falling in Love" in *Dancing After Hours.* I told a priest who is in the workshop about my situation, and I said, "I've got another abortion story, and I've already gone there twice in stories. Do I have to go back again?" He said, "Yes." So I did.

That doesn't bother me. There's a lot of repetition in a lot of writers I love, probably because of their passions, fears, what we love as humans. It doesn't bother me; it's just unintentional.

. . . .

Charles Baxter: It seems to me that, as writers, we always try to capture that telling moment of a culture's history that is going to define the culture to itself in a way that's meaningful to the readers. In my case, it happens to be not about the things that people do with their money, because I know very little about that. What I can do is say something about what happens when people are alone at night and thinking about who they are in relation to everything that surrounds them.

as interviewed by Stewart David Ikeda

ON GOOD AND EVIL

William Styron, interviewed by Jim Schumock

What have you found in that region of the soul you examined in *Sophie's Choice* where absolute evil confronts brotherhood?

I really don't know if I can answer it directly. I think that one of the compelling themes of fiction is this confrontation between good and evil. Possibly the strongest works of fiction have this as an undercurrent somewhere. I know that I'm attracted by it. In all my works, there has been this interplay.

We live in an existence which is utterly baffling and beyond our comprehension. All we have is our lives as human beings to live. We're the only species capable of wreaking ruinous harm on ourselves. Animals don't do this. Animals are not capable of evil. To me, one of the great mysteries is how we survive together without destroying ourselves. At the root of this dilemma is this constant interplay of good and evil. I think it's a theme that I certainly have been compelled to deal with throughout my work, as I think most major writers are.

ON CHANGE AND ENDURANCE

Annie Proulx, interviewed by Michael Upchurch

Change itself is what fascinates me. I am drawn, as a moth to the flame, by edge situations, by situations of metamorphosis and change, by things turning from one into another, by those little magic eggs within eggs within eggs, like those Russian dolls. This kind of thing, this shifting and sliding away—the sand moving under one's feet, the tide coming in and changing the look of the coastline—these are the things that pull my eye. And the study of history satisfies that taste, and that *is* why I studied history, and this is why I happen to write books of stories that deal with change, either in an individual life or on a broad social scale.

It's fortunate for me—or unfortunate, depending on your viewpoint—that I did have historical training and do have something of a trained eye to look at social change, and that's always the basis of the books I write, both *Postcards* and *The Shipping News*, and the one I'm working on now, and the ones to come. Maybe it sounds like I'm in a rut, but that's the kind of thing that pleases me. And it's not specific social changes that attract me. It's really any social change. I just like seeing the situation where everything seems chaos, and only a little is revealed or resolved. But enough is revealed or resolved to give shape and form to the story. I do not like the pseudo-Chekhovian "trailing away."

What I was trying to do with Agnis in *The Shipping News* was this: In the study of history and in reading diaries and accounts of people's lives, particularly in sociological studies of people from poverty-stricken areas and different ethnic groups that are in poverty-line situations, I was struck—one cannot help but be struck—by the human capacity for endurance. One gets through. One gets through.

People do get through, and I wanted a character who was not so much stoic as not going to give up, who would determine to not hang up on the rough stuff, not whine, not go through a twelve step, but to tough it through and get on the other side. I liked that for Agnis, and a lot of people do that. That's how people get through life. Life is wretched for many people, and it doesn't get better as one gets older, so I just wanted Agnis to be toughing the awful stuff through.

The *randomness* of things and the hammer of life is something that intrigues me very much. A lot of vicious, hard, dreadful, evil things happen to people through no fault of their own. The stuff just comes down and hammers them. Life does that, and some people get hammered again and again. And this sense of the inescapability of the hammer, of turning to look at it as it descends on you, is something I do try to catch from time to time. It sounds kind of ghastly. You turn and look at the executioner's axe descending, and recognize, at some point, what it is that's happening to you, what you're seeing—that flying thought has occurred to me more than once when that kind of thing happens in the prose. Yes, looking life in its "shifty, bloodshot eye."

WRITING ADVICE from Jayne Anne Phillips

The minute you write a book that's domestically oriented, you automatically cut your readership, or your serious readership. There's a ghettoization of subject matter that has to do with women's lives. It's the writer's responsibility not to pander to an audience or to a culture or to a publishing climate. You just have to do what you need to do and let the rest of it happen.

as interviewed by Sarah Anne Johnson

ON FREEDOM AND DOMESTICITY

Sue Miller, interviewed by Sarah Anne Johnson

⇒◆⇐

In a *New York Times* book review, Jane Smiley called *Family Pictures* "an important example of a new American tradition that explores what it means, not to light out for the territories but to make a home, live at home, and learn what home is." Do you agree with this statement? Do you see yourself as part of this tradition?

I do. There's been a lot of writing about this, so what I have to say may not be particularly fresh. The novel in English has a long tradition of being about the home. This "lighting out for the territories" was a new wrinkle at a certain point in American fiction, but became the American novel, more or less. The novel as it developed in other parts of the world didn't experience that *On the Road*, let's-throw-domesticity-away kind of thing. Read Leslie Fiedler, *Love and Death in the American Novel*. It was especially true of the period I grew up in, when I was reading people like Roth, and Mailer, and Bellow. But you can write about an awful lot using the home, using elements that are very domestic. They are equally as rich; they demonstrate the human condition fully as much as books which represent fleeing or rejecting domesticity.

In either case, the point is to have a character struggle against himself. Where you put him, what you give him to struggle against, is whimsical and entirely up to you—what you know and what you're most interested in. Whether you have him run off to Mexico, or whether you have him stay at home and make a decision about what to do with his autistic child, what you're trying to do is expose what makes him how he is, and how he thinks about fate as opposed to freedom.

ON POWER AND FEMINISM

Julia Alvarez

interviewed by Mike Chasar and Constance Pierce

Some women got onto me when I was writing about housekeeping, saying that that was regressive and anti-feminist. To hell with it!

All these women that I knew grew up and made a craft of [housekeeping]—that was their art form—and that's a long tradition that I want to celebrate. Sure, I like having other options. I can decide that I don't really want to fold my own clothes, that I don't really just want to cook in a house for a man or a family, that I want other things. But that tradition, that lore, I think, is valuable. How to put a dress together without a pattern, how to cook this or that, how to iron, or how to hang a clothesline.

For instance, Ruth, my husband's mother, was a farmwife in Nebraska with five kids and just couldn't waste a whole lot of time. So there was a way to hang a wash—or *warsh*, as she calls it—so you do the least amount of ironing and it dries quick. Just that you know all of this stuff …

Why would that be regressive? It's a tradition that came out of a certain necessity, just the same way many other traditions do. Many works of art come out of singing in our chains, like Dylan Thomas said.

Lynn Freed: What is "feminist"? I've never been able to work it out. I never think of things this way, never in the abstract. I write about a character in a situation and take it from there.

as interviewed by Sarah Anne Johnson

Lee Martin: I was really attracted to *The Bright Forever*, not only because of the intersections of people's lives and the responsibilities that we have to one another, but also because I was very drawn toward this story of ordinary people whose lives all of a sudden become extraordinary, and how they live with that and how they go on from there.

as interviewed by Linda B. Swanson-Davies

ON PARENTS

Roy Parvin, interviewed by Linda B. Swanson-Davies

What I used to see—and I think that this was a hangover from the fifties—was that parents formed this sort of indivisible unit. And that, you know, one loves one's father and mother equally. This is before the age of divorce, of course, that I'm talking about. In the house I grew up in, the parents were always right. I think that it's valuable to see that parents are fallible, that they make mistakes. To see that one will have a different relationship with each parent. It's only become clear to me since my father died three years ago, three and a half years ago, that I love my parents for different reasons, for the different needs that they fill. I've learned that the relationship with one's mother is completely different from the relationship with one's father. I went through life up until age thirty-eight thinking that there's this sort of indivisible unit that's fused together in some way, this unit that does not have a sex.

Sometimes the families are splintered in my stories. In "In the Snow Forest," I talk about one's relationship with just one parent, such as Darby's father, a lot more. The mother doesn't make an appearance at all. And I thought while I was writing, Is this fair? Should I give the mother any screen time? It was an I-want-to-be-an-equal-opportunity-writer kind of thing. Then I realized, No, it says a lot more that his mother is not in the story.

In my most recent long story, "Mendel's Granddaughter," the woman is going across country to take care of her aging parents. She has a different relationship with each of her parents. It's a very simple truth, but it eluded me for many, many years nonetheless.

ON THE CRUELTY OF HOPE
Pam Durban, interviewed by Cheryl Reid

In that moment on the road with the horse, Martha believes that her mother is really there. To me that's one of those moments when the story ["Soon"] really opens up. Hope is constantly there; not that hope is a positive thing necessarily, but a thing that hounds you through life. It's going to be better, it's going to be different, or I am going to find the answer. It may or may not be true.

That's what I was trying to get at: that hope is not an entirely positive thing. While I was writing the story, both of my aunts were dying of cancer. They were identical twins who were diagnosed with cancer within three weeks of each other. One aunt had ovarian cancer and she went through chemotherapy. Her husband said that it gave her two weeks of good life during her last fifteen weeks. That was the metaphor of hope for me. You do something like that knowing it probably won't help, and yet, how could you not do it?

Even Chekhov, in the last two days of his life, was planning a trip to Italy. He was a doctor. He knew he was dying. But he kept doing those things, and he imagined his own future. That's what I was looking at in the story, that problematic nature of hope. It makes people do bizarre, cruel things as well as positive things.

....

ON MANLINESS

Ernest Gaines, interviewed by Michael Upchurch

One phrase keeps coming up in all the stories, about "being a man." In the last lines of "The Sky is Gray," the mother says to her young son, when he wants to turn his collar up against the cold, that he's not a bum, he's a man. And, of course, in *A Lesson Before Dying*, the whole novel turns on whether Jefferson is going to see himself as a "hog" or a man. For a younger generation, the connotation of this phrase, "Be a man, be a man," can raise a few hackles, suggesting machismo, and might be misinterpreted. Yet it's a consistent connecting thread in your work. How would you handle someone who's bristling at being told, "You've got to be a man"?

Well, manliness is the taking on of responsibility. It's not machoism. Who's a greater man, John Wayne or Gandhi? John Wayne could knock out anybody; Gandhi could not. But how does one live? How does one live with oneself and how does one live with others, regardless of status or color or whatever: What does one do? What does one do? Do you tuck your tail under and go out and drink, or do you stand up for anything? Stand up against pain, stand up against hunger, stand up for someone else, or stand up for an idea. Each and every one of us confronts something like this sometime in our lives, at a given moment. There are so many examples.

For example, the old men in *A Gathering of Old Men* decide to stand up one day. Well, even Mathu, the likely murderer, says, "I never thought of you as men before." And Mapes, the sheriff, feels the same way: "There's only one man here, and that's Mathu. That's the only one who could have killed Beau [the book's villain] out there." And that's only one example.

As you pointed out, the kid who wanted to turn his collar against the cold—the mother was just trying to say, "After the things that we have gone through today, to do that is almost an insult, to turn that collar up. You can take a little more cold, okay? You can be a little bit more cold now. We're going over there now and we're going to get this together. So take a little bit more cold."

I don't know how to explain it to someone who doesn't want to hear the word "man."

Amy Hempel: Safety is where you find it. It interests me that what you think is going to be your home, or what you think is going to be a safe place, often is not, and what you wouldn't expect to comfort you does. Actually, at the time I started the novella "Tumble Home," and all the stories in this book, my husband and I bought a house, and were making a home. It interested me that it was not what I imagined it would be. Perfect in ways, and yet…

as interviewed by Debra Levy and Carol Turner

ON VULNERABILITY

Sigrid Nunez, interviewed by Linda B. Swanson-Davies

If you were a parent of a child of your nature, what would you try to do in particular for her?

I would try to convince her that she was safe, because, if it were a child of my nature, it would be someone who had this constant sense that something terrible was going to happen, this constant feeling of vulnerability, of always feeling threatened. If I had such a child, the most important thing would be to try to give her more of a sense of security—that bad things happen in the world but it doesn't mean that every time you go out the door you're going to get hit by a car.

The question would be, however, why would she have such feelings? I mean, it's precisely because of the parent that the child has these feelings, because the parent didn't [provide that sense of security]. That, to me, would be the most important thing.

With that in mind, would there be a particular thing that you would be inclined to do or say?

Good parents do it by their daily behavior. What creates it, I think, is the child must have the feeling of unconditional love. Too few children have that. The idea that these are my parents, they do not love me because of what I do or how I look, how well I do in school, how well I tap dance, whatever. They love me because I am their child. Unconditional love. If you give that to a child, that feeling of security and safety is going to follow, unless, of course, there's some terrible accident.

How would you finish this sentence: Most people are basically…?

As soon as you said that, I thought of George Eliot. She was talking about the things that people notice—rather, the things that people don't notice. She says somewhere—the passage is in *Middlemarch*—she says that maybe it's better that we don't notice these things, that we're not so sensitive, because if our senses were keener and we could hear the heartbeat of a squirrel and a tree grow, or whatever, it would be unbearable. And then she says, "As it is, most people go about well wadded with stupidity."

So, what was the question?

Most people are basically …

Most people are more vulnerable than they appear. Most people have all these defenses, but they really are more vulnerable than we think.

TIMING AND CONTEXT
Roy Parvin, interviewed by Linda B. Swanson-Davies

There are losses that people grow from and then there are losses that seem to just do a person in. Do you think you can say what about them affects people differently? Does it have to do with the quality of the loss, the person, or the timing of that loss in their lives?

I think a lot of it is timing. I was writing as I was discovering my-self. I was able to take the information that my father was dying and use it to my advantage in a way. That sounds very Machiavellian, but I don't mean that. I was able to say I feel alive right now because I am writing, and I feel alive because I'm experiencing this death in my family. I felt much, much more alive. A lot of days it didn't feel that way—I felt I was rubbed raw, and everything was exposed. I think that was a matter of timing. If that happened at another point in time, I could see myself never having been drawn to writing. If my father's death happened earlier, it might have had a completely different impact.

I think that's a really good question, because it sort of also gets at what causes a story to be a story. And what are the certain circumstances that the writer is going through? What are the certain circumstances that he builds in his mind to build the arc of a story? I'm never quite sure about that. I mean, I think that so much of life is circumstance, but I also think a lot of it is like what Woody Allen says, "It's just showing up." If you show up enough…

Something will happen.

You make your own luck. I think that happens. But it's a very good question. I wrestle with it in my own stories about loss. I wrestle with character—Darby lost too much. I know, in "In the Snow Forest," that what Darby and Harper want is pretty much the same thing, but, after what happens, Darby cannot go on. He was convincing himself the whole story—actually the whole story is him saying, "Not waiting, not waiting." He is finally seizing the opportunity, is convincing himself that he can love a child that's not his, who is physically compromised. And by the time he finally makes that decision, other things have happened, things he cannot get over.

It was a devastating story.

You know it's always a question when someone, when a writer

traffics the idea of loss: When that loss occurs, can you turn it into something positive, or is there no chance for that, is there a darker end in store? That's why I sort of let the story guide me. I'm just really receiving the story at that point.

....

JAYNE ANNE PHILLIPS
interviewed by Sarah Anne Johnson

—————◆————

You write about people coming of age in the context of family, how children often outgrow the constrained and limited world of their parents, and yet cannot fully come to terms with the wider world beyond the family—in the story "Fast Lanes," for example. There is a desire for safety, yet an unwillingness—or inability—to accept or create safety of one's own.

I don't believe in safety. People struggle with wanting to grab safety and hold on to it. When we're children, if our parents do a decent job, we think we're safe. We don't actually know that our parents don't control Ebola or mad cow disease. All that isn't obvious to children. If we grow up inside some kind of safety, there's a period of time in which we struggle with realizing that there was never the kind of safety we thought we lived inside.

Then we come into the situation of trying to provide safety in our lives for our partners, for our children, for our families, for ourselves, and for our own identities. You can't take risks as an artist or a person unless you have a certain safety to start in. That story, and a lot of other work I've done, has been about that struggle to accept the fact that there is no safety.

Carol Shields: I've always been interested in work and the importance of work in our lives. I'm a fan of Studs Terkel. I think work is a human experience. That's what I've tried to write about in my last two novels. That's something about novels that's worried me. People never seem to work. You know, we're told that they're an architect or a designer or whatever but we never see them in their studio or their office actually doing that work. We just see them in their off hours, as it were. This seemed all wrong to me. I wanted to show Daisy actually engaged in this work. I loved writing this section of [*The Stone Diaries*], which is written in letters to Mrs. Greenthumb. It was just pure pleasure for me to do this.

as interviewed by Jim Schumock

WILLIAM STYRON

interviewed by Melissa Lowver

In *Set This House on Fire*, Cass discovers, for an instant, a "continuity of beauty in the scheme of all life which triumphs even to the point of taking in sordidness and shabbiness and ugliness." Many of your novels' characters don't seem to overcome ugliness for more than fleeting moments. Do you see that as inevitable for people in general, or only inevitable in terms of the points of view and experiences of the characters you've chosen to draw?

Oh, I think the two are sort of interchangeable with me. I mean, I don't think I can separate my characters from my own feelings about life. I think that if I reflect that sordidness and shabbiness or whatever it's called, it's because I think that life is often a trial for people, and problematical as to whether it's all worth the candles, for many people.

ON AGING

Ethan Canin, interviewed by Jim Schumock

You write so much about middle and old age.

I work in medicine; I work a lot with old people. I'm present often at the moment of reckoning in their lives. It's the moment from which their lives diverge. In other words, it was one way before that day and it will be different after that day. You see a lot of people at that kind of juncture where they're thinking about what they've done and that's brought on what's happened to them. So I guess that makes me write about that in some way.

Do you think you write more effectively about middle-aged people than about young people?

No matter what I used to write—I could start a story about two lesbians on a sailboat—and it would end up being about a father and a son somewhere. No matter what I used to write, that used to come out. Then, it sort of changed. As you write more and more and more, you begin to find your obsessions or themes. I noticed that there's also a young character in my writing who's always looking up—not quite able to see over the tabletop of things. I guess that's another character I write about. I don't really like to write from a young person's point of view. I would rather be able to use the things I've thought about. If you write from a child's point of view, you can't do that. It's nice to write from the point of view of an intelligent character, because then you get to say everything you think about the world.

And it's especially that way about writing. I think what surprises you, and what seems to be deflected off some hard core at the interior of what you're writing, ends up being what your novel's about, or what your life's work is about. It's not what you thought it was about.

Why are you so intrigued by the failure of characters' will to action? You're such a successful person yourself, yet most of your characters tend to be dominated by their failures rather than by their successes.

I just love that. That's what I'm interested in. Whatever it means to be a successful person, having had books published, if that's what you mean by successful, doesn't change your character at all. I think you're still writing about what you like or what you fear, what you're afraid of. I think fiction is about small ambition, small, failed ambition. That's what I like to write about. To me it's the most noble thing, a teacher who wants to be a headmaster. I think that's a great thing.

Character is put to the test in these little battles.

Absolutely. Napoleon losing Europe is one thing, but I'd rather write about this guy not getting the headmastership.

Stuart Dybek: I will venture to say that if there is a single significant problem for the American story to solve, it is the problem of privilege. Writers who I generally admire address privilege in some way, whether it be thematic or through tone or choice of subject; something about their perspective, on some level, no matter how subtle, recognizes that privilege in America needs to be acknowledged, if not directly confronted.

as interviewed by Jennifer Levasseur and Kevin Rabalais

THE POLITICS OF IDENTITY

Jayne Anne Phillips, interviewed by Sarah Anne Johnson

Writing is very political. You're political in what you choose to write about and the way you choose to write about it. *Machine Dreams* was my looking at the world that had enclosed that small town where I first became aware of identity in myself and in others. I think of *Shelter* as being about the politics of family over the absence of family. I think about the story "Lechery" and *Shelter* as being connected. In "Lechery," a child makes a family out of what she can find, and she operates out of instincts that have been fractured by the world she lives in. Whereas in *Shelter*, I took four with secrets and put them in an extremely isolated, sensual, lush, fierce kind of setting without families. It was a passion play that is a group of children moving through an underworld, a rite of passage, into a survival they created for themselves. It combined a lot of my interests, because it was a book about jarred dimensions, one reality existing alongside another, how perception alters reality. I've always written about the politics of identity/family.

CHITRA BANERJEE DIVAKARUNI
interviewed by Sarah Anne Johnson

⋙⋅◆⋅⋘

Throughout your stories and novels there is a sense of the individuals trying to find home and what home means. They pendulum back and forth between their lives in America and their pasts in India, trying to find some truth that will help their lives make sense. Is this something that can ever be reconciled?

Some individuals might manage to reconcile this, but for many of us, this is the great dilemma of the twentieth and twenty-first century. Where is home? We've become such a mobile society, how many of us live in the homes where we were born? We've moved into a whole new way of life, and the question, "Where is home?" becomes very important. It cannot necessarily be answered. Perhaps the only way to answer it is to create a sense of home inside of ourselves.

ON ASSIMILATION
Chang-rae Lee, interviewed by Sarah Anne Johnson

⋙⋅◆⋅⋘

The theme of invisibility comes up over and over in *Native Speaker*. There is the invisibility of the immigrant, regardless of ethnicity, the invisibility of the non-native speaker, the invisibility that Henry Park assumes as a spy. What draws you to the idea of the individual blending into the social landscape?

It's about the draw and power and attractiveness of assimilation, and then its attending problems. There's a deep-seated human need to assimilate and be part of a group. It's a survival technique. We all talk about being individuals, especially in this country, but really we're not. We're members of many different little groups. For an outsider like an immigrant, the idea is not to stand out because when you stand out you get cut down. To be an individual is to be in a dangerous position. It's about the very overriding desire to join, but then most of that book and especially in *A Gesture Life*, it's about the darker side of assimilation, and what people become when they've given up themselves.

This invisibility is self-imposed, not like that of Ralph Ellison, which is imposed from the outside. This invisibility I'm writing about is a kind of self-protection, but it's not without ill effect.

TOI DERRICOTTE
interviewed by Susan McInnis

Captivity was a new exploration for me, because it was the first time I wrote about issues of race, class, and color. The other two books really don't deal heavily with those subjects. And I think the reason why is that artistically there's a danger in beginning to write about certain subjects. Our literature in the past has been presented as aesthetically bound, as if there is one kind of aesthetic that should bind our literature together—as if there's a kind of universal language and universal experience. In my first two books I was wisely wary about going over into a kind of material which again might put me in a captive position—held in a space and recognized in a certain way that would not let me escape it. That does happen when people begin to write about certain subjects. Often women's issues, often issues about race or class. So on the one hand I feel very driven to explore these issues. On the other hand I am somewhat circumspect about getting into those categories.

Amy Tan says she is reviewed in a cluster, almost inevitably, of Asian writers. What she says is that it cuts her readers off from acknowledging this huge experience she thinks she brings.

Well, take Matisse's statement: The job of the artist is to turn himself—or herself—inside out. Yes, absolutely. But in some way that puts a big burden on the writer of color in terms of being comprehensible. Because frequently, as soon as you begin to talk about these subjects, your reader gets a kind of—a fear, a disease—a feeling almost, maybe, that you are purposefully excluding them.

You as an artist.

You as an artist. And, of course, this is not true. You're using the material you have to get to the deeper things. In a way, for all artists, all experience is metaphor. You're using what you have to uncover the deep human experiences of life, death, birth, loneliness, love—whatever. And that's your material. But it's true that the whole question about the universal has put us—as readers and writers—in positions that hold some tension. And that does have to be worked out. It will have to be worked out, of course, in our country, as we change. As literature begins to hold more voices, we will have to change.

Julia Alvarez: I don't just want to be a "Latina writer" who writes about being "Latina." I want to be able to write about a variety of things that have to do with whatever engages me, or whatever I need to find out more about. And so far it's happened that there are Latino themes in my work, because that's so much a part of my background and what I'm interested in and the way that I see the world.

as interviewed by Mike Chasar and Constance Pierce

THE ETHNIC OBLIGATION
Frederick Reiken, interviewed by Eric Wasserman

Cynthia Ozick once said that while Michael Chabon is Jewish and also a writer, he isn't a "Jewish writer." Have you been witness or victim to this bantering over ethnic literary legitimacy?

So far I haven't, but to me it seems a moot point. While it's clear that there are some brilliant specialists—Cynthia Ozick, for instance—who have built important bodies of excellent work on the basis of writing about Jewish themes, the notion that such a path is more legitimate than the writing of someone like Michael Chabon is in my mind like saying that an Olympic athlete who specializes in, say, the high jump is more legitimate than someone who does the high jump and the long jump and the hurdles. I don't know the context in which Cynthia Ozick made this statement, so it's unfair to guess at what she was insinuating, but so far as my own path as a writer goes, I don't foresee myself being considered a "Jewish writer" so much as simply a writer who is Jewish, and my own particular sensibility is much more suited to the range and flexibility that comes with the latter.

IMMIGRATION

Chitra Banerjee Divakaruni
interviewed by Sarah Anne Johnson

The transformation of the individual that is an inevitable result of immigration is a central theme in all of your books, yet you approach it differently in each story. For instance, in *The Mistress of Spices*, Geeta falls in love with a Chicano and her Indian parents are faced with what they consider a disgrace to the family. In "Mrs. Dutta Writes a Letter" you write about a grandmother who can't adapt to the life in America.

Immigration was a major transformative influence on my life. Immigration, in some ways, is what made me into a writer. Before I came to this country I had no idea of wanting to be a writer. It was after I moved so far from my culture and faced the conflicts that come with such movement that I had a subject that I felt passionate about.

Immigration made me realize something that I hadn't thought about until I came here, and that is that we use the word *America*, which really means something different to each immigrant who comes over. And the experience of America is so different for each individual. For our children growing up here, who are the products of immigration, what does being American mean to them? *The Unknown Errors of Our Lives* is particularly concerned with the move back—immigration begins a movement that really only ends when there's a corresponding movement back to the home country. In this book, I'm focusing in a number of stories on that movement back.

In a way, your writing is like a movement back.

Yes, it's a way for me to revisit, to reconnect, to re-understand.

....

ON SOUTHERNISM

Pam Durban, interviewed by Cheryl Reid

⟾◆⟽

In another context you said, "I don't consider myself a Southern writer in the sense that I deal with people in my work as representatives of any region. In fact, the whole Southernness issue has gotten so tiresome to me that I prefer not to talk about it at all." This is an interesting statement considering how the peculiarities, the structures, the codes, and the history of the place called the South seem to capture your imagination.

I wouldn't make that statement now. I was reacting to this packaged Southernness. I still react to that. What characterizes a lot of Southern writing, and what I am trying to get away from, is a kind of nostalgia for a past. As a white Southerner, you simply can't do that. It's a corrupt way of looking at things. You can't. That kind of nostalgia contains within it an acceptance of a belief in the inferiority of black people and an agreement that this was the right way to do things. I'm not looking to establish guilt or blame, but trying to look at what it means to be a white Southerner and look at the past.

Carol Shields: You know one thing I did worry about in the writing of this book was that there seemed to be no plot in the terms that we usually think of plot. Although, I think "a life" is "a plot." It's probably the elementary plot. I came across a quotation of Patrick White, the Australian writer, just about the time when I needed it. He said that he never bothers with plot. He just writes about life "limping along toward death." That made me feel much better, to keep this in my mind.

as interviewed by Jim Schumock

FREDERICK REIKEN
interviewed by Eric Wasserman

⸺◈⸺

A lot of the new plot-driven, pop-culture-saturated fiction today tends to avoid spirituality. Aren't all memorable stories spiritual on some level? One can't help but think that even a blatantly political novel like J.M. Coetzee's *Disgrace* hinges on redemption.

I think *Disgrace* is a great book, and it's because Coetzee is willing to make his protagonist, Lurie, in the end, a human being. Obviously, it's a book with large political dimensions, but what I remember most are those euthanized dogs that he takes such care with as he's loading them onto the conveyer belt. To me, that really was a redemptive moment, and I agree with you that most, if not all, memorable stories hinge on such moments.

Perhaps this is where my writing will always seem "unhip" to a certain type of reader, but I personally could not even sustain the interest necessary to complete a short story if it didn't incorporate deeply emotional and/or transcendent moments. For me, however, the spiritual is usually not tied to religion or anything of that sort. Often it's tied to nature, but sometimes it's tied to a rotting clarinet found in a landfill in the Meadowlands, as was the case in one chapter of *Lost Legends*.

....

ON MAGIC AND CREDULITY

Ann Patchett, interviewed by Sarah Anne Johnson

One reviewer said that "perhaps a struggle with credulity is precisely what Patchett wants to encourage. Improbable relationships can flourish; strange havens do exist. Becoming accustomed to sad endings may be more naive than believing, now and then, in happily ever after." Do you agree with this?

I don't struggle with credulity. I was raised Catholic and things that seem magical to other people do not seem magical to me. I went to Catholic girls' school for twelve years. I went to mass every day. I grew up loving the saints. I grew up reading *Lives of the Saints*. I grew up believing that St. Lucy's eyes were both in her head and on the plate at the same time. I buy that. In the convent outside of the chapel there was a table of holy relics, which were little tiny bits of cloth and little tiny bits of bone from different saints. That was unbelievable to me, that there was this little eighth-inch scrap of a sheet that had touched the Shroud of Turin and wound up in a girls' school in Tennessee. That's phenomenal. The notion that what is real exists only on one plane, which is what you can see with your eyes in your life, is nothing that I've ever bought.

I love this interview with Gabriel García Márquez that I read a long time ago in which he says that people always say he writes magic realism, but he says he doesn't write magic realism. "These things happened in my time. Everyone remembers the beautiful girl who rose up to heaven with the sheets." I totally understand that. I believe that. I have a looser grasp on reality than most. I don't ever sit down and think that I'm going to write magic realism.

ON THE UNEXPLAINED

Dan Chaon, interviewed by Misha Angrist

In several of the stories in *Among the Missing*, we never find out what's become of the missing people: the mother in the title story, the brother/father in "Passengers, Remain Calm," and Rudy Ormson in "Here's a Little Something to Remember Me By." Is it intrinsically interesting that we don't know what happens to them? Or is it that it's more about trying to call our attention to the living and what they have to deal with as their lives continue?

All of the above, I suppose. I mean, I do think that the stuff you never find out is the most interesting. The stories I remember from the newspaper and TV are the ones where we don't know the answer: Sam Sheppard, JonBenet Ramsey. As a kid, I was fascinated with stuff like the Bermuda Triangle. As long as there's no solution, we are haunted and interested, as opposed to clichéd horror stories, where you read or watch and go, "Yep, he's a vampire. He's a serial killer. I get it." From the other end, I'm interested in the way people deal with the inexplicable in their lives. Things that can't be named, can't be nailed down.

Patricia Henley: I'm comfortable with being called a Catholic writer, but I'll bet there are some Catholics who'd rather I not be identified that way, because I am always questioning the Church, challenging it. I am endlessly fascinated with the Church and suppose that it will always be there as a source of stories and characters. The new novel—the one I'm just beginning, set in Baltimore—isn't concerned with spirituality or religion. So far. But I would say that much of my work springs from a concern with ethics and morality.

as interviewed by Andrew Scott

ON GOOD INTENTION

Bob Shacochis, interviewed by Linda B. Swanson-Davies

Cassius, to me, is the only innocent person in *Swimming in the Volcano*. That's why he's the only one who's born in the book, because I don't know that you can establish innocence unless you go back. It was very important to me to make him also rather malformed and even a possibly evil person. He's still that one innocent. He's still the one who never had a choice in the book.... He's carrying that full burden on his shoulders, and he's an innocent guy. Even though, as I said, events make him misshapen morally and spiritually, he's the only one who never gets to have a choice in his life. This is what *Swimming in the Volcano* is all about. It's about forgiveness and it's about goodheartedness and how even a good heart won't save you.

So what will?

I think that the idea is, just simply, the road to hell is paved with good intentions. My book ends the way Janet Reno ended Waco, with her good intentions, saying, "We've got to save those children." Absolutely correct. And those children are just dust in the wind now. Her good intentions didn't save her from tragedy and I don't know that they save anybody from tragedy.

Whenever I go to Europe and talk to Europeans, and I've had occasion to deliver some lectures there, and I suggest to Europeans that Americans are well-intentioned people, they laugh in my face. They don't believe it. But I still sort of do, with a caveat. The caveat is the road to hell is paved with good intentions.

I think perhaps the point is to not waver and not let it plunge you into grief or self-condemnation, to continue to hold on to the principle that you're nourishing in your own good heart, even if it backfires on you. I don't believe good people make the world better, and oftentimes they make the world worse, despite themselves. One bad person can do so much damage that it takes generations to repair. One good person can't counteract that. But all the good people in the world I think keep the world afloat. That's their role. And they shouldn't worry too much about betterment or evolution because—what's changed? What in the world has changed in ten thousand years? I mean, there are textural things that have changed, but, basically, human nature seems to be the same and it seems to be self-destructive.

I think that the role of good people in the world is simply to keep being good despite all the evidence that being good doesn't help. The problems keep rolling on and expanding and recurring, but good people keep the world from spinning down the drain. I'm convinced of that.

Frederick Reiken: I try not to make judgments in my novels, because I think a well-told story will leave a reader with a very clear sense of the consequences of any action, from which they can make judgments for themselves. In the case of the story "The Ocean," I was intentionally presenting certain loaded questions such as, What are a person's moral obligations in the face of life-threatening illness? If you happen to be in remission from leukemia, does that make infidelity okay? But in asking these questions, it was not my intention to propose answers.... What interested me was that it seemed such a complicated situation.

as interviewed by Eric Wasserman

ON DOING THE RIGHT THING
David Long, interviewed by Linda B. Swanson-Davies

Well, I'm a stewer. We worry with the best of them in my family. My mother was a worrier and her dad was a worrier. I think there are people who are not very self-analytical, who float through life. Kato Kaelin comes to mind. But I think most of us dwell on things. You do ponder who you are and how you fit into the greater scheme, and how you can get around your shortcomings, and what ought to matter to you.

In "Cooperstown," there's a line where the main character, who's a former baseball pitcher, says, "It's wrong to squander so much of your time thinking about one thing you did. But if you don't, what kind of man are you then?" It's a paradox, and there's no resolution to it. But I do think that the stories construct a moral universe. People are worrying about whether they've acted in a way that's moral, although they may not phrase it like that.

If they're consistent with whom they wish to be...

Yes, and trying to see what the right thing to do is. That's the problem. A lot of times, you want to do the right thing and you just can't figure out which that is.

....

THE DRAMA OF THE UNKNOWN
Tim O'Brien, interviewed by Jim Schumock

My job, really, as a writer, is to acknowledge puzzlement and bewilderment at such questions and then try to dramatize what we don't know. My interest, as a writer, isn't in answering questions anymore. It never really was. Instead, I'm trying to go after—to open up the boundaries of—what we don't know. I think of the end of *Huckleberry Finn*: We don't know what happens to Huck Finn once he lights out for the Territories. And we don't know what happens to Jake and Lady Brett at the end of *The Sun Also Rises* after they get into that cab. There's mystery in the world, things we just don't know.

There's this quote from Dostoevsky I use in the book, that there are some secrets we'll only tell to our friends, and other secrets we'll only tell to ourselves, and there are other secrets we won't even tell to ourselves. And I think we all understand that, in a way, there are things we just can't quite admit about ourselves. We jerk awake in the middle of the night and remember: How could I do that? And we'll wake up the next day, and life will go on. We've forgotten it.

Wade in *In the Lake of the Woods* is a man who tries to erase his own shame and guilt so that he'll be able to go on in the world, and be loved. And it finally catches up with him. John Wade does what all of us do with mirrors. We remake ourselves with each step of our lives. We become the person we were not ten seconds ago. Every act we make in life, every deed we perform, makes our lives. He finds escape, in a way, behind his mirrors—hiding his hurt, hiding the desperation with which he craves love, hiding his great secret. Beyond that, though, he's using mirrors to make a new self, a successful politician, a man on the rise, a smooth, clever, sandy-haired, handsome politician on his way to the United States Senate and a career that may end anywhere—who knows? And for him, as for all of us, he magnifies his flaw. But I think we all do this in our lives: We try to present a self to the world and to ourselves that's a little better than what we really are.

CHARLES BAXTER

interviewed by Stewart David Ikeda

In your early stories, so much tension is created by the imminent tragedy underlying our lives—one more drink at a party, a wrong turn of the steering wheel, can ruin us: We are always at risk, life seems hopeless. In *Shadow Play*, characters seem to have more self-knowledge and thus more hope.

I think good short-story writers have to go down a lot of dark alleys—spiritually and psychically. You must have nerve to do that, but sometimes it's just what your fate is. Also, I thought at one time that I would have no life as a writer, and many of those early stories are about futures that never arrive—not for the narrator of "Harmony of the World," or for Kate in "Gershwin's Second Prelude."

....

ON POST-INDUSTRIAL LABOR
Dagoberto Gilb, interviewed by Jim Schumock

⇒◆⇐

One of my favorite stories, maybe even my favorite story, in *The Magic of Blood* is "Al, in Phoenix." It starts off with a bad wheel bearing, but evolves into a tale about a struggle to maintain good faith in a possibly bad faith situation.

Oh, I think that's one of my favorite stories, too. I see that story as a great American story. The thing I happen to love about America and about people who work hard is, even as obnoxious and ugly as they seem on the surface, if you look at them you realize how hard they're working. And they're doing their job and it's something I don't think we respect a lot of times, especially with physical [labor]—what we're now looking at as dirty work. We've reached this era where anyone who does anything physical—it seems that means you're not educated. It means something negative. I don't know what happened. I just have a totally different attitude. I think right now in this country we're setting it up so that people who don't want to sit in front of a computer screen won't have anything to do. There's nothing wrong with these jobs, but it's not for everyone. But I guess we're in this post-industrial period, this new era, where we're losing the respect for people who build or fix. I just don't feel this way. Al is a perfect representative of these people. He is just working and takes his job seriously and does it in an honorable way, even if he isn't the most personable guy. He takes his work seriously. He sticks to it.

All day and night until it's finished.

Until it's finished. Actually, it's based on a real experience I had. I watched this mechanic doing this and I just had to write a story about it.

....

JOYCE THOMPSON
interviewed by Linda B. Swanson-Davies

In several of your stories I notice an absence of safety. I remember in a particular story, the line, "If my father is strong, am I safe?"

I've been thinking about that a lot lately. Actually, in the story, it goes through a progression. It starts out with the premise, If my father is strong, I am safe. Then, If my father is *not* strong, am I safe? If I am strong, am I safe? Am I strong? I suspect possibly that the process of liberation, a kind of ritual liberation, is something every child has to go through, but it may be particularly important to the female child to work through these steps.

I was just thinking that I'm one of those weird people who is rarely afraid on a dark street or in a bad neighborhood, but my sense, I think, has always been of home as the dangerous place. The intimate setting is the most dangerous. The place in which we are anonymous, we are much safer.

ELIZABETH MCCRACKEN
interviewed by Sarah Anne Johnson

———◈◈———

You said in an interview after *The Giant's House*: "I think our lives are constantly transformed by love. Not just by what we think of as romantic love, you know, love with the person you sleep with. But that our daily lives are constantly shaped by the people we love, our friends, our families." How does that belief influence your fiction?

Although I failed to do this, one of the things that I intended to do with *The Giant's House* was write about non-romantic love. *The Giant's House* was not a romance in the early versions, at least not consciously. My readers said, "You've got to face up to this. She loves the guy." I wrote *The Giant's House* in eight months, then revised it for two and a half years, and a lot of the revision was developing that romance in a natural way. I'd start at the beginning and work my way through the book, bringing it a little closer every time.

. . . .

ON VOYEURISM AND INTROSPECTION
Siri Hustvedt
interviewed by Jennifer Levasseur and Kevin Rabalais

———◈◈———

Both of your novels begin with characters watching someone.

I didn't notice the similarity until later. The voyeurism in *The Enchantment of Lily Dahl* is fully carried out in a way that it is not in *The Blindfold*. Lily watching Ed at the beginning of the book leads to an intricate network of people looking at and spying on each other and then interpreting what they have seen, often wrongly.

The two men Iris sees across the airshaft from her apartment never become part of the book's plot. Their presence is atmospheric and erotic, part of Iris's loneliness and longing.

Art itself is a form of voyeurism, of course. You have to stand back in order to see. I'm not plagued by voyeuristic fantasies, and yet it keeps coming up in my work—watching, looking, fascination.

Lily and Iris are both looking out and introspective in the novels.

Introspection is not separate from the drama of looking. I really do believe human beings are formed by and through others. If you lock a child in a closet early in his life, he will never be normal and never have a normal relationship to language. We find ourselves in the eyes of another person. There is no self-consciousness without the other. You are yourself, but you are always also the other looking at yourself. In an important way, we are always doubled.

LOUIS BEGLEY

interviewed by Robert Birnbaum

The care with which you write makes it so obvious that, as you say in another context, there is no Hamburger Helper in your stories. My sense of you is that the precision of your description well serves the focus of your attention—social interaction and manners. Something that is perhaps a throwback to earlier times.

I do write with some care and I rewrite compulsively.

Some care?

Well, yes, by the time I have finished I think I have trimmed away everything that is not essential. I have a very difficult time really, dealing with the question of subject matter of my books. Because it seems to me so very natural and uncontrived. I don't set out to illustrate this kind of manners, or that kind of manners. I am in love with Hemingway's observation that when he wants to send a message he goes to the post office. I don't send messages. So you see I write themes that interest me.

In *Shipwreck*, the theme is betrayal. Betrayal in a marriage, what that does to the betrayer and to the person who is betrayed, and also to the third person in this trio—this could be equally applicable to an adulterous woman as an adulterous man. So that is my theme, and the point of departure in this novel is actually its ending. I wrote the ending before I got going on the beginning except for the first scene, the very first scene. I knew the scene in the café, John North putting his hand on the shoulder of the nameless narrator (but in fact listener) and says, "I have a story to tell you I have never told before." I knew what the theme was and what I wanted to accomplish. I knew the ending, and for the rest I simply used those materials that seemed to come to hand that I know that I am able to handle.

Sure, if you were a different person and had grown up in Wyoming and went to the University of Texas you would be writing about something else. . . .

Yes.

I get that point. I am not suggesting that there is anything inauthentic.

Nor is it a philosophical position that I want to write about this kind of person or that kind of person.

I know you wouldn't be writing about crack addicts and homicide cops à la Richard Price.

Right. I don't know them. The only addicts I know are rather desolate children of friends. It's something that has been dogging me, this question of Why do I write about this, why do I write about that? Why don't I keep on writing exactly the same thing that I wrote about in *Wartime Lies*, my first novel? The childhood of a little boy in Poland during the German occupation, a noble subject, great theme, the inhumanity of the Germans, the inhumanity of Catholic Poles, cosmic suffering, injustice, etc. Well, I have written that book. I cannot write the same book over and over. So I write what involves me as I go on.

....

ON GUILT AND SUPERSTITION
Mary Morrissy, interviewed by Ana Callan

One element in *A Lazy Eye* that fascinated me was superstition. Some of your characters seem to make pacts with the universe, or even with the devil, for want of a better word. In your last story, the final sentence in the entire book reads, "There was a curse on her now." That's a really chilling ending—after a gripping read, to be left with that. I'm wondering if that placement was deliberate, whether you wanted this as your last word.

I didn't consciously decide that that was going to be my last word, although I did decide it would be the last story in the collection, partly because it's longer and I arranged the stories so that the big confession story would be in the middle. In a way, all of them are confessional in mode, and also they're confessional in the sense that they're all about guilt. I mean, these characters are guilty for things they have done or guilty for things they haven't, or not guilty where they should be! Like the two sisters who abandon the baby. There's no sense of guilt in that story.

Yes, that's where you would expect it.

Then you have the girl in the moment of downfall who confesses to something she's not guilty of, and you have the teenage babysitter who goes for a baby with a pin and the curse that's on her is that she's going to feel guilty about that for the rest of her life. Everything after that is seen as retribution for that act of terrorism. That's partly Catholicism.

And a very Irish notion.

Yes, and also the idea that you can bargain your way out of it. Like the woman whose father is ill. She feels as guilty as if she had murdered the young man in the war, even though she hadn't. She had just said to God, "Please take him rather than my father." It is a mixture of perhaps pagan superstition overlaid with Catholicism. Again, it's very hard to get away from Catholicism, but it's a bit like the bog. It has been overdone in Irish writing, too. But the thing is that it's implicit in almost anyone who's been brought up as a Catholic. You may stop being a Catholic but...

It doesn't go away.

It doesn't stop there, no. So you probably find in *Mother of Pearl*—it being set in 1950s Ireland—that there's a lot of explicit Catholicism in it that's kind of inevitable.

Colum McCann: People are sort of surprised that I have gone from *This Side of Brightness*, which was about homeless people in the subway tunnels and the people who built the tunnels, to writing about a gay Russian ballet dancer. And it does sound like an enormous leap, but in truth it's not all that huge. I'm still talking about people who are on the periphery.

as interviewed by Robert Birnbaum

ON LIMITATION

Charles Baxter, interviewed by Stewart David Ikeda

I don't think that there's anything intrinsically more interesting about lives that are seemingly without limits than lives that have them. The proof of that is Chekhov, who is regularly and vigorously interested in the material and social and spiritual conditions that define a life. We might now say that those characters are trapped, but what interested Chekhov was the little side door in every life through which someone escapes the real sense of the word *trap*. It's very often true that his characters are immobilized, or feel themselves immobilized, but it's as often true that the result of Chekhov's observation of them is a sense of the grace—almost the redemption—of those lives by virtue of something that Chekhov has seen or that they have seen.

I've been interested in trying to get into stories a sense of what your life feels like when you recognize what the limits on that life are. To some extent, it's like discovering what your fate is. This may not be such a popular topic in America—de Tocqueville said it's a topic Americans never liked to accept—but it's one of the matters that I think about. The trouble is, it's not very glamorous, it's not immediately compelling—a story about someone who is not interested in destroying the limits.

....

HISTORY AND NATIONAL IDENTITY
Russell Banks, interviewed by Rob Trucks

There's been a recent trend toward the large, historical work. Thomas Pynchon, Don DeLillo, and yourself, three white, male, Northeastern writers in their fifties, have all published large, historical novels in the past couple of years.

You've put your finger on an interesting phenomenon, really. A number of novelists in their fifties are writing ambitious, historical novels, and that's of some interest to me, and I think that it probably has to do with a couple of factors. Something that's true, certainly, for the three you named, and you could add another half-dozen. Charles Johnson. Jane Smiley's got a novel coming out right now that's about the Kansas wars. John Wideman had a historical novel a year or two ago set in Philadelphia, in the antebellum era.

You could come up with a number of writers in my generation who are writing historical fiction, and I have a feeling this is in response to a culture-wide mindset—or a culture-wide confusion might be a better way to say it—a culture-wide confusion about what it means to be American. And for a novelist, that question will send you back in time.

In the late twentieth century we are extremely conscious of ourselves, as a people, of being hyphenated. We're Asian-Americans, African-Americans, Euro-Americans, Native Americans. We're hyphenated. To the left of the hyphen we know what we are—Euro, Afro, Asian, or whatever. What we don't know is what really is embodied to the right of the hyphen. What does that mean? What do we share? Why bother to call ourselves something-American anyhow?

It's historically true, at least for Americans, that when people are unsure about what it is to be themselves, their novelists start writing historical fiction. In the 1830s and '40s it was not that clear what it meant to be American. Fifty years after the revolution you could ask, Why aren't we British? Well, politically we're not, but really, Why aren't we British? And so Hawthorne writes *The Scarlet Letter* and you have Cooper and you have Irving and the major novelists, both South and North, of that era, writing historical fiction. And I think there's something like that going on now. There's a certain kind of confusion and lack of confidence in what it means to be American; and novelists are essentially, at bottom, mythmakers—mythmakers with regard to social identity, the tribe's identity. A storyteller is basically creating, always, a myth about what it is to be whoever you are in this tribe. Why are we in this tribe and living in this corner of the planet instead of some other?

....

PAUL THEROUX
interviewed by Michael Upchurch

Is there a connecting thread that you're aware of in your work? In writing *Millroy the Magician*, did you ever stop and say, "Oh, I've done this before, but from another angle, and here we go again with this particular obsession"?

I think so. Here's what I think is a connecting thread—or not a connecting thread, but a situation I seem to write about a lot: a man taking up with a rather innocent woman, a girl often, or a person taking up with a person who's innocent. I don't seem to have equal relationships. I don't seem to have strong man/strong woman.

Why do I do that? Because *I* haven't had relationships like that. Why, I wonder, do I return to that a lot? I think I write about it from all the different points of view, but certainly the old person and the young person, the master/student, the Svengali/Trilby figure, is something that I have returned to again and again. Another thing that I return to a lot is a fear of death—not always as death but as extinction—because obviously it must upset me.

Melissa Pritchard: My characters are on missions to get at the truth, whatever the truth is. Their ultimate challenge is to understand life. When they're on a mission of this sort, they can't stay within convention very long. They may eventually return to convention, but only after they've explored beyond it. To return home, they must first leave it. To truly learn, they must make mistakes. My characters are on journeys, and their travels take them to actual foreign countries or foreign realms of the mind. They are strangers visiting places they've never been. I want them to take risks, to be confronted by temptation, to touch the forbidden, to break taboos.

as interviewed by Leslie A. Wootten

ON HAPPY ENDINGS

Peter Carey, interviewed by Kevin Bacon and Bill Davis

If you're an American and you arrive in Australia, the first thing you'll feel, I think, is how familiar it is. You've flown twenty-two hours and yet you don't seem so far from home. And yet the two cultures are profoundly different. We have a very un-American history, and will tell ourselves very un-American narratives. Your country tells success stories; ours does not.

I know this is a great simplification, so please excuse me. On the one hand, you have a country that begins with a first fleet of convicts, while the other country's first fleet is religious refugees. There's a major difference. Australia is basically an irreligious country. Certainly we can have a prime minister who says he doesn't believe in God. I think it would be impossible for you to have a president who said that. Also, the experiences of our early pioneers were harsher than yours. Basically, we went west and found death. Our great stories are about people who were lost, who couldn't find food or water, and died. Your stories tend to be about success. Your people went west to wealth and success and so on—not that there wasn't tragedy along the way. So it seems to me that generally our narratives are to do with failure in a way that yours are not. We're suspicious of success, and I think you can look at this also in relationship to our convict past—this underclass group and its feelings about success: When somebody leaves the group and is successful, that's a betrayal for us.

All our heroes, all our great stories are about failure. The military thing that we celebrate most is ANZAC Day, which is about Gallipoli, a peninsula in Turkey where our young men were sent by Winston

Churchill in a doomed military venture where they died—just died and died and died and died. That's our great story. A total defeat, the whole thing. There was no point to it; they landed in the wrong place and they shouldn't have been there anyway.

Do you think you could write a success story?

Pretty tough. It does appear to be difficult for me to do. I was telling my wife my plans for the new book, and she was sitting there listening and nodding, and I could see that she thought it was interesting. I got to a certain point and she said, "Well, don't tell me what happens now. They die, right?"

So I said, "I can't help it."

This is where my personal condition does, in some way, echo, through chance perhaps, the national one. I find it hard to imagine happy endings.

THE LITERARY-CULTURAL CONNECTION
Charles Baxter, interviewed by Linda B. Swanson-Davies

Because I've been on tour with *The Feast of Love*, and because I'm now getting reviews of the book, I've been thinking about the reactions that some people have had to it. One of the things I've noticed is that in the generation of people who are in their twenties and early thirties, the word *love* is almost embarrassing, and I've been trying to think about why that is true. One interviewer said to me, "You don't really think, do you, that people talk about love anymore?" She was about twenty-five. Now, that comment was one that has set off my mind to search for a reason why the comment should exist in the first place.

There was another review of *The Feast of Love*, in a little magazine called *The Barcelona Review*, which said that the title was dreadful. And the reviewer went on to say that it's a dreadful title because no one, neither a man nor a woman, would dare carry a book with the title *The Feast of Love* onto the subway. The sense of it being that it's too old fashioned, it sounds like a romance novel. I don't know how my mind is organized. All I know is that at various times in my life I have certain preoccupations, certain things that I can't help thinking about. And right now I can't help thinking about why it may be the case that we've come to a point, culturally, where a title like *The Feast of Love* could be embarrassing to people. So that's what I'm trying to think through. Whether it's because we have a culture of irony now and of cool emotional responses …

There's a writer named Vivian Gornick, who wrote a book called *The End of the Novel of Love*, and she said in her book that people don't expect love to supply the meaning of their lives anymore, and they don't read novels about love in order to find that kind of meaning. It's an interesting idea that I think may very probably be wrong, but it's an interesting idea all the same.

These questions have a lot to do with the kinds of stories people tell. And the kinds of stories they want to read or think about. I mean, it's one thing to say you shouldn't be talking about love in an abstract way. But it's another thing if you're teaching a class and someone comes in and says you can't write this kind of story anymore. Nobody will read it; no one will care about it. So these are not just literary questions. Literary questions spill out into cultural matters, into theoretical matters. They're all connected.

Do you have ideas about trends in writing that you think we might be moving toward now?

[When he was an old man,] the composer Virgil Thomson was asked where he thought music was going, and Thomson replied, I don't care where it's going, I want to know where it's just been. Though you're tempting me to become a prophet of sorts. I know that recently we have been through a period of fiction in which there's been, for a lot of reasons, a lot of attention paid to abusive behavior and to shame. You have to ask yourself if you have [social] trends that lead to stories about abusive fathers, abusive relationships, stories that are very concerned with obsessive-compulsive or addictive behaviors. I'm sure you see stories like this come into *Glimmer Train* all the time. What is the next stage after that going to be? And I will tell you, honestly, I do not know. I *wish* I knew. I would like to say, Oh, the kinds of stories that I'm writing would be the sorts of stories that we may see next, but I have absolutely no certainty of that. I don't know whether I'm in a vanguard or a rearguard. Whether I'm at the front or the middle or the back.

ANDREA BARRETT

interviewed by Sarah Anne Johnson

Your most recent three books are concerned with the quest for scientific discovery during the nineteenth century and the complications, both difficulties and joys, that quest can bring to relationships. What draws you to this theme and this period?

It was such an interesting period both scientifically and in terms of exploration. It's an easy time and an easy place to make metaphoric sense from. If you're drawn to the shape of the journey anyway, and I am—the journey through our lives, the journeys we all make all the time—then that particular time and place is very rich in interesting examples. People made astonishing physical journeys for such complex reasons, some of which we now deplore, some of which we now admire.

ON FAITH AND VOCATION

Mark Salzman, interviewed by Linda B. Swanson-Davies

I was intrigued from the start by the idea of the predicament that this nun would have of trying to decide what is the right thing to do: What does God want, as opposed to what do I want personally? Is my relationship to God authentic or is it distorted? Is it based on my own selfish fantasies that I'm using to rationalize what's clearly a pathology, or is my test here to determine if I'm willing to sacrifice even my physical health in order to have experiences that bring understanding and joy to so many? During the whole time I was writing [*Lying Awake*], I felt that that character was an exotic, so to speak. Very, very distant from my own experience. I felt that there was no real direct connection between this character and myself. I was intrigued by that problem and felt that was one of the reasons that it was so hard to write. In all the other books, there was something directly related to a conflict in my life that I could work into the story, and the resolution was a way of resolving dissonance in my own life, whereas this seemed to be an exotic problem. I thought, That's fine, writers are supposed to be able to do that. You're supposed to be able to move beyond yourself.

It was only at the very end, after at least five complete rewrites—there was nothing salvageable of the book, and I was so discouraged and so upset because I'd gone through so much and was worried that maybe I had simply written a bad book, that it was time to let go of it. But I didn't want to. I couldn't. I had to figure out what was missing. I remember thinking, This main character is a woman who's devoted herself to a search for God, to living by faith as opposed to by reason. Now, I've never had a religious experience, and I think of myself as someone who lives according to reason, and so it seemed to me that she and I were obviously very different people. But then toward the end of all of this, I asked myself, What have I dedicated *my* life to? I've dedicated my life to art, to writing. What reason, what objective reason, can I give to justify this dedication that I have to writing, as opposed to, say, all the good I could be doing in the world instead of sitting at home and writing? I have no scientific evidence to suggest that art is worthwhile. My life is as much hinged on faith as hers. I believe that art is worthwhile. I believe there is value in trying to be a good person as opposed to being entirely selfish, all those things. But I have no proof that any of that benefits humanity.

That's what the story was really about all along: It's her struggle to maintain faith in her vocation. It's not about her struggle to maintain faith in God—that's not an issue. It's her faith in her vocation, that she's doing the right thing. And that's exactly what I was going through, struggling to maintain faith in my chosen vocation, writing. My last three books have not done very well, and, getting near forty years old and wanting to start a family, I've had to do a lot of deep questioning. My confidence was being shaken, wondering if this was really the smartest thing to be doing. Why did I keep writing books about nichey subjects that only a small number of people can enjoy? Should I be trying to write something that would appeal to a broader audience?

So when I saw that there was this connection between that character and me, that it was a struggle to maintain faith in what you really feel compelled, driven from within, to do, I realized that I'm not that different from religious people. That was a huge revelation for me. In the end, it made me realize the value of what I'm doing, that in spite of difficulty and discouragement, in spite of maybe not getting a lot of response, there is something more important than that: this inner need to try to express something truthful, authentic. I'm grateful to be engaged in that search. I had taken it for granted before, I think.

....

Robert Olen Butler: I'm a Vietnam novelist the way Monet is a lily-pad painter. As with anyone who aspires to art, I write books in order to articulate a deep vision I have of the order behind the apparent chaos of life on the planet Earth. And it's a vision of order that I don't really understand until I create the art object. Discovery is part of the essential process of art. For such a writer then to be called a Midwest proletarian novelist or a Vietnam novelist or now a Southern novelist, all of which labels could apply to me, is to miss that fundamental point. The regionalism, the settings, the kinds of characters that I use are simply vehicles into some deeper concerns about the human condition.

as interviewed by Jim Schumock

ON VIETNAM

Tim O'Brien, interviewed by Jim Schumock

Why did Vietnam spawn such a tremendous body of powerful litera-ture, and Korea almost nothing?

Well, I think, in a way, that Vietnam represented not just a war, but a cultural watershed that Korea didn't. I think of the music that came out of that era; I think of the art, the sculpting, and paint-ing, a monument like The Wall [Vietnam Veterans Memorial]—a beautiful piece of work. Beyond that, I think it was a spiritual wa-tershed for the country. We went into Vietnam with the afterglow of World War II still there: America the White Knight, America the Potent, America the Quick Draw. And we came out of the war like a ninety-two-pound weakling, or feeling that way. We'd lost that sense of efficacy and potency in the world.

And I think we're still sliding down the back slope of Vietnam in a lot of ways. The repercussions of that war remain with us. The music's still with us. I'm writing about it. Robert Stone's writing. Tom McGuane. People who grew up in that era in which cyni-cism mixed with idealism—a very peculiar combination. And we were all idealistic—ending wars and making the world a better place—and yet at the same time, many of us turned a little cynical, a little bitter through the experience.

And twenty-five years after the war [in 1995], my mind, as a human being and as a writer, has settled around the problem of love. I think a lot of the things we do in the world, the ways we behave, have to do with the human craving for love: the jobs we take, the things we say to people in elevators, going on radio programs, writing books. At least, in my case—and I think for a lot of others—love drives us in ways we can't begin to fathom. And it's slowly becoming a major theme in my work.

....

ON CHOICE AND CONSEQUENCE
Chitra Banerjee Divakaruni
interviewed by Sarah Anne Johnson

⟫◆⟪

In *The Mistress of Spices*, Tilo, the one person who is purely Indian and segregated from America behind the walls of her shop, gives up her powers to become an ordinary Indian-American citizen. Do you think this says that the Indian must give in to integration at some point?

What was right for her, was right for her and not necessarily for everyone. Personally, I believe that if one has made the decision to come to this country, one cannot then create an artificial cultural ghetto in which to barricade oneself. What's the point then, of coming out of their culture?

I feel very strongly that some process of integration must happen, between your view of yourself and your culture to the larger culture. At the same time, you can use what you consider valuable. You don't want to give up the wrong things, or hold onto the wrong things. Nor do you want to promote old values that are not positive ones. Integration does allow us a wonderful opportunity to take the best of both cultures, and it would be a pity not to do that.

It's interesting, too, that if Tilo steps outside the walls of her shop onto the streets of Oakland, chaos will come to whomever she is in contact with.

What does this say about the purely Indian mixing in with America? What does it say that she can't resist leaving her shop?

She is responding to a life impulse, which is to move on and not to stagnate. If she stays inside the door, the status quo is preserved, but she is stagnating as a human being. She is responding to a very necessary impulse. In terms of the old culture and the "promises" made through the old culture, stepping outside is a taboo, and she has to pay a price for it. For all our choices, even the ones that are important and positive and necessary, we do have to pay a price.

What drew you to the idea of this woman having to choose between an ordinary life and the extraordinary life of the Mistress of Spices?

That part comes from a number of eastern and western legends where healers have to give up the ordinary joys of life in order to keep their powers. Many times they have to give up romantic or sexual relationships.

The Indian-American immigrants in this story suffer a variety of dilemmas as a result of cultural differences or an inability to reconcile the Indian and American cultures within themselves. For example, Geeta's grandfather, who causes many problems for his family because of his inability to accept their Americanized ways.

The word *American* can mean different things to different people. For many people, it's a wonderful word, to others it's a bad word—"You've become American." It depends on how secure you are with your own identity. One always responds to change from that place in one's life—if you're secure in your identity, the change doesn't bother you. But when you feel dis-ease like the grandfather is feeling—he's lost a whole way of life, just as Mrs. Dutta has lost a whole way of life—and in order to have family, both the grandfather and Mrs. Dutta have had to give up community. That's very difficult.

On the one hand I have a great deal of compassion with their struggles, and on the other hand, I realize that it can cause a lot of tension and bitterness within a family and ultimately break up a family and cause communication breakdowns between the generations.

....

ON LONELINESS, SOLITUDE, AND GRACE
Roy Parvin, interviewed by Linda B. Swanson-Davies

In your stories you have many instances where there is a deep sense of loss. You communicate that very clearly; you probably know some about that. And I wonder if you'd mind if I ask you about it.

That's fine. Toward the end of *The Loneliest Road in America,* my father died—he contracted that Lou Gehrig's disease. And one story in the book is autobiographical. It's a very brief story that started out being a letter to myself. It's the story "Between Knowing and Dying." That really hung like a shadow over a lot of my work, although I think that I had a sense of loss even before that.

I am drawn to solitary pursuits. That's the life of the writer. I don't teach. I'm a full-time writer. I'm drawn to that, but I also find that it's fairly dangerous. You can fall into it. A story can become, if you can't lift yourself out of it, a pit for a writer—something that you cannot get your career beyond. I thought that if I did not write "In the Snow Forest" that my career would not have moved forward. I love the solitary part of writing, but it's a double-edged thing, something that can turn on you at times. It certainly has turned on me sometimes. I know that my writing seems like it's a cry to the world to say, Hear me, listen to me. My characters tend to be desperate because it comes from a desperate place in me. I think that there's a sense of loss, the feeling of never having connected with the world, which I think most people have. For me it seems to be a very extreme need to connect in the world, and knowing that I'm probably not going to do it as well in person as I do on the page. And so I think there's that tension that exists in the work because of that.

I also tend to like dark things, but, you know, it's funny, I don't think my stories are necessarily dark. I think they're filled with grace, and I think that that's what equalizes it. If they were just unrelentingly dark, unremittingly dark, you wouldn't walk away and feel like perhaps you've grown. I want to tell stories of people having met something head on, not blinking and continuing on in their lives. Perhaps being diminished in some way, but having grown in another way.

Mark Salzman: I seem to always find myself thinking and writing about people who are confronted by the gap, the terrible gap, between who they really are and who they wish they could be, who they thought they would be at a point in their life. People who feel that no realistic, practical steps they take toward trying to reach that goal are going to get them there. It's obvious; it's hopeless. They're never going to reach the ideal. So what are they going to do? Are they going to just give in to despair? They've got to find a reason to keep moving.

as interviewed by Linda B. Swanson-Davies

ON FAMILIAL DEBT

Chitra Banerjee Divakaruni
interviewed by Sarah Anne Johnson

In *Sister of My Heart*, Sudha's father misrepresented his true identity and took Anju's father on a dangerous ruby-hunting expedition that cost them their lives. Sudha believes that it's her duty to repay the family debt to the Chaterjees, so when she learns that her elopement with her beloved will threaten Anju's match, she gives up her love and settles instead for an arranged marriage. What drew you to this idea of a child inheriting the karmic debt or unresolved burdens of the parent?

I wasn't consciously doing that, I don't think, but rather, I was exploring this idea of how the past affects the world of the present, and how your understanding of the past can make you feel about who you are today. In our Indian culture, family is so important and the idea of family debt is a very important cultural idea. One of the things that children do for their parents is to repay their debts. This is considered honorable. In this case, it's not a physical debt, but an emotional one. I hope that I've portrayed this ironically. I hope there are points where the reader is thinking, *No, no, don't do it*. I was definitely ambivalent about Sudha's choice.

There's also the larger concept of the woman's role that I'm working with. All over the world, women are taught or brainwashed or conditioned into feeling that they have to be the ones who take care of others, the ones who give up things. Sudha's behavior is an extreme form of that, and I wanted the reader to feel that. On the one hand it's very noble, but on the other hand, you just don't want her to do it. You don't want her to think that she has to make this sacrifice in order to be a good woman. For so many centuries this is what women have been told. I wanted to fight that.

....

ON FAMILIAL RELATIONSHIPS

Jayne Anne Phillips, interviewed by Sarah Anne Johnson

⇒⊷⇐

Many of the stories in *Fast Lanes* are preoccupied with specific family events that shape or permanently shade characters' lives.

Family is endlessly fascinating. It's the psychic map that we use all our lives. We start out with this first pattern, much of it unconscious in the beginning. The mother and father, or the absence of the mother or father, or the people who stand in for the mother or father, are these colossal figures in the beginning, like the sun and the moon. They have that mythic power. They have very much to do with how we first see ourselves, with how we relate to men and women, with what we want, with what we don't have, and with what we have to provide for ourselves.

Then, as we get a little older and identity starts forming, it's always formed in relationship to siblings, to place, to the culture we're in, and all of that is reflected again in that microcosm of family. It has to do with identity, too. Each of us is separated from one another in these separate identities, and we only ever really overcome that in certain moments: in sexual moments, in moments of passion—that is, physical passion—athletics, anything that you forget time while you're doing it and lose boundaries. That blood connection to another person is something you feel with family. We inherit from parents and others not only physical characteristics and mannerisms, but unresolved dilemmas, unresolved losses, dreams that didn't happen. All these things are subliminally communicated inside families and relationships. That's why myths are so powerful. They have to do with identity and who we are in relation to the people who made us. So writing about family is like writing about weather—it's such a big part of the world.

....

SEARCHING FOR AND CREATING MEANING
Andrea Barrett, interviewed by Sarah Anne Johnson

⟹◈⟸

You often write about the inner conflicts and urges that drive people to search for things not known before, and, equally important, to capture what they find. Zeke is a great example of this, and Erasmus, in a different way, but even Max in "Servants of the Map," and other characters. What draws you to this obsession?

I don't know that I have an easy answer for that, almost surely because it is connected to something deep in me. I don't have full self-knowledge any more than anyone else does, and that's why I can't answer that easily. Partly, the material just interests me. It's always dramatic when someone's searching for something unknown. There are always dramatic and metaphoric possibilities when someone is on such a search, so naturally a novelist is going to be drawn to those things. But it's also related to something in me.

Many of the frustrations and challenges your characters face remind me of artistic frustrations.

I think that's part of the link. Artistic discovery, the journey each of us makes as an artist, is nowhere near as dramatic or interesting or heroic, but it is a journey and it can be a hardship and a trial. One is tested in certain ways. There are parallels, even if they're goofy parallels. We're sitting in a comfortable chair in a warm room and nobody's making us do this. So why do I think those things are analogous? Yet clearly something about them *feels* analogous.

In "Servants of the Map," Max discovers his passion for botany and hopes he can make some contribution that will matter, that will save him from the futility of mapmaking. "All he will leave behind are maps, which will be merged with all the other maps, on which he will be nameless: small contributions to the great Atlas of India, which has been growing for almost forty years." What draws you to his desperation to find something worthwhile to do that will distinguish him?

Because I feel desperate, too. We all feel that. Everyone is struggling to find something that makes meaning, that makes sense out of our lives. It's not easy for anyone.

....

ON LIFE AND DEATH
Robert Wrigley, interviewed by Jim Schumock

The narrators of some of your poems, as in "The Bramble" and "Majestic," come across dead people. They seem very interested in the attitude of the dead. What interests you in this?

I have friends who kid me all the time. They maintain that whenever I get stuck in a poem I put a dead body in. I think the reason it attracts me so much, particularly in this book, is the moment of death is a moment of being between worlds. That's supposedly when we enter into what we have of an afterlife. I'm interested in examining that, not what it must be like to go through a near-death experience. That's not what interests me. I'm just contemplating what it's like to look at death, to consider it as a part of life.

....

PHYSICAL CONFINEMENT

Mark Salzman, interviewed by Linda B. Swanson-Davies

≡◆≡

I found it very interesting that you work with kids who are forced to submit to lifelong confinement and to the will of other people, often-times because they have forced their own will on other people in one way or another, and that *Lying Awake* is about nuns who have chosen confinement and submission. You have looked at that sort of thing from a couple different points of view.

There's a wonderful story I have to tell you. One day it occurred to me that I was writing this book about someone who had volun-tarily submitted to live under almost the same circumstances as the kids in prison. They live in cells. They wear uniforms, you know, it's unchanging. They take a vow of silence when they walk. They walk in silence just like the kids. Everything is orderly, ritualistic, and so one day I said to the kids, I'm writing a story about a group of people, and this is how they live. And I even brought some pictures from a male monastery. The monks walking in single file. Their cells bare, just like these kids'. I said these people voluntarily chose to live like this, and here you are; it's imposed on you, and for you it's hell, and for these people it's the opportunity of a lifetime. What do you think about that? There was a long pause. This one kid, he was so smart—he had been labeled dumb because he had some kind of dyslexia so he couldn't read or write—his name was Dale

Jones. And Dale goes, Does the prioress have pepper spray? And that was the difference. I mean he just went right to the absolute core. Oh, man, that was great.

But the question of why that seems to fascinate me—even when I was a little kid I was absolutely taken with the idea of being an astronaut, because I love the idea of the enclosure, and so I made my own little box, and I had a periscope that I'd made so I could watch TV. I had a timer so that every day I could increase by several minutes the amount of time I could stand being in this hot little box. And then with meditation, you know, there's an element of that—the idea of trimming down everything, bringing down stimuli so that hopefully you are able to just appreciate the simple fact of awareness itself. I guess I've always been drawn to the idea of trying to trim away rather than add on. Hoping that by trimming away you then can focus a little bit more, and not let so much of life slip through our fingers. Because when we're distracted doing two things at once, the days just go by. I think we all have this desire to grab life, grab each moment so that when our time comes, we can at least say about our lives, I didn't live just the length of my life, I lived the width of it, too. That appeals to me. Has always appealed to me.

ON CULTURAL CONFINEMENT
Ha Jin, interviewed by Sarah Anne Johnson

One theme in your work is the man striving to define himself amidst a society that wants to constrain him to a rigid role that does not necessarily match his inner experience. For instance, in *Ocean of Words*, the story "Love in the Air" describes the plight of a soldier who falls in love with a civilian, which is not allowed. To make matters worse, she's of another class, yet he pursues his love. Also, Jian Wan, the narrator in *The Crazed*, struggles to understand what he wants for himself in the midst of a society that wants to define him.

There is always confinement in China for every individual. They have to find a way to survive and develop and grow as a human being. For me, the theme of confinement is not a very conscious thing. It's just a part of the story. And it's everywhere, inside, outside. It's part of Chinese society, the culture, the customs. It cannot be avoided. It's present in everything, and so it seeps into my work.

Edwidge Danticat: We live in a world where people float between borders. When you come from such different circumstances and you end up in the United States, it's like space travel. Within hours you're on a different planet. The other effect of migration is that you have these extreme separations and families having to come together again and new communities being created. These are things that have always fascinated me. And because I had that experience of being separated from my parents for eight years, and rejoining a family where my youngest brothers didn't know me at all, those were things that I was working out in my own life. It all informs what I write about.

as interviewed by Sarah Anne Johnson

CHAPTER

4

PLACE AND SETTING

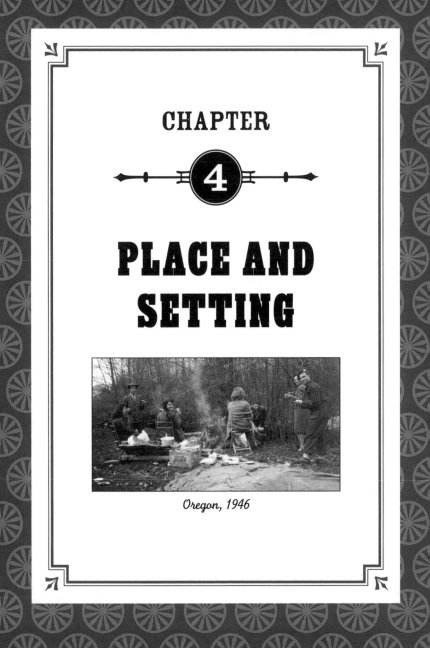

Oregon, 1946

Frederick Reiken: Place is where everything seems to start for me as a novelist. Before I can even begin to think about my characters, they usually have to be attached to a specific place, which is the first step in activating my imagination. In fact, a strong sense of place is crucial to my writing process, precisely because it gives me something to attach imaginatively to long before I know all the quirks and habits of my characters.

as interviewed by Eric Wasserman

ALICE MATTISON
interviewed by Barbara Brooks

New Haven seems to have given you plenty of material.

New Haven is a small city, but not too small. All sorts of connections occur here. The city gave me a place to write about that I could wrap my brain around, but it didn't occur to me to say stories were set in New Haven when I started writing them, although I imagined them here.

The first story of mine that was accepted by *The New Yorker* was called "The Knitting," about a young woman from New York who visits her sister's family. Roger Angell, who accepted the story and became my editor, suggested that I make clear where the story takes place, because it makes a difference whether she's come ten miles or two hundred miles or two thousand miles. He suggested we say it was New Haven. I said I didn't think it was a good idea to set a story in New Haven, because people just associate New Haven with Yale. He said, "I have a friend who lives in New Haven who has nothing to do with Yale." Which was illogical but wonderful. So we set it in New Haven, with the names of real New Haven streets. That was an incredibly important moment for me. I'd been convinced in an instant. I immediately wrote a story called "New Haven" and I've written about it on and off ever since.

YOUR OWN PATCH OF EARTH
Kent Haruf, interviewed by Jim Nashold

I grew up in the northeast corner of Colorado in the high plains and short-grass prairie. I lived out there until I was eleven or twelve. My father was a Methodist preacher and we moved around in towns all with a population of two thousand or less. The towns were named Holyoke, Wray, and Yuma. I lived there again when I was an adult, and I taught school out in that part of the state for eight years in the most rural school district in Colorado. It's a part of the country and part of the world which I call home, and which I have an emotional and almost reverent response to when I reenter it. It's not pretty, but in my view it's beautiful and you have to know how to look at it. Most people drive across it as fast as they can to get to Denver or the mountains, but if you grew up there it feels like home. There's plenty to see. It sort of teaches you how to slow down, how to pay attention.

You've mentioned that you used Faulkner's idea of taking your own patch of earth you grew up on, and concentrating on that, and never being able to exhaust it.

Very much so.

How did you come up with the idea for your first published novel, The Tie That Binds?

My older brother, Verne, had a ranch in northeast Colorado, and one time I was riding around with him in his pickup, and we'd been out checking some cattle. He mentioned that a quarter of a mile away was a house where an old brother and sister lived. A couple years later I began to write about it. What came to my imagination was an old brother and sister living alone out in the country of Colorado in an old yellow house surrounded by weeds. What I knew from the outset was how they would die, and that's all I knew. Rethinking that story, I wondered why they'd end up that way. So I invented their past, and then a male voice who became the narrator, Sanders Roscoe, and he had to have a history and a family. Out of those narrative necessities came the texture of that novel.

So when you describe the beginning of that book, it's the combination of character and place that's the seed of a story.

Exactly.

Was that true of the second and third novels also?

I always come first to character, because I already know I want to write about northeast Colorado. These characters become full blown, so that when I actually begin writing, they are fully integrated people. My effort is to get them down on the page as complexly and as fully as I know them.

Your first book is a quiet but powerful story because the characters are so strong and their relationships are so claustrophobic. Is this the feeling one gets about life in the high plains where people live in physical isolation?

There is a kind of isolation. But maybe that's my character. I may have felt that same way if I'd grown up in Chicago. It's a paradox. Out in the plains you can see forever. You can see your neighbors, their houses, and there's nothing hiding them. You can see people working out in the barnyard. Yet there's this distance between you that's unbridgeable, and that's very interesting to me.

Will you ever exhaust writing about Colorado?

I think of that corner of Colorado as being my material. I feel like I own that in some literary sense. There's so much to write about there that I don't think I'll exhaust it. But I don't think of these stories as separate from the rest of the United States. What I do think is that I'm trying to tell stories that are pared down enough that the skeleton of human behavior can be seen where the distractions of the city are gone.

....

Amy Hempel: People's vulnerabilities are interesting, but I didn't set out to look at that. I started with the place. Place has always been the most—well, maybe the most—crucial thing in my work.

as interviewed by Debra Levy and Carol Turner

THE IMPORTANCE OF LOCATION
by David Long

—◆—

Something that Wallace Stegner said: "We manage to breed saints, brutes, and mudheads in all sorts of topographies and climates." In other words, he's saying that place does not determine character, but we do respond to certain types of geography. I like living in the mountains. I didn't like living in the Midwest. I like the North. Somehow, in my genetic heritage I'm a northerner. I'm English all the way. Rocky coastlines, mountains, pine trees, hardwoods—that seems very natural to me. Italy seems like an awful lot of fun to visit, but it wouldn't be home for me. We're wired, I think, for some kind of experience of place. As a fiction writer, it's been very important for me to make the stories be specific. I don't want a story that could happen anyplace. I want the story to be located.

....

THE MIDWEST
Lorrie Moore, interviewed by Jim Schumock

—◆—

You've been at Madison now for ten years, but the Midwest comes in for a lot of sarcastic comment in your work. How have you made your accommodation with it?

New York and Paris are more harshly criticized in my fiction than the Midwest is—but it's the Midwest that readers seem most defensive of or protective toward. I'm actually fonder of the Midwest than some of my characters might perhaps seem. I'm very interested in the idea of transplanted Easterners in the Midwest and their particular take on Madison. Madison itself happens to be full of transplanted Easterners, so there's a kind of running conversation about the Midwest going on here. And some of my closest relatives are Midwesterners.

So I'm not really feeling like the Midwest is some horrible, foreign country. I came to Madison when I was twenty-seven, as a professor, and I was really quite young and maybe a little puzzled by the place. Now I've found myself here longer than I've been almost anywhere. That should make me a Midwesterner, just a little, but provincial admission standards are strict, you know.

....

LOUISIANA

Ernest Gaines, interviewed by Michael Upchurch

You've lived in quite a few places, and presumably, when you were in the army, you did a lot of traveling.

Well, I was stationed on Guam. And I went to Tokyo. But, really, I don't do much traveling. I've been to Paris a couple of times in the last two years.

Have you ever been tempted to write outside the "Bayonne" area?

That's a good point, because I have lived in California almost forty-six years and everybody asks me, "Well, when are you going to write about California?" And I've tried! I tried to write bohemian stories. I tried to eat the bread and drink the wine, and I got sick on that. Got real sick on the wine. And I tried to write a story about my army experience—something like *Mister Roberts*, during peacetime, when I was in the service. I was in the service after Korea—between Korea and Vietnam.

I've tried to write those stories about San Francisco and the fog and all that sort of thing, but nothing's really come of it. So I tell people that maybe I'll write about some other place after I've written all that Louisiana stuff out of me. But Louisiana is an interesting place: I don't know that I ever will write it all out.

....

THE RHYTHM OF LANDSCAPE
Robert Wrigley, interviewed by Jim Schumock

I've come into Lewiston [Idaho] at sunset and it can be really beautiful there. Have you learned anything new about landscape from living in that environment?

I was talking about this the other night at a question-and-answer session after a reading. Someone was asking me about the rhythms in my poetry. I use a highly accentual line. I like a lot of stresses in the line. I like musical language. I argue—I guess we'd call it an argument—I suggest that, if I had stayed in the Midwest where I was born and raised, my poetry would be completely different. It would have everything to do with rhythm and music. I think that a lot of my love for the landscape, the kind of dramatic variations, the ruggedness of the landscape, is something that got to my soul. It got to me in a way that makes me feel at home when I'm there. In the same way, it's something like the feeling I have when I get into language that's beautifully done: rhythmical, musical. I make a real connection between those things. I value this landscape above all others.

THE SOUTH

Pam Durban, interviewed by Cheryl Reid

In your work, place is important. Often, the place is a layer of the characters and the characters are a layer of the place. And sometimes both lie.

The way I see it, in the South, character and place are both true, but part of that truth hasn't been acknowledged. The South's idea of itself and its racial history exist in some kind of tension with one another, and that's what interests me now about the South. The myth is that people in the South are great storytellers. The myth is we tell stories because we lost the war and because we have the experience of having lost something. I think that experience of having lost something began much earlier when the South accepted slavery as the basis for its society. It wasn't the Civil War; it was much before that. Moral ambiguity was built in.

I am reminded of some lines from *The Laughing Place* that relate to what you're saying about the South. The character Annie Vess says of her father's false representation of himself, "He should have told us how it feels to lie about yourself and make everyone around you swear allegiance to that lie." The same sort of allegiance was sworn to in the South.

Yes, and that's a subject for me. Maintaining one's innocence in the face of all evidence to the contrary. And in the South you've had that over time. To me, that creates evil—insisting on your own innocence. It creates brutality. You can't acknowledge what you really do. In the low-country South, the Southern slave owners were really masters of that. There are millions of pages of sermons and lectures justifying slavery in biblical terms. They were always positioning themselves as being noble, being somehow fully innocent doing this.

Slave narratives uncover that kind of ambivalence. Those narratives report instances of rape and abuse and they break the myth of the kind master.

Mary Boykin Chesnut's narrative touches on that, how everybody was able to talk about the mulatto children on other plantations but remained blind to their own. Who were the fathers of all the children? That's what makes the culture so interesting. Martin Scorsese was asked how he could make all of those gangster movies and then *The Age of Innocence*. He did brilliantly with both. He said it was because both of those societies were the same in the control that both had over their members.

In Charleston, particularly, there was this concern for the hierarchy in society that was constantly being monitored and adjusted. If you were a woman, this is how you acted. If you were a child, this is how you acted. If you were a slave, this is how you acted. Because the society was based on hierarchy, if one role was upset, it threatened the whole. All of this is very rich for me to explore in a novel. They are all moral questions. Not moral in who's right and who's wrong, but an exploration of why people make choices and how those choices work out.

One definition of Southern writing hinges on landscape and place. What do you think?

Landscape is important because particular things happen in a landscape and in a place. That place is important in itself. But in the South, you can love the landscape because it never committed a crime. You can put all your emotion there without dealing with what went on in that landscape. Toni Morrison does an interesting turn in *Beloved* when Sethe remembers Sweet Home. Regardless of what happened there, what she remembers are the beautiful trees. She hates herself for remembering the beauty of the place in spite of the people hanging from those trees. Again, as a white Southerner looking at the place, you can love the landscape because it is innocent. It is not implicated.

The South is rich for me as a place because of the tension there, not because of how much I love it, not because I am nostalgic for it. It's because of the tension. Every aspect of it. Whether it is the landscape or the culture or the city of Charleston and its tourist industry. That's as much the subject of my novel as how history is made.

You are making an important distinction to talk about this culture in the terms of history and not in the terms of nostalgia.

Exactly. That's what I am trying to do. There's a piece I am working on now called "Walking Tour of the Historic District with Unauthorized Asides." The book is set up as a series of documents and pieces and that's one of them.

The knowledge exists that slaves built a historic building or plantation, but this is only mentioned briefly, if at all.

It came to me when I saw these stone walls in Kentucky. That was a defining moment for me. We were living in Ohio and driving from Ohio to South Carolina, and we drove through Kentucky through the back roads, the bluegrass area, through Paris, outside of Lexington, where all the big horse farms are. In that area, you drive past miles and miles of these intricate stone walls. There are two layers of stones and then a vertical layer of stones at the top. Beautiful. This friend mentioned that a company in Lexington repairs the walls, and the company is owned by a man who is a descendant of one of the slaves who had originally built them. If anything was a revelation that was it. It struck me then that these things that the white South claims as its own identifying marks of beauty, from those walls to the iron gates in Charleston, were largely made by slaves. White people have claimed those things and made them their own, but these things are not ours, in the way we think of them as ours. Possession and ownership are always important issues in the South.

ELIZABETH COX

interviewed by Sarah Anne Johnson

My heart is in the South. Eudora Welty says, "Place is where the heart is." I'm beginning to develop a heart in Massachusetts, but when I go back to North Carolina or Tennessee, the air, the sounds, the smells, everything is familiar—it's what I write about. I've tried to write about New England, and maybe one day I can, but I will need to live in the North longer in order to write about it. One aspect of New England that I am beginning to write about is the quality of light. New England light is sharper, it has an edge. In the South, the air is thicker and the light has a milkiness to it, has a softness that isn't in the Northern air. At first, I thought I couldn't stand it; now I love it.

Robert Olen Butler: Vietnam was so ravishing a sensual experience that I recognized finally that the selecting and ordering and reshaping and re-creating of the world through those moment-to-moment sensual details was what I craved to do in my work. Of course, the experience filled me with metaphor and setting and characters that would provide content to much of the work that I would do.

as interviewed by Heather Iarusso

KENT HARUF
interviewed by Jim Nashold

Do you think of yourself as a Western writer?

Only in the sense that I write stories set in the West. It irritates the hell out of me to think anything I write is regional literature. I don't believe that at all. Novels have to be set somewhere, and my novels are set in northeast Colorado because that's what I know. I want to think that what I'm writing about is universal and elemental, so that it applies to people living anywhere.

What's the West's place in American history?

The West is still thought of as a place where new beginnings are possible. Where there are fewer restrictions and fewer boundaries. Where you can go and live life in a more raw and elemental way. A lot of that is myth, but it's still current in American psychology.

THE MYTHOLOGY OF THE WEST

Roy Parvin, interviewed by Linda B. Swanson-Davies

I grew up in the West and I love Western landscapes.

What do you like about them?

I like the physical aspect of the landscapes themselves. The paradox of having land that is so rugged and yet so fragile, fragile as a china cup. There's an internal tension working that I love. I also like the timelessness about the landscape, and—perhaps because I come from the East Coast I can appreciate this—work stops during the winter in Trinity County. The snows get to be so high that, well, how many places are there except for rural America where the weather is almost a character in your life? I find that very intriguing. My writer friends are always asking about my stories, What year did it occur in? I ask, Well, what year did you think it is? And they say it can be any year from 1950 to 1980. Or perhaps even today. I try to work in a sense of timelessness, and it seems like telling a small story against a big landscape gives the story an automatic mythical quality. If I had not gone West, I probably wouldn't be a writer, a fiction writer.

Really?

I don't know. If you look at the way one goes through life, it looks like a whole bunch of lucky breaks, hopefully, and close calls. Perhaps I would have been a writer, but I think that the landscapes spoke to me in a way that made me want to write. In all my stories, all my scenes, I want to frame the scene but also be very interested in what the trees and the mountains look like.

And I don't know if I would have gotten that perspective from the East Coast.

I was born in New York State. We moved to southern Oregon when I was ten, and it took years and years and years to not miss the rolling green. Everything got dry and brown and hard. The smells were different. There were no fireflies. What kind of life was that? What I'm getting at, though, is that I can see how much of an impact a change of place can make.

To me it felt like I had come home. I just read this morning something that Rick Bass, a writer I admire immensely, said: He was a Texan and he moved to Montana and felt like it was the state of his rebirth. I sort of felt that about the West. That this place…there's something about it that is home. It's very hard for me to put my finger on it, and if I were to ever specifically put my finger on it, then it wouldn't perhaps be home. I'm always chasing that in my writing and in my life. What makes it home. What, what, what about these wide-open spaces speaks to me? It's always something slightly different, I think, from story to story. I was talking to a writer friend who said, You know, nature always seems like a character in your stories. It always has its say. And I think people in the West live very, very close to nature. There are earthquakes. There're certainly bad storms anywhere, but the storms here seem to be mythic storms. It snows and that interests me. It's something again that can't be controlled.

Something to be contended with.

Yeah. And I think emotions are sort of like that, too.

ABDELRAHMAN MUNIF

interviewed by Michael Upchurch

⟫⟫◆⟪⟪

One question raised by *Cities of Salt* is whether there is a Wadi al-Uyoun in your own life or the life of your family.

In our country there are a lot of place names that are similar to one another. For example, I am from a region called al-Uyoun. But that doesn't mean that there's a complete identification of the place in the book with the place that I knew in my life. Sometimes the novelist chooses a place that is more suitable as a site to be used in a novel—although sometimes the novel imposes its own choice.

....

EASTERN KENTUCKY

Chris Offutt, interviewed by Rob Trucks

⟫⟫◆⟪⟪

Setting is obviously an important element in your fiction, and, on one level, *The Good Brother* works as a comparison of two states. What are the similarities between Kentucky and Montana?

Kentucky was the western frontier through the 1700s. At that point, all the land was settled and occupied, primarily by Scots and Irishmen. The rest of the country, in its westward expansion, went around Kentucky due to geography, so it stayed with the eighteenth-century mentality, in many ways, for almost two hundred years now, maintaining a frontier attitude about life, self-preservation, relationship with the land, relationship with animals, and relationship with people.

I didn't like most depictions of eastern Kentucky. I especially didn't like the popular-culture depictions: Barney Google, Snuffy Smith, *The Beverly Hillbillies*, *The Dukes of Hazzard*, *Deliverance*, all that kind of crap. I wanted to present a version of Kentucky that was mine, that I grew up with. It was a post-Vietnam, post-VISTA world of Appalachia. I've met incredibly complicated, intelligent people in the hills.

USING DETAIL TO ESTABLISH SETTING

Mary Yukari Waters, interviewed by Sherry Ellis

The story "Shibusa" begins and ends with the character Goto-san and her relationship with the tea ceremony. When you started writing this story, were you aware of the extent to which the tea ceremony would play a symbolic role?

At first, the tea ceremony was just a minor detail. And like most minor details, it came from the life that I knew. As you know, I was born in Japan and lived there till I was nine. Since then, I've gone back every other year, so a lot of details in my stories come from what I've seen and heard. In this case, my grandmother's sister happens to run a school for tea ceremony and *koto*, so I felt comfortable setting my character in that world. It was only after the shape of the story fully emerged that I saw an opportunity to draw a parallel between the concept of the tea ceremony and the events in Goto-san's life. And at that point, the tea ceremony took on a deeper symbolic importance.

WHEN PLACE CHOOSES YOU

Chris Offutt, interviewed by Rob Trucks

=◆◆=

Do the same things that drew you to Montana personally draw you fictionally as well, in terms of material?

I never intended to go to Montana. When I set up this story, Virgil was going to flee to Alaska because I thought Alaska was a genuine contemporary frontier, and I wanted to go there. I was exploring feud mentality in a contemporary time. I was exploring the relationship with land and I thought Alaska would offer me what I wanted. My wife, with two children under six, utterly refused to go with me to Alaska, so we compromised on Montana.

....

REJECTING REGIONALISM

Richard Bausch
interviewed by Jennifer Levasseur and Kevin Rabalais

=◆◆=

You are Southern by birth, but your work has not been received as traditional Southern fiction.

You would get arguments from a lot of people about that. The thing I don't do that other Southern writers do is spend a lot of time writing about place. My landscape is interior. I find terrain less interesting than psychology. There are writers who can do the terrain and the psychology. I'm not short-changing those writers. For me, it's just not all that interesting. I've traveled all over, and it's just land, just rocks and mountains. I like the appellation "Southern" for lots of reasons, mostly because of who else is Southern: George

Garrett, Mary Lee Settle, Allen Wier, Richard Ford, Barry Hannah, Josephine Humphreys, Ellen Douglas, Lee Smith, Jill McCorkle, Madison Smartt Bell, my brother Robert, Shelby Foote, Ernest Gaines, Eudora Welty—good lord, there's dozens of them. Richard Ford has said he doesn't want to be known as a "Southern" writer, but he's really talking in that sense about being regionalized as a writer, and I don't want to be regionalized, either. As Richard put it once, I'm writing for everybody who can read.

....

THERE'S NO PLACE LIKE ACADEMIA
Mark Winegardner, interviewed by Robert Birnbaum

The Paul Auster novel [*The Book of Illusions*] is set in academia, and a lot of first-rate work is set there. I'm like anyone else. I look suspiciously at work that is set there. But it is also true that people that read literary fiction are going to disproportionately be people who were fond of their college years or who have some tangential relationship to writers or English departments. So it's not exactly a limiting thing for your audience. Richard Russo's *Straight Man* is one of the funniest books I ever read.

Michael Chabon's *Wonder Boys*...

There have been books, big commercial books, that have obviously transcended that. Why hospitals and police departments for TV shows? Some things just lend themselves to the genre. Academia is the ultimate contemporary bureaucracy. It's worse than government. Are hospital stories necessarily justified by the countless hours of episodic TV that's been devoted to them? No, but just as a milieu lends itself to TV shows, academia does that to literary fiction.

MARIA FLOOK

interviewed by Sarah Anne Johnson

My landscape and my cultural community are important in my fiction. I think we often pin down writers to their idiosyncratic locales, right? Much of my previous work takes place in Rhode Island, and this is the first time my setting is Land's End, Massachusetts. I'm trying to evoke the odd juxtaposition of wilderness phenomenon and do-gooders with the edgy disenfranchised subculture in a depressed economic setting in off-season Cape Cod. This is a world of lost souls and washashores, loners who collide. But really, it's a comedic, gothic love story.

CONNECTING CHARACTER AND SETTING
Allen Morris Jones, interviewed by David Abrams

Let's talk about landscape and how that influences your writing. Henry [in *Last Year's River*] is so attuned to the natural world. What kind of role do you think nature plays in our modern fiction, particularly that of writers west of the Mississippi?

Landscape is always important, whether you're writing about mountains or cities. You're always going to have to address a setting for your characters. You have to be very careful when you write about dramatic landscape. The reader is not always interested in that kind of stuff. If you want to talk about the landscape, you almost have to have a character who is overly preoccupied with the natural world, such as Henry. As readers, we want to know about other people; we don't want to know about how pretty the mountains are, but we may be interested in knowing how pretty one of the characters thinks the mountains are. If I were to ever teach a creative-writing course—God forbid—then I think that I'd encourage the students not to write about landscape, or to write about it as little as possible. Tell me about the characters—what are their hopes, what are their fears?

CAROLYN KIZER

interviewed by Jim Schumock

Was Spokane a provincial backwater for you? Or was it as useful a place as any for a young poet?

Well, it certainly was a provincial backwater. I think almost every good poet I know came from another provincial backwater, usually in the Midwest. In other words, I think part of what prompted us to write poetry was the need to entertain ourselves because we were bored silly. No inland city, no matter what size, has the degree of sophistication of even a small town on the ocean or on a major river. There's something about the international intercourse and the flow of people to and from other countries.

I know you've traveled widely and lived in a lot of different places. Is there any place you feel as at home as you did in Spokane?

Oh, I feel much more at home anywhere from Vancouver, British Columbia, to San Francisco. That's my area, provided it sticks pretty close to the coast.

ERNEST GAINES
interviewed by Michael Upchurch

One lady wrote me a letter—I got several letters after *A Lesson Before Dying* came out—and she said: "There's so much food in that book that I found myself going to my refrigerator. I was always crying—and when I wasn't crying, I was in the refrigerator."

Several other people pointed out that there's food all over the place. Well, in the South they believe in feeding you, and giving you coffee, of course. Whenever you go in anybody's house, there's coffee. There's always coffee, coffee, coffee, whoever's house you're in.

My mother-in-law—she's ninety-one years old—this lady cooks all the time. We wanted to take her out for Mother's Day in New Orleans this past Mother's Day, but she didn't want to go anywhere. She wanted to cook—for us.

That's why, when Grant says to his aunt, "I'm going to Bayonne," that's the worst thing he could have told her, because she believes, "I cooked that food; you eat that food." And when he says, "I don't want to. I'm going to Bayonne, get away from these people for a while," that's a betrayal. They don't like that. My grandmother was like that. She'd always dish up the food herself. She would never let you dish your own food up. She would put a *pile* of it on there, and you had to eat it. And then you got the cake later. If you didn't eat it, you didn't get the cake, so you'd force yourself to eat the food to get a little piece of cake. And she was a great cook.

She had been the cook in this big house where I grew up on this plantation, just like Miss Emma, Miss Jane, and so many of my older people—Aunt Charlotte. And my paternal grandfather was the yardman. He did all the sharpening of the tools and all that kind of stuff there, fixed the steps and boards that were loose on porches, whether it was at the big house or whether it was at the plantation houses down in the quarter. He would be the one who did that.

When I'm writing, I always have that same house in mind. It's different books—with the same house.

....

MARY GORDON

interviewed by Charlotte Templin

⟹⬦⟸

Your most recent memoir, *Seeing through Places*, is organized around places. Did that organizing principle come easily?

I just began writing about place because I'm interested in writing about place, and then I said, "Oh, my goodness, I have quite a few of these. Maybe if I put a few more in that will work." I can't praise myself and say I thought it up. It came to me. And what about the shaping of the book into a kind of journey? It just seemed to come. Because of my belief that place gives us a lot of information about ourselves that we can't always get to directly. Memory releases information.

A lot of the writing that I love very much has a very strong sense of place, however you define place—as landscape, terrain, house, room. You have to inhabit a space. That relationship between the inhabiter and what is inhabited can be a very fruitful one. And the kind of fiction that I don't like doesn't have much sense of place. It all seems to take place in someone's head.

Annie Proulx: I went to Newfoundland five or six years ago to go fishing. It had been in the back of my mind to go there for fifteen years before that. I went up with a friend, dragged up the canoes and so forth, and the minute I got my hands on a map I fell madly in love with the place names, which were extraordinary, just extraordinary! And stories began jumping off the map at me. A place with such a name as Joe Batt's Arm or the Fogo Islands or the Topsail Mountains or the Annieopsquotch Mountains. Or a place that has a train called the Newfie Bullet. All these place names carried stories that seemed to jump at me.

as interviewed by Michael Upchurch

JAYNE ANNE PHILLIPS
interviewed by Sarah Anne Johnson

Several of your stories take place on the border between Mexico and Texas, and depict the intersection of American and Latino cultures, such as in "El Paso" and "Mamasita." Did you live in that part of the country? What interests you about these intersections?

Any time you have an intersection of one thing smacking up against another, whether it's age versus youth, wealth versus poverty, one culture versus another, something is going to happen. Just as various religions arise from various cultures, different ways of handling language arise within cultures, and that is very rich subject matter.

I did spend some time in Mexico and Texas, and some of those ideas and details came from visual instances. "Mamasita" is set in New York City. You can find anybody anywhere.

....

WHERE WERE YOU IN FEBRUARY?
Elizabeth McCracken
interviewed by Sarah Anne Johnson

⟞⟐⟝

Why did you set *The Giant's House* on Cape Cod?

Because I have a very small imagination and I was living on the Cape. I could write, "It was February and it was _____ out," and stick my head out the window. I remembered from when I lived there the first time that Provincetown held a kind of private joke for me. People left as the winter became deeper; those people would return in the spring, and I had this sense that only the people who were there in February understood the place. I remember walking along the streets on April weekends and running into tourists who were walking slowly. I was unaccustomed to seeing people on the street! A resort town in the off season has a sort of snow-globe feeling that nothing can penetrate. It's an enclosed world. Provincetown is especially like that because it's nearly an island. I wanted that feeling of the outside world not affecting the world of the novel, which I'm sure was partial laziness. I was figuring out how to write the world of the novel, and it was easier to write one in which the outside world rarely intrudes on the lives of the characters. Practically no historical event has any bearing on the novel. It takes place in the fifties and there's a single reference to Elvis. That's about it.

Why did you set the story in a fictional town rather than a real town?

Everyone thinks the novel is set in Brewster, but I wanted Brewster-ville to be a cross between Brewster and Osterville. It's not Brewster. The closest I can say is that it's somewhere along the Cape. The reason I set it in a fictional town is that I didn't want to be beholden to the geography and the particularities of a specific town. Again, this is the snow-globe effect, and I didn't want to have to be historically accurate. The book has a vaguely fairy-tale feeling to it, and because of that, I wanted it set in an imaginary place.

THE LITERATURE OF AMERICA
Paul Theroux, interviewed by Jim Schumock

There's a line you wrote about American books that make you love America. Can you give some examples?

That's a very tough question, but Faulkner is certainly one of them. It's hard to read Faulkner and not think that the South is a living, breathing history and that Faulkner has brought it to life. You can smell the flowers. "The Odor of Verbena" is one of his stories—the air, the trees, the honeysuckle, the way the people talk. I think Faulkner has the South. But there are lots of other stories. All the Chicago novels of Saul Bellow, and *The Man with the Golden Arm*.

Nelson Algren.

Nelson Algren—mainly his writing about Chicago. When I think of Los Angeles, I think of Nathanael West or Raymond

Chandler. It makes you love a place for its smell, the sound of it, for the sight of it. I suppose a place that you come from is one where the smell and the sound are in your senses. I have a quite romantic notion of when I was very young. I saw the movie *Picnic* with William Holden. Whenever I think of *Picnic*, I think of hot summers, the picnics, small towns, something dramatic happening. To me, the quintessential American experience is a summer picnic. It's hot; it's kind of steamy. It's very sensual to me. The way the people are dressed, what they say, darkness falling, the crickets, all of that stuff. And I suppose the film was part of it. That moment in middle America when the corn is ripe. Maybe it's purely fantasy because I've never lived in the Midwest, but that is the sense I have. Sometimes you get it in Wright Morris or Willa Cather. I think of the Midwest and then, of course, for New England I think of Robert Frost. So I think a great deal of writing which is purely American literature arouses a lot of emotions in me.

DANIEL MASON

interviewed by Linda B. Swanson-Davies

The amazing man in *The Piano Tuner* named Twet Nga Lu—the guy with the talismans embedded all over his body. The image of his being killed, having the talismans removed, being decapitated and boiled down to a syrup medicine...

Which was then sold.

Yes, which was then sold.

That true story made me want to write about the Shan States. When I was thinking about where I could set this story, I thought maybe I could set it in Western Burma or Eastern Burma. Or maybe it could be about the French in China. Then I read the story of this man who was boiled down in his death into a potion that was then sold, and I thought this is better than any fictional story I could ever make.

It could leave your mouth hanging open for a week.

Right. It's an extraordinary story. And he's still famous in the Shan States. I met a Shan reader who came to me and said that when she was a little girl, long after he had died, if she was making mischief her mother would come to her and say, Be quiet or Twet Nga Lu is going to come and get you. He's still sort of the boogeyman in the Shan States. I thought it was amazing.

Well, what do you think—is there any chance that a person boiled down to an essence would be a healing substance? Can you think of any possible physical reason?

No, unless there's something paranormal that's going on. You know, unless the man really has supernatural powers and he's protecting you.

That whole thing creates the most incredible image. I just couldn't believe it.

That's why I love history. I've always felt that I didn't need to make anything up because the history itself was so good.

THE CENTER OF IMAGINATION

Pam Durban, interviewed by Cheryl Reid

─═◆═─

There is a connection between "Soon" and the story "All Set About with Fever Trees," especially the setting of both stories.

That place in Highlands was where we held a family reunion. Going to that family reunion was somehow important. It's at the center of my imagination. Over time, I have been trying to put things together around that. Why are those two weeks I spent when I was eleven years old so important? Then I found another piece—the spring before the reunion my mother lost a baby—and put those two pieces together. That time was crucial to me. There must have been something going on there about reconnecting with the larger family. Something about that was very powerful.

In "Soon" the grandniece returns to that place in Highlands that has been deserted. Within that return, there exists an interesting concept about time.

The old woman and the diary made one strand of the story. The other was the feeling I described in the story when we found that house. The feeling when I walked onto the porch and looked through that window. It was such a powerful, strange feeling. It was a physical sensation: joy, sadness, longing, and in the story I was trying to trace that feeling back to its source. Everything worked around that feeling.

And the house is so strange. It's true my aunt died there and people said she haunted the place. The house was littered. Those details didn't make their way into this story. But I have them stored. All of her children had problems, with alcohol, drugs, and periodically some of them would live in this house. So when I saw it again, there were these books, like the Alcoholics Anonymous books, scattered everywhere. A history of lives.

....

LEAVING TO COME HOME AGAIN
Tobias Wolff, interviewed by Jim Schumock

Several stories take place in the Northwest, especially in Seattle. Why haven't you written any fiction about your time at Oxford or Syracuse? The Northwest is still the most fertile ground for you.

Yes, it is. Those haunts of our childhood make an enduring impression on us. I know that's true of a lot of writers. I've written about Northern California, where I lived for years. I started writing about it after I left, though. There's something about leaving a place that suddenly opens it up in a clear way. I have no doubt that someday I will write about Syracuse, which I just left after seventeen years. One thing that's just dying to be written about is the way winter comes there. Any true book about Syracuse would have to have winter as its main character. It's the bully outside everyone's house. That would be something I don't think has really been done yet, and it could be very interesting to have a season as your main character. As for writing about Oxford, there's an immense shelf of literature already. I would want to feel that I was doing something pretty fresh with the whole enterprise. But I'm confident that someday I will write about it. There were a lot of quirky things that happened to me there. I had a lot of very strange friends.

PATRICIA HENLEY
interviewed by Andrew Scott

Place is an important element in your fiction and classroom. What's being praised when a reader delights in a book or story's sense of place?

It's been interesting to watch my sense of place shift. I started writing fiction when my imagination got fired up by moving out West. Those mountains and the tough women and the close-to-the-bone life I led—all that made me want to tell stories, and, more often than not, I found that the stories were bound up with landscape and wilderness and weather and seasonal jobs, which are just a few of the differences I see between that place and, say, this one: the tamed heartland. I cried all summer before I moved to Indiana from Montana in 1987, even though I'd been born in southern Indiana. Maybe it was because I'd been born there. Seriously, I think I just didn't want to leave the mountains and the place that had given me my stories. For a variety of reasons, I've stayed in Indiana, and eventually I began writing about it. Kate, in *Hummingbird House*, is from Indiana, and it appears there in her ruminations. Much of *In the River Sweet* is set here, in a fictional Indiana town named for Booth Tarkington. *In the River Sweet* opens with a love scene at the round barns and several people have said to me, You manage to make it sound romantic. As if the Midwest couldn't be.

My sense of place, though, ranges more widely. I recently set a story in the Bahamas. And *In the River Sweet* is also set in Vietnam and Michigan and New Orleans. I hope I've authentically portrayed those places. They're places I love. There are probably some places I could never write about lovingly or authentically, places I can't feel a kinship with. That feeling is almost like falling in love, a chemical reaction. You are willing to overlook the place's flaws and unpleasantness because there's something in the air that appeals to you. Unless you're terribly cold-hearted as a writer, a technician, I think you need that feeling to portray a place in a way that will delight the reader. We take delight in differences. We want to feel, upon reading about a particular town or mountain or river or street, that we've been to a place we might never have known otherwise.

CREATING MOTION IN A SINGLE SPACE
Ann Patchett, interviewed by Sarah Anne Johnson

Almost the entire novel *[Bel Canto]* takes place in the living room of the vice-presidential mansion, yet it never feels stagnant. How did you keep things moving in this small setting?

It was a very big living room, and I always had that in mind. I pictured the lobby at the Plaza Hotel, which is not just a big room. It's like a microcosm. The lobby at the Plaza is a universe of activity. I never felt claustrophobic in that house, and the characters don't feel claustrophobic. The characters aren't longing to get out, because for so many of them, that's not their country, and they don't really trust the people on the other side of the wall who have the guns. They're not feeling caged or pining for freedom. What they're pining for is for music, for beauty. Everything they want is inside the house. If the characters were pressing up against the windows all the time, it would've felt claustrophobic. The trick was to move the story from one side of the room to the other, to have a conversation next to the piano, then a conversation in the hallway going to the kitchen, then a conversation on the sofa. Keeping it flowing was the harder part.

WRITING ADVICE from Susan Richards Shreve

Part of researching in fiction has to do with knowing what you need to know. When I wrote about an Indian reservation in northern Wisconsin where I've never been, I already knew what I needed to find out for the story. In *Daughters of the New World*, I was quite specific, detailed in history, geography, and even tribal character, but only insofar as I needed to create a place of authenticity. Recently I listened to a public conversation among fiction writers about a sense of place. Some said that the responsibility of fiction is no different than nonfiction. Facts are facts. Others, one in particular, said of a book he had written that it was important to change a road that actually goes through the forest of the Adirondacks. He needed the road to go along one of those dark, pine-skirted lakes. For his story. For atmosphere. For the development of character. In my own work, I would vote to change the location for the sake of the story.

as interviewed by Katherine Perry Harris

ALICE MATTISON
interviewed by Barbara Brooks

You were in the midst of writing *The Wedding of the Two-Headed Woman* when September 11 happened. How did that day affect your story?

I started writing in February 2001. September 11 came along as I was writing, and by then it was fall in the book as well. Of course I stopped and thought, Why am I doing this?—writing, that is—and then, as with a lot of other writers, about two days later it was the only thing I could do that would make me feel any better. And as I said, I was addicted to it at this point—I couldn't stop. I thought of putting September 11 into the book, but that seemed exploitative, and I didn't. Later, though, I realized that the plot made more sense if September 11 happened in the book. I hadn't specified a particular year, but now I made the book take place in 2001. There was quite a bit about September 11 in the early drafts, and some of the first people who read it were somewhat put off by that.

They were reading it very soon after.

About a year later, in fact—it took me a long time to have a draft I could show anybody—and by that time September 11 had been taken over by the right wing, so that it had become impossible to talk about it without sentimental and mindless mouthings about patriotism, which was not what we were all feeling when it took place. In some of the drafts it almost seemed as if I was playing into that, and I included less about it in revision. My editor and I talked at one point about taking it out, and not having the book take place in 2001 at all, but by that time September 11 felt integrated into the book. It's funny about fiction. You get to make it up, but every once in a while you feel that if you made up one particular thing you'd be lying. You get to make it up, but there's truth.

....

IN DEFENSE OF THE IMAGINARY CITY
Mary Morrissy, interviewed by Ana Callan

On the notion of situation: I know you're an Irish writer living in Dublin. But these stories [in *A Lazy Eye*] don't seem to have a particular locus or locale. Even the names aren't particularly Irish. The places are not ones I'm familiar with. Do you just make the names up?

Yes. Even though I'm aware that there is a kind of Irishness about them and about the way the language is used, the obsession with guilt and the whole Catholic backdrop to it, I'm very wary about setting any of my stories anywhere. I mean, I had a real problem in the novel, because it is set in an unnamed city, though it is definitely 1950s Ireland. But I didn't want to get bogged down with, Did this shop stand on the corner of this street in 1950? or whatever. And to me, the sense of place is overworked in Irish fiction.

I actually have this difficulty with using real place names. First of all, it's a bit like a journalistic shorthand. If you say, This character was walking down Grafton Street, well, for most of your readers, you don't have to say anything more. They can picture the street in their heads. It's a kind of laziness.

MARY YUKARI WATERS

interviewed by Sherry Ellis

In your future works do you think you'll continue returning to Japan?

I'm not sure. I've really enjoyed writing about Japan, and I'm not sure if I've exhausted it yet. When I first started writing, I naturally turned to Japan because it was the place of my childhood, which is usually the root of self-discovery. Also, I really enjoy the process of translating the sensibility of one culture into that of another. But there's a whole American side of me that I may want to tap into. For now, I'm comfortable not knowing. All I know is, whatever I find myself most fascinated with is what I'm going to follow.

WRITING ADVICE from Lynn Freed

When the writing comes properly, the place is there, available to me. If I have to strain to know a place, I'm in the wrong fiction. I'm always saying to students that one must colonize the territory of the fiction. It is the only metaphor that seems to carry with it the presumptuousness of fiction, the sense of making a place one's own. In this case, I mean it literally. One has to make it one's own, so that, in a way, it is more than real; it is assumed.

as interviewed by Sarah Anne Johnson

CHAPTER

5

CHARACTER

Blanche Howland, 1960

CHANG-RAE LEE

interviewed by Sarah Anne Johnson

What drew you to his obsession with flying in *Aloft*?

This is one of those things that starts you out on a character. I had this idea of Jerry as a certain kind of person, not knowing the exact details. But once I figured out that he was a man who liked to fly his own small plane, that's when it clicked for me. I began to think of him as not just an abstract character but as the protagonist and teller of the story. Metaphorically his flying seemed right to me, and in terms of language it reflects the kind of yearning he has to be on this other level in his life. It's very different than Doc Hata, whose language is so compacted and careful and constructed. Jerry's is very free and loose. He riffs all the time, and he feels at liberty to talk about anyone or anything. It appealed to me to do something quite different than in *A Gesture Life*.

In *Aloft*, Jerry Battle is preoccupied with Harold Clarkson-Ickes's attempt to fly a balloon around the world in what is both a heroic and foolish adventure. Why did you include this story in the narrative? What did you want to show readers about Jerry?

There's this idea of glamour and danger and daring in what the balloonist was doing. That's the ideal version of who Jerry is or wants to be. In his life, he's just a guy who flies his own little plane over his own patch of land in good weather only. It's very human. He's not an explorer. He's not a dashing, swashbuckling sort of fellow. He's not the fighter pilot that he wanted to be. It seemed natural that he would pin a lot of hopes upon Sir Harold, just silly, private, human hopes, and be crushed when Sir Harold meets his end. Jerry is a very careful guy. He likes his security and comforts, but he still dreams. The book is about the struggle to shake himself out of that comfort, and he does it vicariously through Sir Harold.

THE DYNAMICS OF YEARNING
Robert Olen Butler, interviewed by Heather Iarusso

Fiction ultimately is the art form of human yearning, and that is essential to the work of fictional narrative art. A character who yearns is not the same as a character who simply has problems. A lot of characters have problems, but the problems have not yet resolved themselves into the dynamics of yearning for this writer and this character. That yearning is at the heart of all temporal art forms.

All works of art, I believe, are organically whole down to the tiniest metaphor; everything must resonate into everything else. At the heart of that is that the character yearns for self or for connection. The yearning dictates every other choice. They also are the things that generate what we call plot, because it is the efforts to fulfill a yearning that are thwarted or blocked or challenged that then provide the elements of plot.

The reason the yearning is so rare—and it is very rare, indeed—in the work of inexperienced writers, is that they often have trouble manifesting this yearning in a natural way in their stories. A story is not ready to be written until you have an intuition about the yearning of the character in your unconscious. I think it's a way of averting the eyes: If the passive central character is simply beset by problems, just moving through a world of incident that's really not been shaped by any kind of dynamic from within the character, it's a safe world. It's a calm and detached world.

In a way, the way I teach creative writing is a return to my acting training. There is this thing called method acting, which came about as a way of understanding how actors are in their process. Around the turn of the century, acting was taught and done as a process of willfully and intellectually taking on the external gestures and postures and expressions and so forth of the character being created. You worked from the outside in. Konstantin Stanislavsky of the Moscow Art Theatre challenged this understanding of the actor's art. He articulated the process of acting—and the training of actors—in exactly the opposite way from the prevailing view. That is, you start from the inside and bring the sense memories of the actor into concert with the inner sense memories and sensual experience of the character to be created, and only having done that will the external performance flow. That's method acting. I am a kind of method-writing teacher because everything I've been saying is that you go back to the process, and the process is not one of intellectualizing and putting on something. It's not a matter of technique or craft at the outset. At the outset it must be a matter of the inner self, the unconscious, the dream space, the sensual life of the inner life of the characters that you are creating and from there flows the technique and so forth. That's an important and direct analogy to what I'm doing, which also goes back to the cinema of the mind and my theatrical training.

When you're writing, how aware are you of the essential yearning of your character?

If you're asking me do I sit down and analyze it in some rational way, the answer is no I do not. But I am aware of it with every word I write in the sense that it is the thing around which all other forces are bending. Every choice is being influenced by the dynamic, striving desire inside my characters.

LEE MARTIN
interviewed by Linda B. Swanson-Davies

You're very good at dialogue and I wondered if that's one of the areas you especially focus on in your classes.

There's certainly a spectrum. I mean I break it down into five areas. You've got to know characterization and structure and detail and point of view and language, and of course language is kind of the catchall for a lot of different things, but dialogue fits in. What I try to impress on my students is that the thing that makes you or breaks you as a writer is almost always what you can do with characterization. I often start a fiction workshop by sharing the opening of Tobias Wolff's story, "An Episode in the Life of Professor Brooke." It's in his first collection, *In the Garden of the North American Martyrs*, and I share the first two paragraphs. The opening line is something like, "Professor Brooke had no real quarrel with anyone in his department but there was a Yeats scholar named Riley whom he could not bring himself to like." I tell my students that everything you need to know about characterization is in that line. What he's doing there is laying out a line and then he's turning it, and when he turns it, he makes the character dynamic in the sense that he's capable of emotion in different directions—contradiction.

KENT HARUF
interviewed by Jim Nashold

Certain characters recur in your novels. Is there a conscious re-creation of them, or is it just the type of person that grows out of the story you're trying to tell?

It seems to grow out of the story I'm trying to tell, but there are similarities between the narrators of each book. I'm interested in men who are decent people and who're flawed, but still trying to do the best they can, but don't always succeed. In fact, they don't often succeed.

PUT YOURSELF IN DANGER
by David Koon

There is a danger for writers, especially those who have talent. The danger is that a writer can be so concerned with making a perfect article that she cores out a story's heart, and leaves it grammatically and stylistically perfect, but empty of feeling. The belief in my heart of hearts is that a lot of people in fiction today are simply not taking risks with their characters (I hate it when somebody says this kind of shit to me…. What the hell is risk anyway? You want me to write on top of a speeding car? While bungee jumping? What?), and it is a crying shame.

Let me try to explain. When you pass the age of ten and go to DisneyWorld, nobody rides the teacups. The teacups were cool then, but now—no! As an adult, you want to ride the Screaming Eagle Death Drop with the Double Loop-de-Loops. As adults, for some reason, we want the thing that might kill us and dismember us and spread us all over hell and creation. The reader wants that danger, too. But in fiction, as in roller coasters, the danger for the schmo who simply rides is (usually) all an illusion. The real danger in fiction is always solely over the head of the writer. It hangs there like a big chunk of concrete at the end of a rope. And for many writers, the pressure of that is too much. It is just too easy to move your chair out of the way and write dead fiction.

Push as a writer. Press your self through your fingers and keyboard and onto the page. But—you say—if the writer pushes too far, then she slips over into the pink-chiffon hell of melodrama, and the reader drops the story like a sack of shit and never looks in the direction of that writer again. True. That's why it's hard to let your characters turn back flips and break dance and do all that other stupid crap that characters are prone to do: because there is always the danger of looking stupid, of looking like you are not in control of the situation. (And in writing, it is all about control, isn't it? One of the greatest compliments we can give to a writer is "Look at the control she has over her language/characters/plot/structure/etc.!") But the greater danger—the hidden danger, the siren's song—is in *not* letting the characters do it. And it is so dangerous because, while a writer might feel safe bringing forth a story like that and handing it over to a reader (and the reader might even love it because there is nothing to bitch about), it is quietly dead. It is worse than dead (as they say in B movies), it is *un*dead—a staggering horror brought to life by shoddy means and sent reeling across the surface of the earth.

All in all, people doing writing that matters are easy to spot. They are the ones who—when they sit down to write—frown instead of smile. They are the cool sons of bitches out there on the edge of the cliff, on top of a soapbox, holding a sideshow fat lady in their laps, sitting in a chair tipped up on its back legs and balanced over the void.

PAM DURBAN
interviewed by Cheryl Reid

There is a real balance in your work between the good and the bad things in life.

You have to grow beyond that childish point, as the narrator does in *The Laughing Place*, where everything has to be perfect or it's terrible, that swing of absolutes. Both things can be true, and that's what you learn as you mature. It's what it means to be a mature human being; that is, being able to hold things that are in absolute opposition to each other in your mind at the same time and accept both. Not accept evil, but accept its existence.

When you create a character, do you see these tensions existing within an individual?

If there is anything I am pleased with about myself as a writer I guess it's that I've become more accepting of dimensions in people. I can see people clearly, I think, because I am not committed to an idea that they have to be one way or another. I like what Marilynne Robinson [*Housekeeping*] says, that writers can't get in the habit of seeing people as collections of symptoms that need curing. It's the symptoms that interest us as writers—those things, those difficulties or weird things about people, the things that make them unhappy, or the things that cripple them. Those are the things that make them interesting as characters and not problems to be solved in stories about them. It's people's mistakes that make them interesting.

Charles Baxter has a chapter in *Burning Down the House* on "Dysfunctional Narratives" where he says you don't have to solve their problems.

I love that chapter. He talks about establishing blame, and as soon as blame is established, the story is over. And that is certainly true of a lot of stories.

Karen Swenson: You need to know a great deal about people to write about them, much more than you actually put into your work. You must understand the facts, but much more importantly, the feeling of the person….You build up a great deal of background knowledge, watching and listening, living and traveling with people. The writing is a process of selecting and leaving out, and sometimes inventing—since poems aren't the absolute truth. They're more like epitomes.

as interviewed by Susan McInnis

CHARACTERS MUST WANT

Charles Baxter, interviewed by Linda B. Swanson-Davies

⟾⟾◆⟽

We get in a fair number of stories that don't have enough depth or resonance. How would you suggest writers look at their work to discover and address those things?

There are about five questions you can ask yourself about stories, and they're not foolproof, but they're useful. One is, What do these characters want? Second is, What are they afraid of? Third is, What's at stake in this story? Fourth is, What are the consequences of these scenes or these actions? And the last one is, How does the language of this story reflect the world of the story itself? Now, if a writer is writing a story and looks at you and says: I don't know what my characters want. I don't think they want much of anything. Then, the story is in trouble. If you don't know what's at stake in the story, it means that nothing stands to be gained or lost in the course of it. Something has to be risked. The characters have to want something or to wish for something. They have to be allowed to stay up past eleven o'clock and to make mistakes. If there's a flaw that many beginning writers have, it is that their characters don't risk enough. They are just sitting in chairs having ideas. I had a student a few months ago, when I was in residency at a university, who said, I don't want my characters to do anything, I just want them to think through the problem of nature versus culture.

That's not exactly a story, is it?

That's what I tried to tell her. But she was determined to write a story about issues. I mean, this is an old thing to say, but if you want to write something about *issues*, write an essay. That's what essays are for. If you want to see the consequences of ideas, write a story. If you want to see the consequences of belief, write a story in which somebody is acting on the ideas or beliefs that she has. But that's why it's important to have a sense of what your characters want.

THE ACT OF EMPATHY

Lee Martin, interviewed by Linda B. Swanson-Davies

⟾◆⟽

In your writing, you give the poor, the brittle, the lonely, the unlucky, and the fragile room to suffer as they do in real life, but you don't let readers put them aside. They cannot be simply labeled. Is that deliberate or is that just how they are for you?

I think that's how most people in general are for me. I really think that one of the first obligations of the writer is the act of empathy, to try to understand who these characters are and how they came to be who they are. I am always interested in what information there is from the past that has come to bear as people live their lives forward. One of the challenges that I always set for myself and I think most writers do, is to see characters in all their complexity, as fully and as completely as we can. I like to set myself the challenge of saying, Okay, here's this character. Now, how can I find the opposite within that character?

So you do in fact look.

I think in those terms. The longer that I write, the less self-conscious that is, but I can remember early on in my development as a writer, one of the first really important things I learned was this whole issue of how characters and situations contain their opposites. And as a writer I think about how to look for that and how to dramatize it.

ALLEN MORRIS JONES

interviewed by David Abrams

Some people have said they find it hard to believe that *Last Year's River* was written by a man because you've really gotten inside the character of Virginia and have really pegged how a woman who's going through this traumatic experience must feel. How do you react when you hear that?

I'm very flattered by it, of course. But I didn't sit down and sweat over how to explain a girl to the audience. There are certain things that I consciously did with Virginia—you know, she's a seventeen-year-old girl from a privileged background, she's going to have attitude problems with her elders, she's going to be preoccupied with clothing, she's going to appear more confident than she really feels—that sort of thing. A lot of what you put into a character is subconscious. Every character you write inevitably is a part of you. Where else does it come from?

Oddly enough, Henry was a harder character for me to write. Originally, he was just a foil for Virginia. But soon I started writing scenes which alternated between their points of view. To the extent that he was the strong, silent cowboy type, I flirted with cliché. So I felt I needed to give him some pretty serious hang-ups, and that brought him to World War I and the conflicts with his father and his somewhat ambiguous past. And, in the end, he became a much more interesting character to me.

....

CREATING WITH COMPASSION
Elizabeth Cox, interviewed by Sarah Anne Johnson

=≫◆≪=

How does compassion work in your creative writing and your teaching?

It is everything. I'm not sure we can write about characters unless we are compassionate, which means, of course, seeing everything. Compassionate, I think, means seeing all the sides of a person, all the capabilities, without judgment. If the author begins to judge, then he will begin to ask the reader to judge too, in the same way. The reader will balk when an agenda is felt. At least, I do. So if I'm judging a character I have to back up and look again in order to get myself out of it. A lot of writing, I guess, is trying to get out of the way—to get myself, my small-mindedness, out so that something else can be seen.

In teaching, as I see students create a character, I ask questions that require a different look at that character. Many undergraduate students will write something very judgmental about a father or a mother, with the young person being completely in the right. So I ask them to write from the point of view of the father/mother, and they are forced to get out of themselves as victim and see a different side. That's an obvious way, but also to ask questions about a character that keeps the author from creating only one dimension. That's the kind of compassion I teach: a way of looking that is not narrowly your own. Then of course, I'm constantly brought up short as I try to practice what I teach.

David Malouf: The two main characters in the book *Johnno* are in some ways playing that game we all play. We become different people for whoever it is we're talking to. In a way, when they're with one another, both characters are more themselves, and at the same time too much themselves to be real. Johnno always plays up to the idea that Dante has of him; Dante feels forced to be the kind of person Johnno sees him as.

as interviewed by Kevin Rabalais

MARY MORRISSY
interviewed by Ana Callan

The Irish reviewer and writer Lucille Redmond says that she finds very few sympathetic male characters in Irish fiction. A lot of yours are shadowy, sinister figures who are not necessarily developed but are hovering in the background, often ineffectual. Probably the most sympathetic is Mr. Skerrit in "The Curse." He's at least affable and kindly.

I don't intentionally create them that way, but it does strike me that they tend to be shadowy. Even Mr. Skerrit, who has a good heart, is basically ineffectual in the end. He can't stop the girl being humiliated even though he's understanding. In the novel, there are obviously more male characters, and I like to think they're better developed. But men don't come out very well in my fiction. It isn't a polemical thing with me. That just seems to be the way it is in the fiction itself. I mean, the one story in the book that's written from the male viewpoint—I'm not entirely convinced of it. I think it's quite hard to get inside the male. These stories, in a way, are an indication of that.

ANNIE PROULX

interviewed by Michael Upchurch

In all the books, I've noticed a pronounced fondness for having male protagonists, quite often males who are hooked up with pretty hellacious females. With these male characters, you usually show more sympathy than with the women. What's going on there?

The answer is so simple it will make you throw up: I was the oldest of five girls. I grew up in a family of five girls. If there's one thing I know, it's women and girls. And I don't find them interesting to write about. I find men much more interesting, you know? I didn't know any men when I was a kid, except my father. So it's more fun; it's more interesting.

Also, most of my life the things I've liked to do, the fishing and canoeing and tramping around in the country—this was before everybody got into the outdoorsy number—those were activities where there were not many women; it was mostly men. So I palled around with guys most of my adult life, and felt more at home with the direct approach to things that was then labeled "masculine." Now you can find women like that, too, and I know a lot of women whom I like a lot. Just great women out there.

Anyway, the two novels both demanded male protagonists. They were not set in a time or a place when those stories could have been written with women. I don't *think* of stories around women. And that's undoubtedly, in these days of political correctness, an enormous flaw in my character. But, baby, that's how it is.

A CHORUS OF VOICES
Kevin Canty, interviewed by Linda B. Swanson-Davies

The characters in this collection [*A Stranger in This World*] are frequently denying truth, even when they know themselves better than what they're pretending, and they know how things are going to turn out, but it seems like they still prefer to deny what they know. What do you think would happen to us if we were not able to fool ourselves?

Just look at anybody else. You can see their lives so clearly. In some ways it's like trying to see your own face in the mirror. It's yours. It's too familiar to see. I'm not sure someone without the capacity for self-deception would truly be a human being. I don't think it's intrinsic, but I don't have a version of myself that's fixed, so when I refer to self-deception, I'm not even sure who's doing the deceiving and who's the self and who's the rest of it. It seems more complex than that. I think it's more a chorus of voices rather than a single voice inside. For some people, that might be different. Some people are really driven and they want to go forward. I was struck by that, driving around L.A. Some people get up in the morning wanting to succeed and go to sleep at night wanting to succeed. They manage to shut off a lot of the rest of their lives. That was the feeling that I got when I was riding with people in elevators. I'm sort of jealous of that kind of single-mindedness, but I'm not sure that I wasn't making that up.

And you won't ever know.

I'll never know. That's the thing about writing: You are trying to decide what it's like to live a life that's not your own, and you'll never know. But, on the other hand, if I really thought that you would never know, if I really thought that we were on different planets, that what goes on inside the mysterious caverns of your mind was fundamentally different or fundamentally incomprehensible, then I couldn't write. Not to minimize the difference, not to say that we're all the same or that we all want the same things or all work the same way, but I think that you can understand. I think you can intuit your way into another person's life.

That's really what I'm trying to do: What's it like to live that life? What's it like to be that person?

WRITING THE OPPOSITE SEX
Richard Bausch
interviewed by Jennifer Levasseur and Kevin Rabalais

It has been said that your writing blends the best of women's and men's writing.

I'm very proud of that. It makes me feel good. I have women come up to me all the time and ask me how I know things and how come I can do that. The answer is simple. What you do is think, first, of a *person*, and then write. I learned it with my first novel, where I was writing about a priest. I was going around trying to think what a priest would do or say. You have to be honest enough and open enough to the experience and be whoever this person is and feel whatever he feels. Fiction is empathy. It is trying to feel like somebody else. It is getting out of yourself and into other people. Somebody will say, "Well, a man can't possibly write from the point of view of a woman very convincingly." And, of course, they've never read Henry James or Leo Tolstoy, or Chekhov or Shakespeare.

RUSSELL BANKS
interviewed by Rob Trucks

In *Trailerpark*, I was trying to write a novel that wasn't a novel, but that was, in an important way to me, a portrait of a community.

Which is not all that dissimilar to your attempt with The Sweet Hereafter.

Exactly. I think it's much more successful in *The Sweet Hereafter*. I was trying to avoid having a hero. I was really playing with the whole idea of having a hero by avoidance. Can you write a novel without a hero?

Can you use the term *protagonist* in the same sense as *hero*, or do you have to stay with the classical term?

I think you can say protagonist. A single, central figure. What James called the emotional center of the narrative. A single person where all values are tested. Any action which occurs is important insofar as it affects that character. And so *Trailerpark* is kind of a crude attempt to do what I think I did much more successfully in *The Sweet Hereafter*.

EVERYONE SPEAKS A LITTLE TRUTH
Charles Johnson, interviewed by Linda B. Swanson-Davies

One of the things I noticed in Middle Passage is that each of your charac-
ters speaks some substantial truth. There are no unnecessary characters.

Although I think that in most fiction there's one character who
bears the author's message or burden necessarily, and all the others
are foils or straw men, my characters pass through a social world in
which everybody they meet has a truth which they pick up on and
learn from—sort of Hegelian in that respect—so that by the end of
the story, there is a grand vision, a larger truth, that the main character experiences. So the truth is not static, but is something to be
achieved. It's always a process and the more people you encounter
the more your sense of understanding about the world deepens. I
think that's one of the reasons the characters all speak something
that's important to whoever the protagonist is.

Captain Ebenezer Falcon is a hateable guy—but not totally.

He's a loathsome character, a monster of the ego, but he is, I hope,
interesting. And he has reasons for being who he is and thinking as
he does. John Gardner used to emphasize that with all of his writing students. It's John who put it in front of me in a very clear way
when he was looking at chapters that I was writing for *Faith and
the Good Thing*. There is one character—the husband of Faith—who
was based on a good friend of mine; but I objected to many of his
ideas, and so I used him as a straw man in the novel. John wrote in
the margins: "Shame on you. Why present this character to us just
for us to dislike this person, or to disagree with him? Why not dig
as deeply as you can into his motivation, his background, his biog-

raphy, his thought process, so we can understand how someone can inhabit this position?" And, you know, I think he was quite right. You have to see each and every character in their totality and from their own perspective. We can disagree with them, but they have integrity as human beings that has to come through at some point in the fiction. I think writers have to do that with every character. You have to walk a mile in everybody else's shoes within that book, every major character's, at least.

THE DIFFICULTY WITH VILLAINS
Ann Patchett, interviewed by Sarah Anne Johnson

Was it difficult to create sympathetic yet realistic characters in the terrorists in Bel Canto? *How did you go about this?*

I have no idea if they're realistic, because I don't know any terrorists. It's never any problem at all for me to create sympathetic characters. I'm an absolute bomb when it comes to creating villains. I have no villains in any of my books. I have a villain-free oeuvre. Carl, in *Taft*, is the closest, and I don't think anyone would consider him a villain. He's a kid who's trying and messing up. Any character I get my hands on becomes a sympathetic character. I'm a bleeding heart.

In The Magician's Assistant, *at first Parsifal's mother loses integrity in the eyes of the reader, because she tells Sabine that she had her son sent to a reformatory because he was gay. Only when she reveals the truth of why he was sent away do readers see her as protecting her son by not unveiling his history all at once. This interplay between the sympathetic and the not-so-sympathetic aspects of character come up in your other books as well. What interests you about this?*

I don't agree with that, really. I think that when Dot tells that lie, she is sympathetic in that moment because she's saying that she did a terrible thing, she made a terrible mistake. I may be wrong, but I don't think the reader is coming down on her. Her grief is in the fact that she let him get away after all that happened, that she didn't do more to mend the break. Her remorse is real. A good lie is always a lie that is based in truth. Her lie is believable because it's so close to the truth—she knows that she made the wrong choice, and she's been punished her whole life with the loss of her most beloved child. So I don't think that the reader condemns Dot, but maybe just I don't condemn her because I have such a hard time with villains.

....

IT CAN'T BE HELPED

Carol Roh-Spaulding
interviewed by Linda B. Swanson-Davies

In the story we published, "White Fate," there's a line that's so beautiful: "It was a bright and breezy morning, the kind of morning when his heart always lifted with a little chirp of abandon, filling him with the brisk promise that some of the things he had always longed for could still be his." How did you ever write that sentence?

That's simply an autobiographical experience; I've had that very feeling and I put it into Mr. Song. I don't have it all the time, but it's this sense of hope and vitality and freshness that sometimes hits me on good days. There's a lot of longing involved in there, too. I want to be cautious because I can't speak for Korean culture or for Korean–American culture, but there is this state of being called *han*. It means lots of things. There's a river, you know, named Han, and it's also a surname. There are whole books on *han*—it's this sort of psychological state that is characteristic, they say, of Korean people, because of their history. China trampled through, and Japan, and over the course of centuries they've always been occupied by one country or another. It's a little like the Japanese sense of *sho no na gai*: It can't be helped. It's a little bit fatalistic, but what's more, it is longing, a deep-seated longing that never really goes away. A deep, wistful kind of longing where you can experience other emotions, but still feel that at the bottom. I think I've inherited that, and, even though it can be productive in some ways, it's a difficult thing to live with. I tried to get that into Mr. Song's life—that he is a loving person, a compassionate person, and a burdened person at the same time. You can be very loving and burdened.

YOU CAN'T PROTECT THEM

Stephen Dixon, interviewed by Jim Schumock

There's a fair amount of Nat's stream of consciousness throughout *Interstate*. He's an equivocator and a worrier of near epic proportions, isn't he?

Yes, he is. I wanted to make him a complex guy by having him think of every possibility in perspective. And it's a book where the crime is done through happenstance. It's just they're on the road and two horrors pass by. He's trying to think how he could have avoided them. He finds that there's no way to avoid it. He can't avoid bad luck.

He realizes there's no human action that isn't honored by his daughter's death, ultimately.

Yes, that's right.

One thing that I really appreciated about *Interstate* was Nat always instructing his daughters in the subtleties of getting through life. It's really amazing to me how much we have to teach children just about crossing the street. We're always speaking directly and giving them these little nips with the elbow trying to get them to go the right way.

Sort of a manual, my book, for children on how to live in the city or how to live in the contemporary world. But the irony, and the book is filled with irony, is that no matter how much you instruct your children there is something that might happen that you have no control over—a madman, a car accident, a needle in an apple that they got for Halloween. That's the irony. He overdoes his advice and protection for the kids. There are things that are on the road that you can't protect your kids from.

There is a little confusion in their lives as to whether he might be just a little bit physically abusive. Maybe he's a little bit that way. His children are kind of giving him some feedback. It's difficult for him to comprehend and process, isn't it?

He's more emotionally abusive, or psychologically abusive, than physically. He is at times physically abusive. He pushes them and he shoves them. There's a scene in the Baltimore Aquarium. He denies it immediately. I do this to show that he is a fallible person. This is one of the things he might learn from this long car trip which he might be imagining. He might be imagining the circumstance that carries this book, and that is the death, the violence. He might learn that he, too, has potential for violence. Maybe not, certainly not the kind where you shoot guns, because he's against the gun. Maybe at the end of the book, he's learned something about himself. That's why I put it in. I put it in to show that he is not above the violence. He is a victim of it but he's not above it. He's above the worst kind of violence but he, too, has a violent nature. He, too, was a rat when he was a kid, and he beat up guys and things like that. That he's aware of, and he hates himself for it. He's guilty about it but it's too late. It's already done its damage. He might be doing some emotional damage to his children, and he's aware of it. That might even be initiating the thought about his children's death through violent means. It could be something like that which turns into something worse in his mind.

There's a term you use several times in the book, *paterfamilias*, the old Roman idea of a father as master of the family. It seems like Nat's life is so over-examined and he's always in such flux that he really can't be a good paterfamilias.

But he is a good paterfamilias. He's a good father. He cooks for them. He's usually there for them. He loves his kids. He shows them what love is. He's good to his wife. I think he's a good father. He has faults, but he's not a bad father.

Do you think his children will turn out to be over-examiners of life like him?

In the book, they tell him about his over-examination. They say, "Come off it, Daddy," several times. They're hip to his problems and to his frailties. He takes it on the chin many times from them. It seems that they're pretty healthy and they will remain healthy, if they live.

EDWIDGE DANTICAT
interviewed by Sarah Anne Johnson

How did you handle the challenge in *The Dew Breaker* of writing sympathetically about a man who tortured and murdered?

He becomes like every other character—he becomes a man. You don't have the luxury of passing judgment when you write a character like that. You just write his life. You go into his head to write about him. He's the father of one woman. The husband of another. When I started writing that first story, it was going to be a more traditional immigrant story in which the father didn't understand the artist daughter's choice. Then these other pieces emerged. I didn't know myself what direction the story would take until I was writing. All of the characters who have encountered the torturer know a different aspect of him. Even the ones who were tortured by him were approached in different ways, and they deal with the aftermath in different ways as well. That's the complexity of human beings—what do we show and what do we hide? The Dew Breaker hides a lot, but at one point he becomes tired of it and begins to confess.

You hold off on telling how her parents came together until the last story, and with that revelation you let readers know why it's so complicated and difficult for the parents to explain their past in any way that will make sense to their daughter, Ka. Why did you hold off on revealing the powerful connection between the parents until the end? What does your narrative gain from this?

It's not an attempt at mystery. From the first story you know who the Dew Breaker is, and Ka thinks that that is the biggest news she'll ever be told in her life. If anything, the book holds the information off in the way that the mother holds it off. It's the last truth she wants told. She's agreed to let the father tell his daughter about his past, but she doesn't want to confess anything herself. The mother doesn't know how to confess, except at church. She holds things in. You get a sense in the story that this would be her deathbed confession. She may never tell it. She thinks there's no point to telling that kind of story. The reader only finds out as the mother is telling us about her inability to tell.

In "Night Talkers," Claude tells Dany that he's lucky because in killing his father, he has done something bad enough to make him want to live better. Claude is the voice of redemption in that his presence suggests how a person can redeem himself after committing horrible violence. Is the Dew Breaker redeemed in the end by living his life differently?

I try to avoid easy judgment because I don't think redemption is a one-time thing. For the wife and the husband, it's a daily choice. She sees that forgiveness is not a one-time event. She has to keep forgiving him. I had to keep forgiving him, too, as I was writing, and had to keep forgiving her for loving him.

ANTONYA NELSON
interviewed by Susan McInnis

How do you work between inner and external landscapes, so that the plot develops, the characters follow their own idiosyncratic paths, and the issues nonetheless stay in focus?

I think that the internal and the external have to play off each other. I'm frequently telling students to make use of what I call "Acts of God" to establish a character's identity. It's hard to come up with a character who hasn't got anything to react against.

What do you mean by "Acts of God" in this context?

I can use an example from the first book [*The Expendables*], actually. Three characters are in a car. As they are driving along, they witness children mistreating each other on the side of the road. They drive right by a disturbing spectacle, something that should make them stop. That's where a story in that first collection began for me. I wanted to know, Who *are* those people? For any real, coherent answer, I had to back up from the question, which becomes the last scene in the story, and consider what kind of people simply drive by instead of stopping. I had to consider what was compelling to me about people who would not stop.

In the end they are people who are exceptionally messed up in their own relationships, particularly in the moment they drive by what's happening at the side of the road. And what's happening there in some way reflects the relationships in the car. Two men and a woman in the car, two boys and a little girl on the side of the road. Characters are created quite frequently by how they react to an event. The novella, "Family Terrorists," begins with a family that's gone through a tornado. The youngest child in the family was in the womb then, fully formed, but still inside. She's always felt somehow separate from the central drama of the family, out on the periphery. The story begins there—with that notion of a storm and her being protected and not present, and, though formed, still not fully formed. Her sense of being just in the shadow of the family's life prevails. She has that sense of being the shadow child, and she's formed by that more than any other thing. "Acts of God" doesn't always mean storms and traumas and floods and famine. They're frequently much more mundane, like illness in a life. All of us are formed by what happens to us as much as by what we do to exert ourselves in the world. Maybe more so. As writers, we tend to think we have to keep coming up with outward-directed action—plots that move from the inside out—rather than having the character react to the external world. But much can happen in the world that can generate equal movement within a character's psyche.

....

Valerie Martin: I want my characters to be as complex as possible, and I don't think of them as good or bad. I make a case for them. Because that's really what you do when you write a novel, you make a case for the way a person is, the way you apprehend them.

as interviewed by Janet Benton

CAROL SHIELDS
interviewed by Jim Schumock

⟹◈⟸

After Daisy goes into her depression in The Stone Diaries, *several people theorize about why she's depressed. Why do you think she went into the depression? It's more than losing the column, isn't it?*

Of course. Although, I think that's a very big part. It's the theory of one of her children. All these people have different suggestions. Her son thinks that she's thwarted her intelligence. Her old girlfriend, Freddie Hoyt, thinks that she just didn't have enough of a love life. I think that all these surmises are right and they're also all wrong. But coming together, they form the whole sense of her loss. I don't think people have breakdowns for one particular reason. I think it's when several events, or several memories, coincide and bring about a failure of nerve, which is what she suffers. Curiously, one of her daughters guesses that she is partly enjoying her anger. For the first time, she is letting herself feel. In fact, it has given her a kind of intensity of experience that she has never had before. I think that's true.

....

INCORPORATING HISTORICAL FIGURES
Andrea Barrett, interviewed by Sarah Anne Johnson

⟹◈⟸

It's interesting that you weave actual historical figures into the cast of "Ship Fever" and other stories. What does a narrative gain from this?

A certain verisimilitude, I suppose. There were doctors and politicians who were very important during the Grosse Isle epidemic, and any person invented or real might have brushed by or known of those people at the time. It seems helpful to include those persons in the frame, not so much in the center in the direct action, but to put them around the edges so that the whole fiction will feel more real to the reader.

....

GEORGE MAKANA CLARK
interviewed by Linda B. Swanson-Davies

"The Pit-Bull Drill," "Astral Navigation," and "Politics of Rain." Was there really an Uncle Blas? Were these stories his, yours, or did they come from other sources?

I meant, as grim as it was, for there to be some humor in Blas's story, in the way he told it, the offhanded way—it jars. That's how the novel will be. Uncle Blas came from a photograph of a black butcher, which I thought was a fitting occupation, who had fought in the Bay of Pigs. There were lots of Cubans in Angola who were fifty years old, unlike the American Army, where most retire after twenty years. I wanted a soldier who had fought at the Bay of Pigs and in Angola. In the photograph, he had this enormous goat belly, one of those tight bellies, where if you hit it, it would hurt your hand; but the rest of him was very fit, and he was jet black with a huge cigar and a beret. He was bare chested, wearing dark blue dungarees and combat boots, and I thought, He's perfect! I can't just make up a character. Some people can, but I can't. There has to be some element, something I've read or seen.

THE NEW KID AT SCHOOL

Roy Parvin, interviewed by Linda B. Swanson-Davies

I go through a funny process with my characters, and I do care about them. I love them, even the villains. They all need love. They need my love. I frankly can't write any other way. I go through a process, though, in the beginning, with the characters. I feel like they're the new kid in school, in grade school. I make fun of them, in my writing.

What do you mean?

Well, I mean that I'm condescending toward them. It's because I don't understand them. Just like you don't understand a new kid at school. It takes me a long time to understand their particular humanness, and once I do, I fall head over heels for them. I feel like they need my protection. I like to know everything that they're thinking, and there's a lot of stuff that happens off the page that you don't see.

....

Kevin Canty: There are some characters that I found it very easy to spend time with and I sort of miss them and wish I could go back and write those stories again and spend time with them. I like the woman in the last story, "A Stranger in This World." She's good company—she smokes, she drinks, she weighs too much.

as interviewed by Linda B. Swanson-Davies

THE REASON FOR CHARACTER

Russell Banks, interviewed by Rob Trucks

≈◆≈

I guess with the recent publication of Cloudsplitter, *the most obvious question to start with is, Why John Brown?*

Well, I think that's a question you can ask about any novel, in a way. Why a school-bus accident? Why a fourteen-year-old mall rat? Or, Why a white whale, Mr. Melville? And you're going to get a similar answer from most writers, because there's a braid of reasons. There's rarely, if ever, just one reason, if you look at it honestly and try to understand it, or try to speak about it honestly.

I can say that, on a personal level—this is one strand in the braid—Brown was in my life in a vivid way when I was in my twenties in college in Chapel Hill in the middle sixties, because he was sort of an emblematic figure like Che Guevara. Very much like Che Guevara. He was a man of action whose ideals one could identify with. And his picture would be up on the wall of the SDS office or the SCLC office, and he crossed those racial lines that a lot of us white kids were trying to cross during that period, trying to do it in a thoughtful and respectful and committed political way. He was also, at the same time, uniquely connected to the literary figures that meant a great deal to me then, and still do. Which is to say the mid-nineteenth-century New England writers—the Transcendentalists, Thoreau and Emerson and so on. I loved Melville's poem about him, and even lesser poets like John Greenleaf Whittier wrote about him. So he was a figure who was a part of my literary constellation, too. In addition to being a part of my political and social constellation, he was part of my literary constellation. And unique in that regard.

ALICE MATTISON
interviewed by Barbara Brooks

The intersecting stories in *Men Giving Money, Women Yelling* relate to one another much the way people in a small town do.

Yes, or a small city. Each story raised questions that the next one answered, sometimes about the plot—why something happened—and sometimes about the characters. In a story called "The Hitchhiker," there's a woman named Charlotte whose friend Daisy tells her about something going on in her life. Daisy is a teacher, and she's slept with a student. I thought Daisy was an interesting character, and I began to suspect that she knew something she wasn't telling. This has happened to me a number of times: A minor character becomes more interesting to me than the major characters. The more I thought about it, the more I thought Daisy was lying when she talked to Charlotte; that she hadn't told her the whole story. And sure enough, when I got her to be the spokesperson—in a story called "Selfishness"—the story she told was quite different, much more complicated. She stayed in my mind after I finished that book, and eventually she became the main character of *The Wedding of the Two-Headed Woman*. I knew Daisy was going to do something bad, something destructive. And then I started thinking about a headline that I had once seen, years ago: "Two-Headed Woman Weds Two Men; Doc Says She's Twins." Then it took me months to work out the story.

RECURRING CHARACTERS

Andrea Barrett, interviewed by Sarah Anne Johnson

I've been working with some of the same characters now through the last three books. You've probably noticed, in *Servants of the Map*, that there are things that hark back to previous books. Often these days, as I'm working on one story or novella or novel, I'll get a glimmer of somebody else in this gigantic family and what might have happened to them in some other time. Actually all the people are related, but you can't see it yet.

It's thrilling when they come back. I loved seeing Ned and Max again in "The Cure." It adds a new dimension to the work.

Most of the people in *Servants of the Map* and some of the people in *The Voyage of the Narwhal* are actually related, sometimes in complicated and distant ways, to the Marburg sisters in *Ship Fever*. They are various ancestors of theirs. The book I'm trying to start now will show more clearly how everyone fits together. I have a big chart in my office that's quite insane looking, all these wings and people through all these centuries over all these countries. But I don't think it's actually important to the stories. They stand alone, as do the novels, so it's not that it's some endless saga or set of sequels. More that this has been important for me as an idea-generating device. It's very fertile for me. When I'm writing something about Max, I can wake up one morning and think, "But what about Clara?" Then I'll be writing about Clara and her daughters, and I'll wake up another morning and think, "What was Gillian doing when she was eighteen?" And on it goes. And that's nice. I don't seem to run out of material.

Throughout *Servants of the Map*, *The Voyage of the Narwhal*, and *Ship Fever*, several characters recur, and their stories unfold in new and intriguing ways. For instance, Nora, Ned, and Denis Kynd first appear in the story "Ship Fever," then Ned is the cook in *The Voyage of the Narwhal*, and Ned and Nora are reunited in "The Cure" in *Servants of the Map*. What draws you to revisit your characters and continue to explore their lives?

They're alive for me. I spend so much time with them that when a book is done or a story is done, the characters don't disappear from my brain. I made them, and I live with them for a long time, and then I send the story or the book off, but they're still there. They seem, in some senses, to continue to live their lives without me. Sometimes, years later, it's as if I can go back to the barn in Pennsylvania where they have all been living and open the door and catch up with them. I don't know what that's about either. I seem unable to dismiss them. It does feel like death to me. Not to revisit them feels like killing them off. To lose those people from your life when you've had such an imaginative connection with them is too difficult. This way, I refuse to let them die unless I kill them off on the page.

The appearance of these characters throughout successive works, their individual growth and development as characters, gives them the sense of having a life beyond the pages of any particular story or narrative. It gives them a sense of individual existence that engages readers more deeply in their unfolding stories. How much of this is intentional?

It wasn't intentional at first. It surprised me and I went with it, and for a while I did it more or less unconsciously. But since the publication of *Servants of the Map*, which came out in February

2002, a lot of people have asked me about this. Inevitably, I've had to think about it consciously, to try to understand what that linkage does and what I'm doing. That's been interesting for me as a writer. It wasn't a planned thing, but I've been brought to consciousness about it, so I'm much more aware of it in what I'm writing now. I've had to admit to myself what I'm doing. That's often true for us as writers, not just with regard to this question, but with regard to all sorts of things we do, the characters we make, the themes we revisit. At some point in reviews or conversations someone will point out to us what we're doing. Often we're not conscious of it, and then we're forced to become conscious of it and to integrate that more deeply. That's interesting. I learned a lot this spring as people pressed at that point and made me think about it.

RICHARD BAUSCH
interviewed by Jennifer Levasseur and Kevin Rabalais

You really get inside your characters and make them come alive. The two older men in your novel *The Last Good Time* are older than you, but you seemed to have had no trouble creating their voices. Do you become close to all your characters?

Oh, yeah, all of them. I understand perfectly that they are constructions and that they are made up. But it's like when you were a kid and had imaginary friends. You were always thinking about them. You saw with their eyes, and you had some of their memories, which is really a kind of wonderful thing. Mary Lee Settle talks about her characters like it's gossip. She'll say, "Guess what she did today," about one of her characters. I sort of picked some of that up from her. I wish I could tell you something that could be revealing about this, but I really don't know how it works. It just comes with the character, thinking about it, dreaming it up.

CAROLYN CHUTE
interviewed by Barbara Stevens

Is it easy for you to get inside the heads of your characters?

Once I've got them together. Those last few months I find myself so immersed in that world that even [my husband] Michael joins me, and we start talking about them.

Because it's so real?

Yeah.

But how do you get to the point where it's real?

I don't know. I don't know how I finally get there.

Is it hard?

Yeah. It's awful. It's so frustrating.

Are they as real to you as real people?

In the end. In the end. But not for a long time. Right now they're not too real. Kind of like shadows. It's awful.

Andre Dubus: I do sometimes plan to have several stories with the same character, but I have never thought of the advantages. It could be a limitation; I don't know. I prefer reading stories. François Mauriac said, "I don't know why anybody writes long novels. You could always write another novel about the same people."

as interviewed by Jennifer Levasseur and Kevin Rabalais

WHEN IT'S OVER

Charles Baxter, interviewed by Robert Birnbaum

⇒◆⇐

Why are you so sure you are not going to revisit Saul and Patsy? I have heard other writers say that they are done with a story: Julian Barnes with *Talking It Over*, which he revisited with *Love, etc.*, some ten years later. He now will not foreclose on another installment of these characters' lives. Richard Ford said he was done with Frank Bascombe after *Independence Day* [which is a continuation of *The Sportswriter*].

I would not revisit them because I am no longer as interested in them as I once was.

Today. At this moment.

Today. I don't find them, now that I have written about them at the length that I have, as interesting for me as they once were. [Long pause.]

There is a certain kind of inner resonance that I feel about characters when I know that I am about to write about them. I feel full of them. And the process of writing often feels like an emptying out

Character 199

of that fullness: the knowledge I have of them and also the feelings I am going through on their behalf. I feel as if that's gone now with them. That it was not gone before—but it is gone now.

....

IMPOSING YOUR WILL

Thomas E. Kennedy
interviewed by Linda B. Swanson-Davies

⸺◈⸺

I wondered, with a character like this who presents himself in many of your stories, if you ever want to just make him give over to his better inclinations. For instance, Michael Lynch—it drove me crazy how worried he was about his family, and yet he did not act at a point when he felt they were in extreme danger. He didn't just go home. And I also worried he'd drop into real alcoholism. It sounds maybe silly, but once a character comes to life, what sort of feelings do you develop for that person, and how do you feel about him? I mean, is he a real guy now?

You're talking about *The Book of Angels*. I hold very much with those who say that writing is a process of discovery, and that if there's no surprise for the writer, there'll be no surprise for the reader. So I just followed Lynch, and did my best not to impose my will on him, because that would kill it. When I try to impose my will on my characters, it kills the story. Someone asked Beckett about *Waiting for Godot*, when it first came out, to please explain a little bit about the characters, to help the audience understand, and his answer was something like, "What I know about the characters in *Waiting for Godot*, such as I know it, only came to me because of my scrupulous desire to remain free of the desire to understand them, and to only know them through what they do and what they say." And I would say the same thing. Of course, after I'm finished writing, I begin to interpret them. Also in the revision process, you have to get a little bit more conscious understanding of what's going on in order to make sure that things are functioning as they should.

It's interesting that you mention that—I've had one or two people ask me why didn't he go home when he knew something was wrong. I think the reason is that he was caught in the complexity of this mystery, and it was something greater than him. I think he was basically powerless to go home at that point, and was just hoping beyond hope that his friends would protect his family. I think he felt that if he didn't continue his journey into the darkness that he was lost. There was no other way for him.

Does this feel like a person to you?

Yeah, when I'm writing it, it does. Definitely.

When you stop, when you're done, do you miss him? Or is that just gone?

Usually it's just gone. It's funny you say that, because there was a story in *Unreal City* called "Murphy's Angel," about the angel in the basement that dies. I had a student at William Rainey Harper College in Chicago ask me, "What did they do with the angel's body?" I was utterly stumped. So I went home and wrote a story called "Angel Body." Two moving men come and take the body and deliver it to Lauren—that was the student's name—and they dump the body on her carpet and it's her problem now. "Murphy's Angel" just ended with the angel's death. That question was beyond my ken, although it was a wonderful question.

But with *The Book of Angels*, it didn't just end like that. Those people do still exist for me. All of those characters. And in fact, a number of people now have asked if I'm going to write a sequel, because it seems to have been left open-ended. I want to write a screenplay of *The Book of Angels*, and I might consider a sequel to it. I would not have thought that before this tour, but so many people have mentioned it, and mentioned, for example, the character Nothing, who's left standing against the wall at the end. It would be interesting to follow her and see what happens. Maybe her life would loop back to Lynch's.

AN AFFECTION TOWARDS CHARACTERS
Carol Roh-Spaulding
interviewed by Linda B. Swanson-Davies

My story "Brides of Valencia" is an exact retelling of a Eudora Welty story. I told the editor [at White Eagle Coffee Store Press] this is what I'm doing. I'm stealing this story, basically—it's a tribute to her, and maybe I didn't get it right, but that story is one of my all-time favorite stories. It gets me closer to the sensation that I'm always trying to articulate, but can't really articulate. The young woman is on a journey. My theory is that what she has in her life is joy, and she is not large enough to contain it. She needs to get away from it for a while so that she can get some perspective. We think of other emotions as being too much to bear, but they're usually negative emotions. The capacity for joy is something that many people don't have, and we're only given it in moments. No one has it all the time, not even the Dalai Lama, you know. How do we as humans sustain the largest emotions even when they're beautiful ones? To me the story is a journey, a way for her to get away from that, to step out of it, because there's every sense that she's going to return to the life she has and be fine.

I don't want to get on a big crusade about this, but so much fiction that's considered good right now—well, I don't want to generalize, but Welty has a quality in her writing, and I think to a certain extent Katherine Mansfield has this, too. It's an affection toward their characters. I'm not sure that's the best description of it. They're quite as capable of irony and wit as anybody writing today, but there is this other quality that I just don't see in contemporary fiction. It's a kind of freshness and innocence she has toward her characters—a wiseness that is not jaded. I love that quality.

Welty's story, "The Bride of Innesfallen," was published in *The New Yorker* in 1955, and I don't think anyone would even bother to read it today because it doesn't do what fiction does nowadays. I know there are literary fashions, but I don't think people have the time anymore for a story that does what "The Bride of Innesfallen" does. People also don't know how to respond to "Brides of Valencia," because it's really sort of plotless, and yet it's telling, I think, a very important story.

William Styron: There is a strong trend in modern literature known as "post-modernism," which tends to minimize a story and character—in terms of profound introspection—and that kind of writing I'm neither terribly attracted to nor do I want to write. I think that the traditional writing I admire is writing that has a narrative thrust, and a narrative momentum, and also has believable characters.

as interviewed by Melissa Lowver

ABDELRAHMAN MUNIF

interviewed by Michael Upchurch

One thing I've been wondering since the end of *Cities of Salt* is when Miteb al-Hathal will come back in from the desert.

Everyone asks me that, and I always give the same specific response. Miteb al-Hathal is the hero of bygone times. There is no need for him to return. If he came back it would be as a poor, miserable man. For him to remain a phantom or a conscience is the best role for him, because he's incapable of providing a solution to the future.

....

RICHARD BAUSCH

interviewed by Jennifer Levasseur and Kevin Rabalais

Is there a particular character who has stuck with you?

The ones who stay with me longer are the ones I write about again. I wrote a story, "The Fireman's Wife," and the couple in that story appears again—although they're not quite identifiable—in the novella "Rare & Endangered Species." And they also show up in a story called "Evening," as this fractious couple across the street continually breaking up and getting back together. I kind of always want to put another face on it or another name because I don't want readers to think they are going to be looking at the same characters all the time.

Pam Durban: I don't see how you can write about somebody who is alienated and doesn't believe in or care about anything. What's there to write about? That's part of the problem with a lot of stories I see. There is only so much you can say about that condition. All of my characters want something or are trying or struggling with something. And maybe that's just an old-fashioned sense of fiction. The alienated stuff strikes me as sentimental, finally.

as interviewed by Cheryl Reid

YOUR CHARACTERS, OUT IN THE WORLD
Vikram Chandra
interviewed by Jennifer Levasseur and Kevin Rabalais

In *Red Earth and Pouring Rain*, Sanjay says to Abhay, "The stories cease to be yours the moment you write them down." What is your relationship with your characters after you have completed a book?

It's like sending children out into the world, really. It's difficult to control how other people see them or react to them or engage with them. I did mean that when I wrote it, that stories cease to be yours the moment you write them down, and I still agree with Sanjay. What the characters become when they are out in the world is sometimes strange and foreign from what I intended them to be. They get rewritten, reinscribed, in the lives of my readers. I still feel close to those characters, but they change, and I change. I was looking at *Red Earth and Pouring Rain* the other day and thinking that it feels like it was written by somebody else. You get distant from the person who started the book.

SUSAN RICHARDS SHREVE

interviewed by Katherine Perry Harris

≫•≪

In *Skin Deep: Black Women & White Women Write about Race*, the anthology you co-edited with Marita Golden, you talk about Prudential, an African-American woman who keeps recurring in your novels, including *The Visiting Physician* and *A Country of Strangers*. You write that "Prudential Life Insurance is the only character I have ever imagined who has appeared more than once in a book of mine, and always her role in the story is to witness the action with clear eyes that see the world for what it is." The character, you say, is a gift who clearly has the role of seer. Why do you think this particular character stayed with you, in this role?

The first time I used Prudential was in *Dreaming of Heroes*. She's in her thirties, a survivor of segregation in Washington, DC, during the late sixties. I liked her but she wasn't central in that book. I didn't imagine using her again, although I was fond of the name Prudential Life Insurance, taken by her parents from a sign advertising life insurance. Then I wrote *A Country of Strangers*, about a family of whites and a family of blacks in the early forties in northern Virginia; Prudential is a main character. That book is her best role. She's a cranky, daring, sassy little girl compromised by fate with nothing to lose. I loved writing about her. She appears again in *The Visiting Physician* as an older woman. She's there more as a salute from me because three is magic, so I wanted her to have one more story.

BRAD WATSON

interviewed by Robert Birnbaum

The person in *The Heaven of Mercury* who comes closest to being evil and a villain is Earl's sister. Everyone's flaws still seem to be worthy of sympathy. You don't seem to revile your characters.

In that these characters grew out of relatives I either knew or heard a lot of stories about, I knew how those people were flawed, and yet very sweet and kind and generous at the same time. If I have a vision of humanity, it's that. Rarely do you see what you perceive to be pure evil. What you see are people making mistakes, being blinded by their anger or frustration. And doing harm to other people not so much with the long-term intention of doing harm as simply expressing themselves with their limited ability to act properly in any given situation. Selfishness, greed, pride—all of this figures in, but at heart you have a decent human being who has made a lot of mistakes and probably has a great deal of regret over those mistakes.

I see myself as being a very non-judgmental person. It probably serves me well as a fiction writer. Sometimes as a human being you can get in trouble if you don't become judgmental to a certain degree. I'm sympathetic to all these characters—I'm even sympathetic, to a degree, to the Junius character, who is, to my mind, probably the least redeemable character in the book. He has fewer regrets, but at the same time he is a character about whom I told a story about his younger days when he kills his brother-in-law in a fight. He is doing it to defend his sister, who has been abused by this man, so even he has a modicum of redeeming qualities.

This is the character that, at his sister's deathbed, refuses her request to forgive her.

Yeah, he's the hardest character in the book. That's why I see him as the least redeemable.

....

THE HUMAN CAPACITY FOR SUFFERING
Mary McGarry Morris
interviewed by Linda B. Swanson-Davies

⇒◇⇐

There's a great deal of pain in the world. And the terrible reality is that some people have more pain in their lives than they will ever have happiness. I have no idea why this is so. It mystifies and confuses me. It seems to mock my religious faith. All I have to do is wonder, Why them and not me? and it necessarily undermines my own happiness, my own success and peace of mind.

But what this terrible reality does do is it makes me write. It makes me explore such lives and question the limits of human endurance. And what I've found, what I keep finding, and what is most reassuring is the unbelievable resilience of the human spirit in even the most deprived, the most fragile, among us. In *A Dangerous Woman*, the character of Martha Horgan experiences a terrible dichotomy. She is as fully aware of her limitations brought on by her emotional instability as she is of the normal life that goes on around her—but she can't change either one. She can't make herself "normal" no matter how hard she tries, and she can't make people like her. She can neither solve her dilemma nor be free of it. She is driven by her absolutism, by her maddening insistence on truth, the one truth. Her concept of right and wrong is so clearly defined and painfully dogmatic that, with her peculiar zeal, she often manages to make morality seem like an aberration. Martha's need for truth is as basic, as innate and propelling a force as is her need for love. And yet, vulnerable as she is, she possesses a great power over her community, a power she will never understand or effectively harness.

ROBERT STONE
interviewed by Jim Schumock

Your characters generally choose between the flawed path and the very flawed path. What so intrigues you about these moral lowlifes and self-destruction?

I think in a way these people are perfectionists. They're people who are driven to spite. What drives them to spite and what drives them to spiteful self-destruction, I think, is not so much a despair as a refusal to settle for things in near imperfect reality. I think these are people who have never recovered from illusions and refuse to accommodate a world that is not as good and beautiful as they would like it to be.

The character of Owen Browne in *Outerbridge Reach* is different from those who usually populate your work.

He's a character who's different from the characters I've written about because his self-destructiveness is really very much more subtle. He's a guy who lives a conventionally successful life. He went through the Naval Academy. His experience in Vietnam was not ultimately destructive to him. He didn't feel like he was doing the wrong thing. He didn't feel like he was burned out. It left him, in fact, with a sense that he had been trained for accomplishments that he had not yet made because he wanted to be tested even more. In a way, his self-destructiveness was unbeknownst to him. He was a character without very much insight, and my characters are often as dynamic as their insight. Browne was a guy capable of insight, but who had never in the course of his life had to cultivate it. He really comes to it in the course of his voyage. He's also a prickly character. He's a fussy and demanding man. He's not at all a hipster; quite the opposite. He's a different sort of character than I've written about before.

REACTING TO THE MARGINALIZED
Elizabeth Cox, interviewed by Sarah Anne Johnson

In each of your novels and many stories as well, there is an outsider, a marginalized character who gets by on the kindness of the people around him. In *Familiar Ground* there is Soldier, in *The Ragged Way People Fall Out of Love* there's Zack who lives in the cabin, and in *Night Talk* there's Capp. I love these characters, and they work to inform the narrative in many ways.

I always have these characters in my books. I think that the other characters might be defined by their relationship to these marginal people. I don't know, maybe I think that we are defined by this relationship—whether we ignore it or participate. These characters work more like an image, though I use them as characters. They come from a recurring dream image I've had. The character was first an animal, mute but with enormous vulnerability, dependent on those around him. I'm glad I'm not a critic, because I don't know why they keep showing up.

STEPHEN DIXON

interviewed by Jim Schumock

Poet John Hollander, in blurbing your book of collected stories [*The Stories of Stephen Dixon*], credits you with describing your own special anomie. Do you think that's true?

The unfortunate thing about that quote is that every time I hear the word *anomie* I forget what it means and I have to look it up. So I don't know quite what he's saying. What does the word mean again?

It means a kind of a social isolation or dislocation.

I would never contradict John Hollander. Certainly not when he's saying something nice about my work.

Why is it that so many of your characters are distressed in that particular way? They're not quite able to gather their lives together and force them through into the next stage.

I discovered a long time ago that they're more interesting to write about than characters who have it together. I like to write about losers more than about successful people. Successful people bore me as fictional creations. I know that popular fiction is filled with successful people, in love, in money, in power, in business. I don't read those guys. They're jerks to me. To me, it's the little man who is facing the worst things in life. This time, the most unspeakable, unthinkable thing, the death of a child. But also a guy who loses his job, a guy who is desperate for money, a guy whose wife is going to have a baby and they need a room to have it in—these are the people that I find interesting to write about. I'm writing about the things that people suffer through rather than the things that people have success with. It just generates more creativity in me.

THE MADNESS THAT IS UNCONTAINED
Ha Jin, interviewed by Sarah Anne Johnson

Little Owl is an interesting character in *The Crazed*, retarded and therefore crazed in a different way than Mr. Yang. Jian Wan's room-mate said that "China was a paradise for idiots, who were well treated because they incurred no jealousy, posed no threat to anyone, and made no trouble for the authorities—they were model citizens through and through." Little Owl's presence is at times a source of irritation to Jian Wan. Besides the obvious social commentary, why did you include him?

I wanted to show that madness is quite prevalent. When I was an undergraduate and a graduate student, I ran into men like Little Owl. They were banished to the countryside, and then the schools took them back. They were crazy. The schools didn't know what to do with them, so they would just roam around the campuses talking nonsense all the time. It was quite common. Little Owl's presence shows the kind of madness that is not always contained.

....

LONG JOURNEYS LEFT BEFORE THEM
Maria Flook, interviewed by Sarah Anne Johnson

━━━➤◆◄━━━

How does a story come to you?

I start with a character who intrigues me. I want to invent a world around him, but he's somehow demanding it. I didn't pull him out of a hat. He comes from all my demons. He takes over the page. He takes form and becomes his own man, almost, but he's that edgy, relentless anxiety made flesh again.

I'm interested in writing about risks people take to attain something that's out of reach—love, safety, family bonds that have broken. There are a lot of walking wounded out there with long journeys left before them. These are my characters, I think. I'm comfortable with them. I don't choose who I write about. They just surround me. I'm interested in writing about risks people take to attain something that's out of reach....

Did you know Willis would be a driver for WASTEC in *Open Water*? How did you come up with that?

I have a real interest in working-class occupations for my characters. I guess because I've had my fair share. I mean I wouldn't know much about Wall Street situations, you know? If you can give some realistic information about the working lives of characters, you are giving them footing in their worlds in a larger context than they might have if you kept them in their kitchens and living rooms. I've worked in banks, in fish processing plants, as a waitress, as a corrections officer; I worked in a factory that makes velveteen boxes for the jewelry industry in Rhode Island. They weren't real velvet, but some kind of stinking resin they sprayed onto these little boxes from high pressure nozzles. It wasn't good to breathe it.

If you can put your character in some sort of job setting or working conditions a lot can happen. WASTEC was a very low-end and ill-suited occupation for Willis. You wanted him to get out.

One of my favorite work settings in recent fiction is the emergency room in Denis Johnson's brilliant story "Emergency." He has his characters working beyond their job capacities. His main character is lovelorn and doped up and has deeper problems than the hapless patients he attends to, but putting him in that setting, with the hospital routines and familiar details, skewed just right by Johnson's relentless wit and edginess, helps the reader see him as a hero.

. . . .

ANTONYA NELSON
interviewed by Susan McInnis

When you carry characters forward from story to story, do they become even more real over time?

Well, yes and no. If they have a history in my fictional consciousness, I think they emerge on the page as more complex characters, because I feel more confident of where they've come from. But by the same token, they're confounding. Frequently they won't do what I need them to do in a particular story because that "action" wasn't a part of their past. It can be annoying when I don't have the freedom to make them behave in certain ways because that's not "who they are." I've had to rearrange lives.

Of course, that's a bother.

It *is* a bother. Characters can be a little like family members, you know. There's always someone you like a lot, or even love deeply, but you can't help wishing they'd just settle down and do what they should be doing in life.

....

ANN PATCHETT
interviewed by Sarah Anne Johnson

Bel Canto hosts a huge cast of characters, yet each is distinct and leaves his or her own impressions on the reader. How do you create unique characters without running the risk of one character blending into the next, or falling out of the reader's consciousness during the story?

I read a lot of Chekhov. Honestly, there is nobody who does a better job with a one-sentence walk-on character having a complete and distinct personality than Chekhov. It's something that I've studied for years and years. He never lets anybody fall through the cracks, no matter how tiny. If it's just a postman bringing a letter to the main character, you know that postman. No one is a throwaway character. You don't have to present a full life history—we're all distinct. We're distinct at a glance, and your characters should be distinct at a glance.

THE VOICE OF THE AVERAGE
Carol Shields, interviewed by Jim Schumock

Daisy Goodwell Flett, the main character in *The Stone Diaries*, is really involved in the process of reinventing herself. Tell about her shifting voice in the book.

The voice varies from first person to third person here and there. But it's always Daisy's voice. It's always her consciousness. Even when other people offer their versions of her history, they're all filtered through her consciousness. This was the trick of writing this book which purports to be a kind of autobiography. At the center of Daisy's life there's a void. She is, in fact, like many women this [previous] century, erased from her own life story. There are no photographs of Daisy in this book. There are lots of letters in this book. But they are letters she receives. The letters that she writes, no one saves. She's one of these women who never quite achieved what she might have, certainly not in the eyes of other people. In fact, I had a letter from someone after this book came out. She said, "I wish Daisy had tried a little harder." I wish that, too. But I think that, like ninety-nine percent of the women of this century, she felt the full weight of social and political constraints. She did not make the record. She was unable to try harder. No one gave her permission to try harder. We have novels about those women who tried harder and made it. But we don't have many novels about this great milk that lies beneath the thin layer of cream. That was the life that I wanted to look at.

Andre Dubus: I want to use physical details and spiritual light and darkness in such a way that a reader experiences them and becomes the character, goes through what the character goes through. But when I'm writing, I always become the character. I just go through the story with the character to see what is going to happen.

as interviewed by Jennifer Levasseur and Kevin Rabalais

BRINGING CHARACTERS TO LIFE
Elizabeth Cox, interviewed by Sarah Anne Johnson

You teach the importance of drawing characters that are not stereotypical, but are whole and real and inhabit an emotional world. Can you talk about how you achieve this in your own work?

When I first work with a character he or she is flat. The character begins by speaking in ways that feel directed by the author. The dialogue is horrible and no one seems to be speaking convincingly. I have to stay with these people until they come alive on the page, until they begin to speak and act in ways that are more their own. But sometimes a character comes in whole. Anytime I write about a seven-year-old boy he comes in as a complete person. Seven-year-old boys are easy for me. Maybe I am (actually) a seven-year-old boy disguised as a woman.

The more difficult characters have to be lingered with, like staying around people you know until you know something more about them. You might think you know how they would behave, then they surprise you, and your idea dissolves—they become alive outside your ideas of how they are. I create scenes and go with these characters to different places. Maybe we go to the zoo and I see something they are afraid of, or maybe they have an argument, or someone comes to see them. The more places (scenes) we go, the better I understand their behavior.

How do you keep characters sympathetic, that is, not too good or too flawed, but a realistic combination of both?

If a character is too nice, then I have to wonder what he or she would do to reveal selfishness, envy, jealousy, meanness in order to make the personality real. If a character is too demonic, I have to create vulnerability. I don't usually realize what needs to be developed until I get far into the story. For instance, I'm working with a man now who is probably too good. I don't know when I will see a side of him that makes him a little more human—maybe something he fears. I always wonder what a character's secret is. I'm curious about people's secrets. Even sitting by someone on the plane I'll ask what their secret is, and often, to my horror, I am told. I don't ask that question as often as I used to.

Some of the scenes [in *Night Talk*] depicting racism are written with such clear detachment that they truly make me cringe, or blush with embarrassment for the characters. How do you create such empathy in your readers?

I try to put down truthfully all the ways small and large that we are intolerant of each other. If the characters are human enough, the reader recognizes those places. I wanted to bring the reader close enough so that they could not see the character as racist, but as someone who was human and intolerant. Both girls were intolerant in certain ways. They had to figure out a way to be friends and still accept the difficult parts of each other.

What do you do to get to know your characters on and off the page?

Sometimes I eavesdrop on conversations in public places, and I am struck by a phrase or a sentence that I know a certain character would have said in exactly the same way, or I'll see a gesture or some expression that I know belongs to a character. The more of those I get, the more the character is developed. Then I bring characters into different situations. The other day an argument took place between two sisters, and I learned more about them. One sister is having an affair with the husband of the other sister. They are arguing about something else, but the affair is always foremost in their minds. There's great anger and meanness in what they say to each other, but at the end the sisters are united against the man, and though nothing is said directly, indirectly so much is implied. Seeing how people react to each other, what they lie about, what they admit or deny, these quirks tell us who the character is, and what is important to them.

EXPLORING THE DARKER SIDE
Mary Morrissy, interviewed by Ana Callan

I think what most of the characters in *A Lazy Eye* have in common is that they're pretty ordinary people but they're emotionally *in extremis*, and they have a skewed vision of the world. I didn't actually set out to write disturbing stories. I suppose I am a bit taken aback that people find them so disturbing, because I think they're verging on normal. Except in obvious stories like "Rosa," where they abandon the baby in the department store, which is an act of complete moral abandon. But generally speaking, I think the characters are the darker side that everybody has. What I've done in these stories is to indulge the darker side and explore that.

My characters long to be the center of attention and even long to be at the center of their own lives, which they somehow cannot manage. They haven't taken possession of their own lives and there is that feeling of remoteness from their own lives, let alone being the center of someone else's life. For many of them, it'd be impossible. When they try to be that, they fail. Like the girl in the story about petty theft at school: She is so longing to be this other girl that she is willing to take on her sins. It is that yearning to be at the center, and yet when she has a chance to be at the center, she can't move in and take center stage.

WRITING ADVICE from Thomas E. Kennedy

One of the things that I suggest in workshop when people are having trouble with a story and a character is to just follow the character. Stand behind or to the side, be a fly on the wall, follow that character through some familiar route down a street, into a hotel, whatever, and see what that character encounters. Because the things the character comes upon will be meaningful objects, meaningful encounters, and bring out what's interesting about the character. Just follow the character through a day. What you come up with might not be pages that you'll use, but might lead you into the place where the story starts.

as interviewed by Linda B. Swanson-Davies

KEVIN CANTY

interviewed by Linda B. Swanson-Davies

In *A Stranger in This World*, the first story that I read is the second story in the book: "Dogs." I was thinking that I would go have lunch, sit with a glass of wine, and relax with the book. Well, I read the first page, and I had to stop and collect myself. I think it was because you were using language that was exactly representative of what you were saying—I felt very unprotected when I was reading that story.

That's one of the things that I try to do as a writer. I think most of us think that we're here, and people who do bad things are a different class of people, separate from us somehow. I don't really believe that. I think that we have a lot of capacities in us. Often it is very hard to say in advance, "I am the sort of person who would never do that," because then you do that and you discover things inside yourself that you might not like. Anyway, that's sort of a fancy way of saying that a lot of what I'm trying to do is reduce the distance between the reader and the character so you can't say, "Oh, that poor idiot! I'd never be like that." My experience has been that, even though most of us stay on the rails most of our lives, trouble isn't only visited on other people. There are ways to get off the rails, and people do.

Harry Crews said that all fiction was about people trying to do the best they can with what they got to do with—you have to say that in a deep Southern accent to make it sound profound. In that striving is where I find the movement for my stories that there is. Most of my characters want something. They sometimes choose odd or perverse or ineffectual ways of getting there. That seems to echo the experiences of my own life and people around me, too. If I want to go from Portland to Tigard, Oregon, I tend to go by way of Seattle. You end up putting obstacles in your own path, or you end up not being able to see things around you that everyone else can see. I think a character has to want something to be worth writing about. I think the relationship between what they want and what they get is pretty complicated. Kundera talks about this—the complicated nature of action. You're trying for something and you reach for it, and in the course of reaching for it, you get something entirely different. You're going along in a relationship and you decide that you want to stir things up a bit, and so you have an affair with somebody outside that relationship—and, of course, you've succeeded magnificently at what you started out to do, but you find yourself back out on the street or living by yourself again. Characters start out in stories wanting things and the world decides whether they're going to get that or not.

THE VELCRO FACTOR

Charles Baxter, interviewed by Stewart David Ikeda

What qualities do you find appealing or compelling in people and in characters? Do you demand the same things of both? Is it fair to say that you must love your characters as they develop?

You must try to love them. People whose company I enjoy in life would quite possibly bore me if they were in stories. Generally speaking, fictional characters have to be on a road that's going to lead toward some kind of interesting trouble. They must be pleasingly guilty of various kinds of misjudgments and good judgments. I think this business of "lovability" is a dangerous area for writers; more than a few writers have been seduced into thinking that characters should be charming and lovable. I don't think so, you know; I think they have to be interesting. They have to have enough of, let's call it the Velcro factor. We have to be able to attach ourselves to them and they must attach themselves to us. So there must be things in them that we discover and recognize.

They must be flawed, too.

Well, they have to do something in order to make themselves worthy of our attention. And I mention this because I think that, in American literature, there's often a missing middle. You have characters who are utterly charming, funny, sweet, and utterly uninteresting; then there are characters at the opposite pole, who are sort of dingy and awful; and few fall in between.

Carolyn Chute: In fiction you have to create characters to be living beings. It's like being God. You can't mess with them. You have to let them develop and become what they want to be. If you don't approve of something, you've got to let them do it, whether you like it or not.

as interviewed by Barbara Stevens

BATH OR SHOWER?

Andre Dubus

interviewed by Jennifer Levasseur and Kevin Rabalais

Your stories are driven by character, and you've said your characters often control the fate of the story.

In my story "Miranda over the Valley," the character gets so bitter, and I kept rewriting the ending, but she kept doing the same thing.

It sounds like you feel your characters hold the ultimate responsibility.

Yes. I only got nineteen words today, and I don't even know what the characters are doing in this story I'm writing. I've got to take a couple days off until they show me something. If I would have finished that section today, I would have been screwed. It's a new section, and I don't know what's going on, so I'll take a few days off and then see what happens.

So do you see your characters as somewhere outside your mind? Where do they come from?

I think they come from their actions and what they are thinking and feeling. My job is to figure out what they are feeling. I will have a physical description and some history in my head before I start a story. I'm writing a Western now, and I know this character who is a black cowboy in Southern California. I know his family went from Chicago to California during the gold rush, and his father set up a church in Los Angeles. That's not the story, but I know that.

Do you feel you know more about your characters, even things that don't get put into the stories?

I want to know about their religion; their sensual habits; how they feel about death, life; where they are from; whom they are kin to. But that's not always what I get to know. I'm thinking about my story "Dancing After Hours." All I had with the female character was her age and that she thought she was not pretty. I don't know where she's from, and I don't know anything about her family. Since she doesn't mention much about religion, I assume that is not part of her life.

If I can finish this Western, I'm going to try this one again: a Catholic family, French one side, Irish the other, with a martyred nun. I wanted to have her martyred in El Salvador. I either copped out, or I made a tactical decision. I've never been to El Salvador, and I don't know any Spanish. I thought, why go through all that work to find a violent country when we live in such a violent country? I try to see the characters, to know some of their history. I will think about characters for a long time rather than just start the story and see what they do. I like to feel I can get inside of a character. I used to tell students to write sketches. I told them they should know if their character prefers a bath or a shower. I like to think I know that. Now, with this story I'm writing set in 1891, they don't take many baths. This is a sequel to one I wrote last year, and nobody has taken a bath yet.

CHAPTER

6

DESCRIPTION AND DETAIL

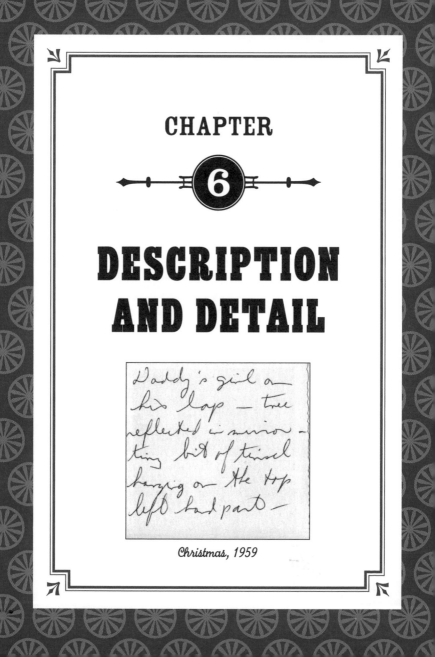

Daddy's girl on
his lap — tree
reflected in mirror -
tiny bit of tinsel
hanging on the top
left hand part —

Christmas, 1959

Ernest Gaines: I'm looking for something beyond what the average person will ever notice … my antennae are out for sounds, for physical things that I can see, and they pick up all sorts of things. I suppose that's what makes the writer different from the other person, that his antennae can absorb these kinds of things.

as interviewed by Michael Upchurch

USING SPECIFIC DETAILS
by David Long

You never want to supply something the reader can supply for herself. Descriptions of places, for instance. If you're going to set something in a café, you don't need to describe the café very much because people have been in cafés. It's like a Japanese painting—you just need to do a little of this, and that's a mountain range—what I call getting past what people already know. Your job is to provide those few critical details that supplement what people already know, and make it specific.

Push your sentences until they say something interesting. Here's a tiny example, from Denis Johnson's story "Work." A badly hung-over man is helping a friend salvage copper wiring from his ruined house: "I felt weak. I had to vomit in a corner—just a thimbleful of gray bile." Picture the second sentence stopping at the word *corner*; picture it minus the word *thimbleful*. Keep coming back to your work. Sneak up on it. You don't have to solve all the problems at once. The more sittings, the more likely you are to find unusual things to add.

Name names. Make your writing physical. Use lots of exact nouns. *Food* is an idea; *black-bean soup* is a thing. Naming not only makes the writing more visceral, it makes the reader trust you. And use your own expertise, whatever "insider information" you have. Use words like *soffit*, *draw shave*, *spit valve*.

....

FROM WATERCOLORS TO DELACROIX
Edwidge Danticat, interviewed by Sarah Anne Johnson

What were the challenges in writing a story not only set in a historical time and place, but in the midst of an actual event?

Action scenes and journey scenes where people have to cross the mountains were difficult. The scenes where I had a big crowd were challenging as well. I had to write much broader scenes than I ever had in the past. It was like going from painting watercolors to painting like Delacroix. It was a leap for me to describe this crowd and the long journey. I had to create a sense of the journey by offering specific details about the rocks and the mountains and how the landscape changed. For the crowd scene, I had to pick out a person, and then another person, and I was only able to write the scenes when I was able to visualize it for myself so that I could go back to it again and again.

In both cases—the scale and the fact that it was set in a time I hadn't lived in—I found that writing details helped. Certain details added authenticity and I made use of lots of them.

How has addressing these challenges helped your work as you move forward?

Well, having done it once, it's less intimidating to try it now. So I feel I have a little bit more range. But as I was writing, I read a lot of books with large, almost epic scenes and watched how the writers handled them. That helped a lot. Movies, too, were helpful in that I would watch where the camera goes during a particular scene. When you're watching or reading with a writer's eye, you can't help but observe certain techniques. When you're in story mode, you learn from everything.

CREATING REALISM IN GRITTY CONTEXTS
Jayne Anne Phillips, interviewed by Sarah Anne Johnson

No matter what the voice or style or technique of a piece, my work is always grounded in very physical, sensual detail. That has to be present because the work tries to go so far spiritually, and the reader can't move inward without being extremely grounded in the physical details of the piece. The piece can't move off without first being completely real and convincing. We're all concerned with what reality means. Does it mean anything? Is there anything besides this moment or this room? What are these dimensions that we inhabit in our thoughts, which are not physical, or in our dreams, or in our memories?

Literature is operating in that territory, in a dimension that isn't real, yet it can connect with the real in a way that's sensory. It can trigger memory that is actually sensual, such as memories of smells or feelings or tastes. You work your way into a psychic understanding through the real world. You do it every day in your life, and you do it in your art.

ANNIE PROULX
interviewed by Michael Upchurch

What is useful is eavesdropping, listening, talking to people in an informal way, sitting around tables swapping stories, listening to kids. I might take notes, too. And I keep huge notebook sketches. I have one that's just physical descriptions: faces, postures, walks, the way somebody's elbows point outward, their complexion, the cast of their eyes, any scars, pockmarks, peculiar gaits, accents, odd ways of holding the mouth. So all these things I'll write down at odd moments as I travel.

When I approach a new novel, I know the characters I want and will look through to see if I can find a physical description that fits. I also work a lot from photographs, especially when I'm doing something that is set in a particular period. I'll spend weeks with books of photography from the period and place, and study them very carefully, again to get the right kind of bone structure and build and clothing.

THE POWER OF INDIRECT DESCRIPTION
Amy Hempel, interviewed by Debra Levy and Carol Turner

⟹◈⟸

I have tremendous impatience and lack of interest in conventional description. It tells me absolutely nothing. Sometimes I can better describe a person by another person's reaction. In a story in my first book, I couldn't think of a way to sufficiently describe the charisma of a certain boy, so the narrator says, "I knew girls who saved his gum." So you're describing through somebody else....

Compression has always been hugely attractive, and rhythm, whether it's in a sentence or a line.

Why do some people dislike compression?

You mean they like everything spelled out. Certain critics go after you for that. I don't understand it—I really don't understand it. Because to me, I pay the readers the compliment. I mean, I'm acknowledging that they're smart enough to get it. They don't need everything spelled out. They live downtown, they've seen tall buildings. So I don't understand it. Because you don't hear—or at least I haven't seen it—the same complaints brought to poetry. I think that my concerns are more a poet's concerns and always have been. I don't understand why these things in a story would be criticized, whereas in a poem it's the norm, it's what you expect. But I guess some have certain expectations of what a story is—that a story can be this, but not that. I think it really has come from a more provincial sense, a restricted, limited sense of story, and what it can do.

RON CARLSON
interviewed by Susan McInnis

In "Blazo," and in every story I write, I try to approach human problems step by step, in whatever situation the characters find themselves. In Kotzebue, Burns is put up against what he finds and doesn't find there—his mission, the cold—and what happens to him and in him creates the story. But if the story is about a man and a woman changing a tire on a remote highway—less inherently dramatic perhaps than a storm blowing up in Kotzebue—you've nonetheless got to convince me of the highway, the tire, the night, the margin, the shoulder, the gravel under their knees, the lug nuts, the difficulty getting the whole thing apart and back together, and the smells. You must do that. But that's not what you're there to deliver. That's the way you're going to seduce me. What you're delivering is, Who are these people?

Think of it as a two-person quest story: Two people on a highway changing a tire. Two people in space trying to fix the solar-star dish that powers the huge space vehicle taking refugees off the doomed planet. Either way, it's the same story. You have to convince me of the star dish and space suits, but after you've got my shirt caught in the machine of the story and you've drawn me in, what you're really going to crush me with are these hearts and these people. Who are they? How are they affected by the pressure they're under?

INVENTING NEW METAPHORS
Mary Yukari Waters, interviewed by Sherry Ellis

In the story "Seed," radishes serve as a metaphor. You write, "But these radishes had no juicy crunch. They were as rubbery as boiled jellyfish and required rigorous chewing. Shoji didn't seem to notice— he was often exhausted when he came home—and lately Masae fancied that he was absorbing the radishes' essence. Since they had come to Tai-huen, something about him had shrunk in an indefinable way, as if an energy that once shimmered right below the surface of his skin had retreated deep into his body." How did you develop this metaphor?

I think it comes down to using details that you're familiar with. I happen to love food in general, so it's always fun to use it as metaphor. Grated radishes are actually a common dish in Japan— you mix them with dried whitebait and a little soy sauce. Fresh radishes have that nice juicy crunch, but old radishes get tough and rubbery because they're trying to conserve what little water they have left. When you're exposed to something all the time, it's much easier to see them as metaphor, to find fresh parallels.

DRAWING FROM LIFE EXPERIENCE

Kent Haruf, interviewed by Jim Nashold

—◆—

There's quite a bit of understated humor in your books. In *The Tie That Binds*, one of the funniest scenes is when Edith is milking the cows and the cow's tail slaps her in the face.

I intended that to be funny, and corrective of the romantic notion that milking cows is glorious or fun. Part of it was also my own revenge for when I milked cows as a way of making a living for my family once. It was a good education, and it was hard work. I started milking at three in the morning and went back again at three or four in the afternoon. What I describe in that scene actually happened to me. An old cow wrapped her tail around my head and I wanted to kill her. So it was my literary revenge on an actual cow.

You lovingly re-create the detail of ranch life, which is fast disappearing. Such details as cutting hay or taking care of cattle are integral parts of your writing.

I've been interested in ranch life since I was a kid and heard my dad talk about it, and then spent time with my brother on his ranch. I do know something about that, but I'm no expert. It's very important to me to get those details accurate. The passage of the cow wrapping her tail around my head was read aloud to me by a dairyman on New Year's Eve. We were both drunk enough that he called me out to the kitchen, opened *The Tie That Binds*, and read that passage to me, and then stabbed his finger on the page and said, "That's exactly right, goddammit." That to me was the greatest compliment I've ever had, because it came from somebody who knew exactly what I was writing about and who was an expert.

A FRESH EYE

Annie Proulx, interviewed by Michael Upchurch

Have you kept up with friends or acquaintances you made in Newfoundland?

God, yeah. When we were talking about the details of things, I was going to tell you this story about a couple who came down to visit. *This* detail never would have occurred to me. I haven't written it down anywhere, but it's a great story to tell. This couple lives up on the Great Northern Peninsula, at the far end where the only trees are low-growing tuckamore, no trees higher than your waist; it's all bare rock. They came down two falls ago and stayed at the house when the leaves were at their height, and the day they came we had a big hugging and squeezing and so forth. It was nighttime and we ate a big dinner and all that. And the next morning they went out onto the deck, or the wife went out onto the deck. She came back in with her eyes on stalks and she says to her husband, "Come out 'ere!"

"What is it?"

So he goes out there, and they're talking excitedly, and I thought, What the hell is it? Maybe they're seeing deer up on the hillside. They have moose in Newfoundland, but not much else. And I went out there, and they turned to me with this expression of ecstatic surprise on their faces and they said, "They makes noise!"

"What makes noise?"

"Leaves! The leaves is making noise!"

You know? The wind blowing through the leaves? They had never heard that. Here are two adults who had never heard wind blowing through leaves. And that's the kind of thing you want to watch for. You've got to find these things out. There's nothing like a fresh eye—and that's my best example of a fresh eye in a place. No one who lives in New England would have noticed wind in the leaves ever, ever, ever. It took someone from away to see it: the value of the outsider's eye.

CHITRA BANERJEE DIVAKARUNI
interviewed by Sarah Anne Johnson

You choose physical details that draw your characters quite distinctly and also serve to create an intimacy between the characters and the reader. For example, in *The Mistress of Spices*: "Geeta's grandfather still walking like a military major though it has been twenty years. His shirt ironed stiff with pointy collars, his steel-gray pants perfect-creased down the front. His shoes, midnight-black Bata shoes spit-polished to match the onyx he wears on his left hand for mental peace." How do you arrive at these carefully placed details?

Often I get a very strong visual image of the character. I'm always happy and thankful that it happens, because it doesn't always happen right away. Quite a lot of the characters in *The Unknown Errors of Our Lives* don't have physical descriptions. In that case, what I'm doing instead is focusing on their mental habits. It's not so much their physical attributes that I'm concerned with but their mental states. This is another way of making a character come alive. In that book, I realized I was moving toward something different—not consciously necessarily, but I noticed that I was more interested in describing characters through their thoughts or internal habits. In this book, you're very aware of the *tone* of a character, and the whole tone related to the work. I'm thinking particularly of a story like "The Blooming Season for Cactii." We see everything through Mira, the main character's eyes, and it's not until almost the end of the story, when she looks in the mirror, that the reader sees what she looks like. Yet by then we very much know who the character is.

....

MARIA FLOOK
interviewed by Sarah Anne Johnson

You often use the lyric image to reveal character and to instill a deeper resonance in your narrative. For instance, in the story "Rhode Island Fish Company," a teenage girl has a tattoo that's oozing. The narrator, her aunt, recalls seeing statuary in Greece. "I had seen marble limbs discolored, worn concave at the wrist and fingertips, marred by centuries of human touch. Unchecked, these habits of adoration can wear away their subjects." Readers feel the narrator's struggle to give the girl space and not smother her with love. How do you arrive at a particular image? How do you then develop the image into a revelatory statement about character?

That's like asking how a poet writes poetry. It's an eruptive and only partly controlled mechanism in its first manifestations. The psycho-intellectual disturbance that an image creates works to engender a parallel between external and subconscious elements in the narrative. The lyric image evokes an instant recognition, unlike exposition, which accrues differently. Image is *supreme statement*. It's the lightning-bolt instant when perception crosses over from intellectual wisdom to spiritual knowledge. En masse, lyric details are a magic adhesive in fiction; they are the marrow jelly in the skeleton, and without it a narrative would seem staid and anemic. But there's always a risk that the lyric detail will be disruptive or distracting, so it's a constant struggle to find the image that propels the emotional current, but doesn't sweep you off course.

Regarding the image you mention, I have seen ruins and art treasures that have been deformed by tourists' manhandling—and I suppose this goes into the image bank that writers have stockpiled and nurtured throughout our lives. The image surfaces, it *strikes*, but it's not a conscious decision. We recognize the immediate connection it has, and then we try to write it down as well as we can.

Of course physical description must be impelled by real experience and by real-life sightings of our world around us. But there's another element in writing physical detail that has to do with sensibility, vision, even attitude. Writers have idiosyncratic, even idiopathic ways of *seeing*. The writer John Berger writes, "Seeing comes before words.... The relation between what we see and what we know is never settled...."

Recently, I reversed a familiar idiom in conversation. By accident, I said, "I'll see it when I *believe* it." But this reversal makes sense to me. Seeing requires belief. Belief informs our vision. To *see* requires we have unity with our subject.

In regards to the actual "things" and "stuff" that I notice and later put into writing, of course I'm always eyeing the curious, threatening, or compelling instants I might witness. These come from both urban life and from the natural world. In my memoir, I describe burrowing beetles, insects that climb into a mouse or small animal corpse and make it wriggle and twitch so it looks like it's come alive. They're also called marionette beetles because they can move a dead animal as if it were on puppet strings.

THE THIRD ELEMENT
John McNally, interviewed by Stephanie Kuehnert

What was your writing/rewriting process like with "The Vomitorium"? Can you compare it to what you went through with other stories?

I wrote the first draft longhand over a series of days while sitting up in bed at night. It came together relatively fast for me. The Roman theme didn't come into play in the first draft until about a third of the way through the story. Ralph was originally going to be dressed as something other than an Etruscan. While I was writing that story, my wife was taking Latin, and her professor was telling her things about the Etruscans. She would tell me these things as I was literally writing the story, and on the third day or so of writing, I realized that Ralph would be the perfect Etruscan. After that, the Roman stuff threaded its way into the story and ended up playing a large part. It's what one of my professors, Allan Gurganus, called the story's "third element"—that is, the sort of detail that can be removed from a story, but with it in the story, you end up with something richer, more three dimensional (hence, "third element"). I can't imagine the story without the Roman details. It, of course, affects how the story ends.

I bring my own obsessions and/or quirks into my stories. That's why, say, *Planet of the Apes* references might show up in my fiction. I was a huge *Planet of the Apes* fan when I was a kid, and you can't shake that sort of thing. As an adult, people give you odd looks when you reference a movie like that; but in a short story, it's funny and weird and maybe a little obsessive on the narrator's part, but it's okay. My own life works its way into my stories more and more these days, but in quirky details, rarely in obvious, autobiographical ways.

THE DETAIL THAT MATTERS
by Monica Wood

You should certainly strive to make your reader see what you see; the trick is in finding details that allow for an accurate vision. Learn to include only the details that matter—the ones that suggest more than they describe. Say your character is a wino living in a refrigerator box. You could describe him from head to foot, including his missing teeth, the corrugations on the cardboard box, the broken laces in his boots. But who are you really describing here? Any wino, that's who. What's interesting about this particular wino, however, is that he is vain. The only detail that matters, the only one that suggests to the reader a character rather than a caricature, is that he wet-combs his hair every morning with a carefully placed part. That's the detail that will let your reader see beneath the surface.

Elizabeth Cox: When I'm writing a story or novel, I don't think about craft. When I'm editing I think about it, but not when I'm writing it. I use detail in order to see the moment. To be inside the moment we must use the senses, to see the cloth someone is wearing, to feel a breeze or the brush of a hand, to hear a door open, to taste an apple or a lover's neck. The use of the senses brings the physical experience closer. That ends up being craft, but when I'm writing I'm not thinking about the physical sense, I'm actually smelling, tasting, hearing, seeing, touching. Later, during the editing process, I make the moments more clear.

as interviewed by Sarah Anne Johnson

IT'S IN THE EYES

Charles Baxter, interviewed by Robert Birnbaum

I've written an essay about how most writers now don't describe faces anymore, either as an index to character in the way the nineteenth-century novelists tended to do, or as a dramatic inflection. You are more likely to get descriptions of clothes or body language than you are of faces. I just wanted to ask myself why.

Some of the great scenes that I recall from movies were where an actor said something with eye movement—some facial gesture that might have lasted a nanosecond.

The Quiet American is a good example, the way Michael Caine uses his eyes in his acting. And two of Charlotte Rampling's most recent films, *Under the Sand* and *Swimming Pool*, are all eye acting. In the essay, I was particularly interested in what Paula Fox does in some of her novels. She likes to crowd her characters, get them into very narrow spaces, put them under a great deal of stress, so that they are constantly having to look at each others' faces to see what the subtext is of the remark that each one has just made.

THINK LIKE YOUR CHARACTER
Chitra Banerjee Divakaruni
interviewed by Sarah Anne Johnson

You often use a metaphor as more than just a point of comparison. You use it to further paint the world of the characters that exists beyond the page. In *The Mistress of Spices*, for example: "But today the light is pink-tinted like just-bloomed karabi flowers," and "Saturday comes upon me like the unexpected flash of rainbow under a bird's black wing, like the swirl-spread skirt of a kathak dancer, fast and then faster." While the narrative isn't talking about the kathak dancer or the karabi flowers directly, here they are adding a glimpse at the world of the characters. Are you aware of this as you work?

This comes fairly organically. What I'm trying to do is to think the way the character is thinking, and what are the connections the character will be making depending on their background. Human beings often think by analogy and by remembering and by comparing. So that when we're faced with something new, we think, not even consciously, but subconsciously, "This is like..." And not every character will do that. Some characters don't think that way.

CHAPTER

7

USE OF LANGUAGE

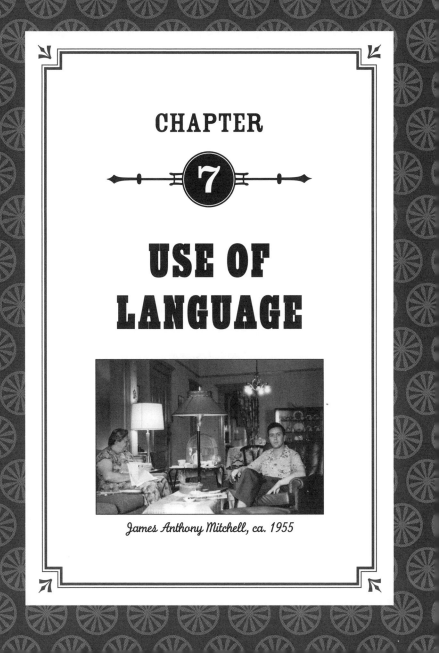

James Anthony Mitchell, ca. 1955

Joyce Thompson: I think we approach our work as writers for different reasons. Some people are called by the language, and then they have to learn to see the stories and find out what they mean and all those other things. Some people are called by story and then have to learn to love and use the language. When it's language that calls, it tends to be an early call. This is a gross generalization, but I think that people who are called earlier are called by language; people who are called later are usually called because of the stories they have to tell.

WORDS TO WATCH

Charles Baxter, interviewed by Linda B. Swanson-Davies

Nouns and verbs. And cut the adjectives, unless you absolutely have to have them. Make sure the verbs are the very best ones that you can find. Make them direct. Make them forceful. Make them to the point. If the tone of the scene requires a slightly unusual verbal texture, use your thesaurus. Use the dictionary. Vladimir Nabokov said that a writer who didn't spend time just paging through the dictionary looking for good words was not a real writer.

I think when stories rise to a moment of great tension or release or traumatic revelation, the language is absolutely crucial, and you have to make sure that the emotional temperature of the language matches the emotional temperature of the scene. Of course it's possible to have a highly charged emotional scene that is narrated in completely flat and affectless language, and that can work once or twice, but it won't work all the time.

AN ARGUMENT AGAINST MINIMALISM
Lynne Sharon Schwartz, interviewed by Nancy Middleton

You've noted minimalism as a trend that you're not all that crazy about.

It's true, I don't especially enjoy it. I go to reading for an experience of richness and intrigue and I don't find that in minimalism. Besides that, it's not fun to read. I don't mean that it's depressing; I rather like depressing books. By fun I mean that it doesn't give you the pleasures of reading, the sort of rich, panoramic sweep—the whole battery of what language can do. In many ways it is like an acrobat who jumps up and down, and that's the only trick he knows. Whereas a writer like Proust does every trick in the book. And that's what I enjoy.

I understand the aesthetic of minimalism: seeing how large an effect you can wring out of very small means. It might work in the hands of a very good writer like Raymond Carver, yes. But there aren't too many Raymond Carvers out there. Mostly what you get is small means and small effect.

I also think that there's something not true about it in that I don't perceive life as minimal. I think life is pretty terrible and difficult—I'm not an optimist—but it's also rich and full and soupy and frothing over with sometimes awful, sometimes beautiful things. There's a lot happening, and minimalism does not reflect that abundance. So when I read it I think, This is not the world I know.

MATTHEW SHARPE
interviewed by Sherry Ellis

In his *Village Voice* review of *The Sleeping Father*, Ed Park comments on the "aching absurdities, word salads, inspired semicolon deployment, golden-eared teenage monologues," that you utilize in this novel. To highlight a few of your inventive descriptions, Dr. Lisa Danmeyer "smelled of lilacs and competent sweat." "Chris and his mother's sex partner were walking through the woods" is another description. Can you describe how you get into a mindset where you shut out the world and use language so creatively?

I would say in some ways I shut out the world and in other ways I let the world enter. I mean, thank you for complimenting my linguistic prowess. I have to say that the review by Ed Park is about as good a review as an author can ever have hoped to get. If I die before I get another review like that I'll consider myself well reviewed in my life. I suppose I shut the world out in the sense that I'm not a person who, say, writes with music on. I know there are some people who write to music, who allow the music to infuse the work, but I need a quiet writing space, which is hard to come by in New York City. In terms of letting the world in, I'm a real big fan of Mikhail Bakhtin, the Russian theorist. His idea was that any way that speech gets used out there in the world can make its way into a novel, that novels are omnivores of all kinds of speech and writing. So I actually try to let the acoustical and rhetorical properties of all the other forms of language used in the world inform how I write. TV and radio, legal documents and bumper stickers, other people's novels, prayers and apologies, emails and letters, political speeches and medical jargon—I try to welcome them into my novels.

Your language in the short-story collection *Stories from the Tube* seems more simple. Do you believe the change in language from this story collection to *The Sleeping Father* has to do more with your evolution as a writer or the topic matter of the work?

It's funny about that. I always thought of myself as a Baroque, fancy, wordy kind of writer, a "putter-inner" as Stanley Elkin called it, instead of a "taker-outer." So I think it must be the topic which dictated the simpler form of most of those stories in *Stories from the Tube.* Again I was dealing with TV as a discourse, and I suppose that the discourse of TV is fairly simple because they're trying to reach as large an audience as possible. But there are a couple of stories in there—"Doctor Mom" and "A Bird Accident"—that I think are probably closer in style to *Nothing Is Terrible* and *The Sleeping Father.*

THE IMPORTANCE OF THE SENTENCE
Richard Bausch
interviewed by Jennifer Levasseur and Kevin Rabalais

It's everything. I have such trouble getting students to understand that. If you can't make the sentence, forget it. Sometimes students think they don't have to pay any attention to punctuation. I like to make a big fat sentence that's held together by a semicolon and make it hang there and support itself. I love to take a page of sentences and make them different, give them variety. I like to have a different kind of sentence in each paragraph. It's like writing music. You are going to do this in a minor key, but then this other thing is going to come in. It's all in there. If you can write a good sentence, then you can write another one, then another one.

I hate it when people say, "Well, in poetry, you have to pay attention to every word, and in short stories you have to pay attention to every sentence, and in novels, you can ramble." It's not true. A novel is written sentence by sentence, word by word, if you are any good at all. That's the fun of it. I couldn't do it any other way. I carve it out a little bit at a time. Some mornings I don't get any more than a page. Today I got about a page and a half. It's fine: a day's work.

....

THE PERFECT WORD

Annie Proulx, interviewed by Michael Upchurch

➤◆◄

I use an old Webster's unabridged. I do collect dictionaries, and I do read them, and I do keep word lists, and I do make notes of language. I have big notebooks, page after page of words that I like or find interesting or crackly, or whatever. And from time to time I will also, if I feel a section is a bit limp, take a couple of days and just do dictionary work and recast the sentences so that they have more power because their words aren't overused. Often the search for the right word can consume a lot of time, but usually it can be found. I've put a lot of effort into finding the right word instead of using a scattershot approach.

The milk "firping" into the pail in *Postcards*? I assumed you were coining some of these, but no?

No. There are enough words there for me. There really are enough wonderful words to be used. Some of them are not used much, and they ought to be.

....

SENSITIVITY TO LANGUAGE

Sigrid Nunez
interviewed by Linda B. Swanson-Davies

⇒◈⇐

When you are teaching, are there particular qualities that you see in a student's writing that you get excited about?

Yes. Sensitivity to language.

Give me an example, if you could.

Most of the students don't write well yet, and it doesn't matter in the sense that you can write really terrible stuff at the age of nineteen or twenty or even twenty-eight and produce something divine in your forties. It is not necessarily a relationship between how you write when you're young and how you write later on. Because the students are so young and because they've never done this before, their ideas are often not that interesting. They're sentimental. They don't have much experience. They tend to see things in a certain way. They don't know how to develop a story. They tend to use stock characters in their stories.

So I don't expect from them wonderful characters, wonderful plot, or wonderful structure. That takes a long time. But if they have a sense of the language as a tool, that's everything. I don't care if they've given me a page that is just a description of a room as long as there's a rhythm to the sentences, and they know not to rely heavily on adverbs, and they know what a verb can do. That's what I mean by understanding language. Also, I think you can see—the truth is, you see in some of their work that they have no respect for the English language and no sense of it as a marvel. There's no beauty or mystery in it. But occasionally you see a student who—you see that when he was writing he was relishing the language and does recognize what its beauties are. Without that, it's just not possible to write.

....

DOWN TO THE LETTER

Alberto Ríos, interviewed by Susan McInnis

We know how to use things and use them well. But we don't know what they are. My favorite example is the alphabet. We use it to form words. We write sentences and paragraphs, but we build them on a foundation that we truly don't understand. We don't know what the letter *A* is anymore. *A*, going back to the Greek, is *alpha*. We say it's the beginning of the alphabet. Or it's just the beginning. Or it's a sound. Or it's a symbol. But we don't know what it's the sound of, or symbol for. In fact, it comes from the Phoenician, maybe two thousand years ago when it was upside down, a V-shape that represented the horns of an ox. An ox, for the Phoenicians, was food, and that's the first letter: food. It's the first thing. It had meaning all by itself before there were other letters. As I read it, the crossbar on the *A* was a sign that the ox was domesticated and yoked.

My favorite is the letter *Z*. It's the sixth letter of the Greek alphabet, but it's our last letter. One of the first things you do when you conquer somebody is take away their language, because inherent in language is culture, everything about living. And when the Romans conquered the Greeks, they wanted them to become Roman, to live like them, to follow their laws. So they took their sound away. But when they used the Greeks as tutors, I can imagine the Greeks saying, "The only worthwhile literature is Greek literature. We'll teach your children, but we need our sound back to do it." And the Romans would have said, "All right, we'll let you have the letter Z—that sound—but, because it's Greek, it's going to the end of the bus, the end of the alphabet." Because it's Greek. To me that's a lesson. That's immediate. It's right in front of us. It's right there in the alphabet we use. And that's where, I think, the work of staying in place, staying with the alphabet until you understand what it is—before you start to use it—makes sense. And that "staying in place" is part of my job as a writer.

David Long: To me, it's all about sentences. Good writing is good because it has good sentences, the way good movies are good because there's good cinematography, light through plastic. Now if there's no story there, that's not good, either. Because of this, I work slowly. I haven't produced a lot of work. So that's the negative side. On the other hand, I haven't had to look back on things I published years ago and say, Boy, was that stupid! I still feel pretty good about most of it.

Jayne Anne Phillips: I started writing as a poet, so I've always written line by line, and with a real sense of the sound of a sentence and the rhythm of words against one another. My early sense of narrative had more to do with trying to get across perception itself rather than telling a conventional story. That very short form was a good way for me to intensify writing. They were narratives, but they moved out from an image and they worked very much according to language. I'm still a very language-oriented writer.

as interviewed by Sarah Anne Johnson

READ THE POETS

Thomas E. Kennedy
interviewed by Linda B. Swanson-Davies

The way I write fiction I think is maybe similar to the way a poet writes, because I'm very concentrated on the language. I love poetry. I think most fiction writers would profit greatly from reading poetry, very deeply. I see some people who come to workshops who just don't read poetry. I think it was Flaubert who said a really good line of prose has all the qualities of a line of poetry, and I think it's true.

You take a great poem like "Dover Beach," [by Matthew Arnold] for example. You read the opening—that could be the opening of a short story. It's so elegant, so rhythmic, without being intrusively so, and that's what I try to look for in my fiction. I look for rhythm and evocativeness of language, a certain flow. So I think what I consider good fiction is related to poetry in that way. Wasn't it F. Scott Fitzgerald whose advice to young writers was, "Read the poets"?

Some people allow their stories to serve their language skills rather than having their language serve their stories. Do you ever struggle with, Gee, I've got these great words—I really want to use them.

Yes. Really, that is a lethal tendency. I think it's something you learn your way through. You see it in workshop when somebody has a real facility to write, and really wants to use that facility, and it becomes overblown and inflated. I'm a great believer in less saying more. Sometimes more says more, and sometimes less says less, but usually less says more.

....

MARY MCGARRY MORRIS
interviewed by Linda B. Swanson-Davies

Aubrey Wallace [in *Vanished*] is a distinctly disadvantaged person, essentially kindhearted, largely incapable of independent action, even at critical moments. It's interesting that one of his clearest, bravest moments involved expressing himself in writing. What effect does your writing have on you?

It was with a real sense of my own wonder that I wrote that scene when Aubrey realizes that, for the first time in his life, he has finally been able to express himself in writing. It was my way of honoring the story, for which I have great reverence. Aubrey thought that the letters were magic and the words had powers, and they do! They absolutely do.

Andre Dubus III: I like movies, but for me the thrill and the majesty and mystery still lie in prose. It's those sentences I'm drawn to, the ones that yield the images and the sounds and the people in them that are a constant surprise to me. That's when it feels like it's going well, when it's all one big surprise.

as interviewed by John McNally

LANGUAGE AS IDENTITY

Chang-rae Lee, interviewed by Sarah Anne Johnson

This narrative touches on the themes of language and identity when young Hata first speaks with K in his native Korean. "I found myself listening to her closely, for it was some time since I had heard so much of the language, the steady, rolling tone of it like ours and not, theirs perhaps coming more from the belly than the throat. It was almost pleasing to hear the words, in a normal register. But her talk was also not vulgar or harshly provincial sounding as was the other girls'; she was obviously educated, and quite well, and this compelled me even more, though it shouldn't have." He discovers her through speaking to her in Korean.

This is not a huge moment, but it's important. Her speaking the Korean language calls him out and reminds him about who he is. He's not this pure Japanese, and he can't have the same kind of detachment and detached view of her that other people at the camp can have. He knows his origins, and those origins still have a very visceral effect when he talks about her language and he hears it. There are things that we hear from our childhood—sometimes in different languages if we're immigrants—that are like powerful old songs. Hearing her speak Korean transports him and makes him a different person, and makes possible his connection with her.

··

DIFFERENT LANGUAGE, DIFFERENT SELF
Julia Alvarez
interviewed by Mike Chasar and Constance Pierce

I think that in Spanish I'm a different person than I am in English. I understand myself differently, and I put the world together differently. I asked Marilyn Hacker, who lives part of the year in France and who writes while she's there, "Marilyn, how do you write in English hearing French all around you?" She said she has no problem with that at all; but her friends who have a native language that they don't write in, if they go to their native land and try to write in their adopted language, they find it hard, because they start to be absorbed in their mother tongue—back into a world they knew before they even started to write. And I find that happens to me in the Dominican Republic with Spanish. So I think that different selves get expressed in different languages. I think that because I understand something about the rhythms of Spanish, I can hear my Latino friends' Spanish in the way they write English. And one of the interesting things for me is what the rhythm of another language does to the English language: Southern writers and their sense of a sentence versus Heartland writers or a New York City writer. I hear different rhythms in their prose.

Sandra Cisneros said a similar thing about her voice in *The House on Mango Street*—that as much as people say it's a child's voice, it's also an English-informed-by-Spanish voice. Is a similar thing going on in *García Girls*?

I don't even hear it, because it's like a native tongue becoming merged with my writing tongue. People who know me will say to me, "Boy, I can hear your voice in the prose, the way that you put a sentence together, the way that your voice goes up or the way that you move from one thing to another," and I'm sure that's because my Spanish is part of my rhythm in English and the way I speak. I like long sentences—once, a guy in a writers workshop asked if anybody had ever told me to write shorter sentences. I thought, Well, that's probably part of my Spanish rhetoric taking off, all those Faulknerian sentences, all those embellishments and asides that don't give you time to breathe.

Contemporary writers' inclusion of Spanish with English can seem very in-your-face. It seems aggressive sometimes. And then at other times writers parenthetically translate the Spanish, as if to be helpful, or maybe in way of initiation. Or maybe they just want to be sure that they're understood. These seem to be very different approaches.

And sometimes that, I think, annoys me—when I feel the heavy hand of the writer. So I think it's such a balance, because you are writing in English. How do you keep a rhythm and a flow and at the same time introduce what, for us, is part of English while we're talking, our little *ays* and *carambas* and *asabaches* and *Hoolias*?

I tend to think, "Get used to it," that the United States is becoming more Latinized. "Get used to this. This is America."

And at the same time you want to include the reader, so to do the right kind of balancing is important. I think it's exciting.

I came to this country pre-bilingual education. English became the language that I learned things in. I was ten—that age when you start creating a sense of yourself and your understanding of the world—and it all happened to me in English. Plus, English gave me that necessary space to pull away from a way of thinking of myself, and of being, which didn't credit my wanting to be a writer. English gave me a certain freedom, I'm sure. That was a part of it. Then all my training came in English—all my training, all my reading, everything—and that's the language I learned to master. I feel like, in Spanish, I can't reach the gas pedal and I can't always work the steering wheel. I don't have that sense that I can really fine tune what I'm saying. It's much more what I call my childhood language.

ROY PARVIN
interviewed by Linda B. Swanson-Davies

Your writing makes me think of a fruit, a fig, maybe, because it's very thick, very fibrous and snug. What do your stories feel like to you?

Well, they don't feel like figs particularly, but I can understand that. I always say that I want the words in the end to be etched. I want to have the sense that they're etched in metal.

I try to write sentence by sentence. And that might sound ridiculous because who doesn't? But I try to think about every sentence, the architecture of every sentence. I want to make it as spare as possible. To me it feels like a mixture of something that's very, very spare, and something that also is very lush.

Ha Jin: Because I'm not a native speaker, there's a lot of flexible room for me to abuse the language, so I have to be very careful and accurate. There are both advantages and disadvantages to coming to writing in English so late. It's hard to write with the full weight of the language and with the natural spontaneity. The advantage is that I may write with a different kind of sensibility, and a slightly different kind of syntax, idiom, and style.

as interviewed by Sarah Anne Johnson

GEORGE MAKANA CLARK
interviewed by Linda B. Swanson-Davies

You speak dozens of languages?!

Well, no, I shouldn't say that. The Romance languages: I mean, oftentimes you can speak Spanish in Italy and you can get a good set of directions and perhaps figure out the menu. I know some Xhosa, and a patois they speak in the South African Defense Force which is a mixture of Bantu words and English and Afrikaans. I know some Afrikaans, and English, of course. I also know some German, but I really want to learn a language the right way, using proper grammar. I don't want to speak like a four- or five-year-old. There are so many bits and pieces of language in my stories, but that's all you get because that's all I've got.

I grew up in a very chauvinistic, English-is-the-right-language way. I would get in trouble for speaking Xhosa, even sayings which would find their way into everyday life. Afrikaans was not spoken widely in Rhodesia because that's a South African language, but there were lots of South Africans in Rhodesia, so certain words would come out in slang. I wasn't allowed to use them at all. It was considered an inferior language. I remember my mother would not let us use glottal stops.

Forbidden sounds!

Yes. My father grew up in London—my family left South Africa before moving back to Rhodesia—so he had the cockney accent where you kill the middle consonants of a lot of words. I wasn't allowed to do that. Contractions were somewhat suspect as well. We were supposed to speak proper English, really no other languages. It bothers me now because in later life, it becomes much more difficult to learn a language.

. . . .

USING MULTIPLE LANGUAGES IN TEXT
Daniel Mason, interviewed by Linda B. Swanson-Davies

You used a lot of Burmese words and phrases. How did you decide when to use them?

Ah, that's a wonderful question. I usually kept words that have no English translation, or no good English translation. And so, for example, the women with the wood paste on their faces, *thanaka*. I could have explained it, but I wouldn't want to write that into the story.

Of course. I mean, how would you do that?

I would call it "the women whose faces were painted with sandalwood paste." That sounds terrible. So I said *thanaka*. Another instance would be when there's a job that's specific. At the beginning of the book I use the word *Bedin-saya*, which is the type of fortune-teller that they have there. The term *fortuneteller* here has a particular connotation. So I didn't want to use the word *fortuneteller*.

What type of fortuneteller is that?

They are very different, from the role they play in people's lives to their form of divination. They may divine by casting tea leaves. You may tell stories to them and they interpret them, looking at encounters with animals or other events for prophecies. My image of a fortuneteller in the U.S. is very different. Other times I chose to keep a word just because it sounds different. For example, now I am writing a book on Brazil, and I've decided on some of the Portuguese words I'm going to use. Part of it's set in an ecosystem called *caatinga* in Portuguese. *Caatinga* is what the word feels like: dry and scratchy and harsh, with spines on the plants. It's a very difficult land. The word *caatinga* is so much more evocative than *scrub brush*.

....

A STORY IN EVERYTHING
Edwidge Danticat, interviewed by Sarah Anne Johnson

You've said that in Haiti, "Everything is a story. Everything is a meta-phor or a proverb."

Haitian Creole is full of so much nuance. Even a groan can be so monumental and have so many layers and meanings. People can say a lot with a proverb. There's always a turn around with a joke or with the stories. For example, Colin Powell goes to Haiti, and his name Powell is close to a Creole phrase, Pawèl, which means "don't see," so people call him Colin Pawèl because they don't think he sees or understands anything that's going on there. There are so many ways that the language can be maneuvered to be funny or sad, so that indeed there's a story in everything.

SIRI HUSTVEDT

interviewed by Jennifer Levasseur and Kevin Rabalais

Does using multiple languages allow you to see things in more than one way?

I think most bilingual people experience both double-ness and between-ness. With two languages, you never situate yourself quite as firmly inside the culture you are living in. I am American and I live in America, but I have a Norwegian mother and a father who grew up speaking Norwegian in America, and the presence of that other language in my life has had a powerful influence on me. When I'm in Norway, people can't hear that I'm not Norwegian, but it doesn't take long for them to realize that I'm outside the nuances of the culture.

In the end, the outsider view is a good one, however. It works against provincialism and against complacency. It can also give you a useful distance from language itself. People who are learning a language, for example, are able to see words as arbitrary objects. When you get to a certain stage of proficiency in a language, you see puns everywhere because you are still far enough away to notice those linguistic twins. People who live entirely in one language can become so buried in it that they lose that happy distance.

THE MUSIC IN WORDS

Siri Hustvedt

interviewed by Jennifer Levasseur and Kevin Rabalais

There is an interesting word choice in the beginning of *The Blindfold*. The word is *relieve*: "It would relieve me enormously if you could keep books out of this for once." On the level of language, the weight of each word within your sentences is carefully chosen.

When you live a life with books and stories and ideas, they never go away. Like the character, Mr. Morning, I often feel that there's a lot of chatter in my head—all those voices yelling for attention. You get filled up, loaded down. There's so much in there that you long for peace and emptiness. Iris hopes that Mr. Morning will *relieve* her by keeping books out of the discussion for a moment. Of course, he can't.

As for choosing words, a lot goes into making a sentence. There are writers who have great ears—Beckett, for example. His language is wonderfully musical. It has something to do with Irish English and its melodies. Part of being a writer is hearing the music in words while keeping an element of surprise in the language. Varying diction is one way to do this, dropping from high to low, borrowing from ordinary speech as well as elevated language. At the same time, my idea—and it's not an idea shared by all the writers I admire, by any means—is that the prose should be so lucid that you're not looking at the sentences. I want the reader to look past the sentences and see the pictures that bring a story to life, that make it real.

CHAPTER

8

DIALOGUE

Harold Wyman and
Caroline Burmeister Wyman, circa 1927

AIM FOR TRUTH

by Melanie Bishop

Dialogue should do two things: It should sound like people talking, minus the pauses and *umm*s and stumbling, and it should move your story forward. A couple of carefully chosen lines between two characters are much more effective than a long conversation back and forth. Try to include the couple of lines in any conversation that are most crucial, most key. The rest is often better paraphrased. Let dialogue be like subtle arrows shot through your story. Characters come alive on the page through what they say and what they do. Dialogue and action, therefore, are your vehicles for showing readers who they are dealing with in a particular story.

The best advice for preparing to write good dialogue is just to listen to the ways people talk and to the lines that come from their mouths. Write down memorable lines loved ones or not-so-loved ones have spoken to you. You know, those lines that we can't forget, that are etched verbatim into our minds. Use these lines in an appropriate story.

As interesting as the ways people understand each other are the ways we often misunderstand. Being able to write an exchange between two people where this lack of understanding is revealed is a sign of a skilled writer. Are the two people in the conversation listening to each other or not? Are they wanting to hear or not? Are they coming to the conversation with opposing personal agendas, and if so, what are they, and how do they drive the conversation? Aim for truth, which is what I would say in response to most any question about writing.

PACING AND SCENE

David Long, interviewed by Linda B. Swanson-Davies

You don't want to put in a lot of stuff that people already know. If every conversation has a beginning, middle, and end, you don't want to include those parts that are just perfunctory stuff. It may be important for people, when they're first meeting, to greet each other, and if there's something significant about the way they greet each other, then you might use that. Otherwise, you'd want to just jump in. So I think the key to the thing is having most of the conversation be middle, not much getaway, and not much lead-in.

And there are rules in dialogue. You can't tell the reader things the people wouldn't say out loud. This is something I used to tell my writing students. You'd have these conversations where John comes back, and Mary says, "Oh, I've been visiting Rose down on the third floor. You know, our neighbor Rose, who grew up in Boston." In other words, people don't say that stuff, and so you can't use a patch of dialogue to feed information to the reader. I mean, that's your job as a narrator. Beyond that, I just try to listen real hard. I try to hear the words being spoken and to get the rhythm of the sentence and try to use how it's laid out on the page to capture the pauses—so you can break it up. You can indicate a pause by putting the *said* in the middle of the sentence. You can leave words out, you know: "Run get me that roll of VisQueen." You just want to say what somebody would say.

I'm really impressed with the way you do that. It seems to me that dialogue is one of the places where people can easily go wrong.

For me, along with writing place description, it's the most fun there is.

You know, the other nice thing about writing dialogue is, if you've given yourself a quota for the day, it takes a lot less words to fill up the page. If you look at days that you wrote three pages, there's a good chance some of it is dialogue. The days that are, like, one-and-a-half pages, are pretty dense-pages days. I'm being about two-thirds serious now.

Dialogue can be used to open out a page. Pacing is really critical for the flow of the story. You always get a choice in how you handle a piece of material. You can either give it a full scene, you can summarize it, or you can account for a long patch in somebody's life in just a sentence, if you want: "And things went pretty smoothly for the next three years." You've covered three years in one sentence. In the next sentence you move to when things are not moving smoothly again. Sometimes, for pacing purposes, you'll decide that a scene needs some air let into it, so, where you've had a long passage of exposition or a long passage of summary, you'll try to zero in on a moment and give two or three little exchanges of dialogue—little half-scenes, you might call them—and then you can go back to what you were doing. It just breaks it up. It's like when people have been sitting too long and they need to stretch a little bit or they need to see something that's here and now. Scene is always inherently more interesting than exposition. It's more vivid and more immediate, so you want to get into scene as often as you can.

Charles Baxter: I wrote an essay about dialogue called "The Elephant in the Living Room." Some of the most interesting dialogue is that in which the characters are either not listening, or listening selectively, or are hearing things that haven't actually been said. It's not as if great dialogue represents the care with which people listen and respond to each other. It's much more often the case that good dialogue in plays and novels calls your attention to the way people are not listening. Or are listening in light of their own needs at the time.

as interviewed by Robert Birnbaum

WHAT'S LEFT UNSAID

Amy Bloom, interviewed by Sarah Anne Johnson

I've heard you say that you're interested as much in what people don't say as in what they say. You even have part of a story, "Faultlines," in which the dialogue contains what the character didn't say, or should've said. What interests you about this dynamic? Why is it important to show?

It's because I'm interested in people. I don't know anything more interesting than the difference between what people say and what they feel. There's a whole universe there below the surface. I'm always interested in the way that feelings underneath leak out and shape behavior. People try very hard to have them not show up or change anything or affect anything. But our defenses leak. That's how we know they're there. I love that.

THISBE NISSEN

interviewed by Linda B. Swanson-Davies

You're very sure-footed in your delivery of dialogue. What is your approach?

This summer I'm doing a little talk at the Iowa Summer Writing Festival, and then another talk at Bread Loaf later on in the summer, and somewhere along the way, I've taken on dialogue as my thing to talk about. I can't quite figure out what I'm going to say yet, but I am fascinated by it. Why dialogue works or doesn't work. I don't know how aware I am of what I'm doing when I'm doing it. I really am hearing people talk and writing down what they say. I don't think I edit out as much crap as some people do. There are a lot of real dialogue tics in my stories. People don't speak in full sentences. They pause, repeat phrases; you know, there are so many tics to real dialogue.

Often when dialogue doesn't work, it's because people are using dialogue as a vehicle to get something across, instead of putting people in a room together and watching what happens. What comes out of their mouths? Often the things that come out of our mouths are not what we want to say, or what we're thinking. Or what would propel the action to a logical conclusion. We're all a mess. The things that come out of our mouths are gobbledygook. Occasionally someone is able to say what they're thinking, or they accurately represent their emotion in what they're saying. I really just go about hearing what people are saying and finding a way to get that into dialogue. Cutting out enough of the *um*s and repetitions, but keeping enough of them in that it's real. But maybe it's the things that go along with the dialogue, the gestures that belie the dialogue, the things that someone is thinking that are so different from the dialogue, or how they're actually getting out what it is that they're thinking. That somehow feels very natural to me. I wonder if it's a theater thing a little bit, too. I started out writing one-act plays in high school. I was part of a theater troupe that did that sort of thing, and when you're doing theater all you have is dialogue. You don't have the luxury of exposition. You have action and dialogue. I wonder if that's rooted in there somewhere, too.

Do you ever face the problem of how to get some bit of info out there that you feel compelled to use dialogue for?

My instinct is to say—and I'm not sure if this a blanket truth—but my instinct is to say that if there's something I'm really trying to get out there, usually what I'm writing is crap and I have to toss it anyway. It's too leading. I'm using my characters instead of letting them do what they're going to do and get to the place that they get to. Maybe I have an idea of where I'm trying to get them to go, or something I want them to grapple with, but I follow them and see what they do, and they take me down different roads because they don't say what they're supposed to say. If you're trying too hard to guide them—I want you guys here—and they want to go over there…

You cripple them.

Yes, and what they're saying isn't real because you're *making* them say it. There's too much manipulation going on. I've never actually taken a workshop class with Ethan Canin, but I have a lot of friends who have. He talks about deeply imagining your world, being inside it, and transcribing it rather than being the puppet master. Because if you're the puppet master, your characters are puppets.

If you can be a fly on the wall, who happens to have a laptop, you know you've got it made, because you can just scribble down what those people are saying.

. . . .

EXPRESSING THE SUBTEXT
Carol Roh-Spaulding
interviewed by Linda B. Swanson-Davies

Your dialogue is just wonderful; it's like hearing the clearest bink of a bell at exactly the right moment; it's right on.

Wow. That's my weak spot! I have a terrible time with it and try to avoid it as much as possible. When I have to do it, it's very controlled, and there's not a lot said. It's one of my weak spots. It's not my only one.

Well, that's very funny. I wanted to ask you how you teach dialogue to your students.

You know, the main thing that comes to mind is Hemingway's "Hills Like White Elephants," because I remember reading that and thinking, Well, there's nothing here but dialogue and some stage direction! I thought I had to figure out which one of them is speaking, etc. And then I realized that you didn't have to do that—if you were paying enough attention, you could tell who was talking! It was surprising in that at first you don't know what they're talking about; you feel like you're eavesdropping. There's so much subtext. It's a superb story to teach dialogue with. I will have students stage a tableau of what they see as the quintessential scene that expresses the subtext. They don't talk, they don't do a dramatic interpretation of it, they just stage a tableau. Different groups choose different moments. I ask them to try to express through their bodies and their alignment and positioning what the subtext is. There's just so much to teach with that story. Anyway, that's the main thing I do with dialogue; other than that I try to stay away from it because I'm scared I'm going to lead them astray.

....

RICHARD BAUSCH

interviewed by Jennifer Levasseur and Kevin Rabalais

The many characters in *In the Night Season* are given equal weight within each segment of dialogue, but who is speaking is never questioned. Each character has a life of his own, and that life is presented through his voice.

That has to be done extremely carefully. You don't want to repeat too much who's talking, so you try to make it clear to the reader by the way it's laid out on the page. When you are writing narrative—what people are doing, what the weather is like—you can dream that up without thinking about it a lot. It's not the same with dialogue. You really have to go over it and over it and make sure nothing is wasted, that every single line is doing more than one thing. The trouble people get into with dialogue is they allow the line to do one thing only, whether it is to sound realistic alone, or to carry forward exposition alone, or to give character alone. None of these by itself is enough. It's got to do all three of those things at the same time or else you have to find some other way to get it done. Dialogue has to sound like people talking without being like people talking. If it is like people talking, it's incredibly dull. You really have to think about it, step back and look at it, and go over every single syllable.

CHAPTER

9

BEGINNINGS

Susan on farm,
Dushore, Pennsylvania, 1960

Amy Bloom: I spend a lot of time looking out the window, walking around the house, watching daytime television, talking to my friends, going to the grocery store. There's probably material anywhere you look. Everybody's lives are full and mysterious and unexpected. It's just a question of whether or not you're paying attention, whether or not you want to stand around long enough to let them tell it to you, or imagine it.

as interviewed by Sarah Anne Johnson

ELIZABETH MCCRACKEN

interviewed by Sarah Anne Johnson

Your library work is probably where you formed the idea for Peggy in *The Giant's House*. Where did you find the idea for the giant?

I remember finding the idea for the giant in my special libraries class at Drexel University in Philadelphia. I had a teacher who I adored. I didn't adore many of my teachers, but she was a real librarian, a "librarian's librarian." Nevertheless, I spent a certain amount of time daydreaming in her class. I remember thinking in the special collections class, I want to write a book about a librarian in the nineties who is the archivist at a museum housed in the house of the world's tallest man. That was the initial idea for *The Giant's House*. You can see the difference between the initial concept and the final book.

Why a museum in the house of the world's tallest man?

I always loved the *Guinness Book of World Records*, and I'm fascinated with the Human Extremes: the oldest mother, the youngest mother, the longest fingernails, and the longest mustache with two women holding each end out. There was Mrs. Ethel Granger, who had a thirteen-inch waist. I always thought that was her natural waist. It was reduced from twenty-two inches over the course of several years, and I thought that meant dieting. Much later on, I discovered that Mr. and Mrs. Granger were famous fetishists, and she was a corseter. She'd corseted herself down to thirteen inches. If you go back to that picture you'll see this very 1950s looking housewife touching her hair, but her ear is pierced all the way around. Someday, I want to write something about Mrs. Ethel Granger. I love the idea of her. There she is, standing so innocently in the *Guinness Book of World Records*, but still, there's the danger of her ear.

I always liked house museums. The Maxfield Parrish house in New Hampshire, for instance, looked like he just stepped out of it, as if they never changed anything. It was dirty and homey and sweet. I like bad museums—well, not necessarily bad museums. I visited a museum in Niagara Falls, the Houdini Museum, this unbelievably cheesy, horrible museum. I always thought I'd write something about a museum like that, a two-bit museum where the people who came in were always disappointed by what they found. I thought if the museum housed the world's tallest man, it would be physically interesting. I wanted a house that belonged to someone you had never heard of, but was still intriguing enough to enter.

RON CARLSON

interviewed by Susan McInnis

For those who aren't familiar with it, Kotzebue is stark and wind-riven. It lies on a spit of Alaska's northwest coast, just across the Bering Strait from Siberia, and is home to about three thousand people. Inupiat people have lived on and around the same land for over six centuries. How did you happen to visit Kotzebue? Were you researching or writing, or both?

I was living in Utah in the eighties, working for arts councils in Idaho, Utah, and Alaska, and the work took me north twice. I went out to Aniak—which is quite a bit south and inland from Kotzebue and Nome, but still in western Alaska—and once for two weeks to Kotzebue. I was teaching in the local schools in both towns, and spent my free time just tramping about. People took care of me in both places. They took me out for plane rides and showed me their world. Both towns struck me as being very serious ventures, both having serious elements of the frontier about them. That atmosphere and the unforgiving nature of weather there marked me.

I suppose, without knowing it, I was gathering data. It certainly came back for me later. It's interesting to consider what rains back down on you from your life—the things that come get you and haunt you and bother you, things that may or may not end up in the writing.

That's where "Blazo" got its start: I actually did hear dogs barking in an airplane once. I was flying from Anchorage to Kotzebue, and the flight out was terrifying. Somehow the dogs were a comfort. Later, when I was in Kotzebue, there were dogs loose around town. Two or three were rogues, and they were raising hell with the sled dogs, very valuable working dogs. The sheriff was out hunting them. From time to time I'd hear gunfire, and it lent an edge to my sense of life there. I wasn't used to any of it—the barking, the rogue dogs, the gunfire. It all stayed with me, and then it came back in "Blazo."

THE SOURCE OF STORIES
Chitra Banerjee Divakaruni
interviewed by Sarah Anne Johnson

How do your story ideas come to you?

They come in many different ways. Sometimes I'll overhear something. As you know, writers are great eavesdroppers. Whenever I'm at a gathering, I'm participating, but a lot of times I'm just being quiet and listening. I get ideas from things I see in newspapers and magazines, from other writers, from things that happen in my life, in the lives of other people I know. But ultimately the source of all writing is mysterious. It comes from some deep place. We call it the imagination, or we could call it the creative mind. The ability to transform these nuggets from life into art comes from the creative mind.

What is your process like for writing a short story?

A lot of times I'll start with an image. I'm a very visual person, and in some ways I have to see the character doing something before

I start the story. It's the same way for my novels. For example, in *The Mistress of Spices* I got a series of strong visual images of an old woman in a little Indian grocery. It was a sensory experience: I could smell the spices, I could see the place, and I could *feel* it. That began the writing process. With many of my stories, it works in the same way. The image I get won't necessarily be the beginning image of the story when the story is complete. It could be the ending image. Sometimes I have to figure my way out backwards.

···

THE WORK OF THE UNCONSCIOUS
Siri Hustvedt
interviewed by Jennifer Levasseur and Kevin Rabalais

⟹◆⟸

How did the ideas for your novels begin?

Ideas usually begin as a single image, feeling, or a real event. *The Enchantment of Lily Dahl* began with a real suicide. There is a café in Northfield, Minnesota, where I grew up, called The Ideal Café. The real suicide did not take place there, but I used it in the novel to bring together the book's characters. That novel is written almost as a stage piece. It unfolds visually, a fact that reverberates with *A Midsummer Night's Dream*, the play inside the book. The café was a convenient place for characters to enter and exit. The real Ideal Café was like that. People dropped in and out, even when they weren't eating. Two of my sisters, Liv and Astrid, and my best friend, Heather Clark, worked there, and I heard lots of stories. There were stories I thought I had invented, which turned out to have their origins in real life. For example, Boomer Wee, a minor character, is an Elvis fanatic.

After Heather read the book, she pointed out to me that the café's owner had a bust of Elvis in the restaurant. Obviously, I knew it, but couldn't remember it. Something similar occurred in relation to *The Blindfold*. When I was in Germany, a journalist pointed out the wit of using the name Klaus as the hero of *Der Brutale Junge,* because Klaus is the name of one of Thomas Mann's sons. I thought of Mann when I wrote the story, but hadn't made that connection consciously. The unconscious does a lot of work for you in a book.

ANDREA BARRETT
interviewed by Sarah Anne Johnson

How does your research kindle your imagination and get you writing?

Oh, in all sorts of ways. Sometimes things really do grow from the reading and the research, but it's always in such odd ways. Often it's a picture, a visual image; sometimes it's an image in words, a sense of somebody on a dock or in a room holding a bandage. Sometimes a whole area of subject matter will seem interesting to me. That's what happened with "The Cure" in *Servants of the Map*. I used to drive through Saranac Lake a lot on my way to someplace else. I never stopped to look around, but it imprinted itself on me. I got curious about the porches, and then curious about the people who would've been on the porches, and then curious about the state of society that would've led everybody to be clumped in one place on the porches.

DORIS LESSING

interviewed by Michael Upchurch

I'd been wanting to write a version of the changeling story for a long time. You know: The fairy people put one of their babies in a human cradle. I had it on my agenda to write for some time. And then I read some casual remarks by a scientist saying that it was impossible that the Neanderthals and Cro-Magnons did not mate, and that meant that their genes must be in us. So I thought, if Neanderthals and Cro-Magnons, why not one of the little people?

Because every culture has the myth of the little people, and I personally think it's quite possible there *were* little people that vanished. There *are* little people! They're the Pygmies and they're a good yard shorter than those extremely tall people on the East Coast, the ones who are doormen in New York. So I thought, Okay, we'll have a dwarf fall into a human cradle—or a goblin or something—and see what would happen.

....

Roy Parvin: Usually the impulse to write the story is a very tiny thing. In the story "In the Snow Forest," I had bought a throwing knife, an antique throwing knife. I was walking around and I thought, Well, wouldn't this be wonderful to put in a story? It's really a minor part of the story, but it was one of the keys that opened the door that got me started.

as interviewed by Linda B. Swanson-Davies

STARTING WITH CHARACTER

Pam Durban, interviewed by Cheryl Reid

⟹◆⟸

How does a story start for you?

Sometimes it's an image. Sometimes it's a thought. It's been a while since I've written stories. I've been working on this book.

So you don't write novels and stories at the same time?

It depends. When I was writing *The Laughing Place*, I would get so tired of what seemed like the endless process of writing it. I would take a break and write a story, just to be able to finish something.

What about the story "Soon"?

I have a friend in town who's a collector of folk art and Southern memorabilia. He bought this huge collection of family possessions from a woman who was a descendent of a major plantation owner. People have said it is one of the most important collections of Southern artifacts. It's got everything: diaries, plantation ledgers, slave-sewn shirts. He made me a copy of the diary and gave it to me and also told me about the old woman whom he'd bought this stuff from. He basically courted her for a year in the nursing home. She was a mean woman who had disowned her children. I started looking at her diary and her diary literally opens with that scene of being blinded by the doctor. And that started "Soon," along with that woman's character. I think all of my stories start from character. Something about a character will catch my attention or my imagination.

WHAT IS PRAYER?

Patricia Hampl, interviewed by Susan McInnis

In preparing for *Virgin Time* there was another catalyst, a book called *An Interrupted Life*, by Etty Hillesum. Like Anne Frank, Etty Hillesum lived in Amsterdam during the war. She was also Jewish, also kept a diary, and met the same fate. She was older than Anne Frank, in her twenties, having love affairs and being a graduate student. A worldly, secular, sexy young woman. She experienced a spiritual awakening during the years of the war, just before she was carted away, and became fascinated by and immersed in prayer. In her diary, she wrote about the instinct to bend the knee and to bow the head.

When I read that passage, it lifted right off the page. I have always believed in the experience of awe, in that instinct to bend the knee. At that moment, prayer was redeemed for me, from habit, from a lot of words you just say, to a life force. One doesn't need to ask, Is there prayer? Once it is pointed out, as Hillesum did for me, it is clear that prayer is an instinct. This was an eye opener. And at that moment, I realized that the scriptural line, "The kingdom of God is within you," means that instinct for prayer, for crying out.

The revelation also related to my understanding of poetry, which says speech has to do not so much with communication as with utterance, what we cry out to the universe. It was a significant moment of personal discovery, and it gave impulse and trajectory to *Virgin Time*. It gave the text its questions, and the context for its retrospective pieces. It focused my thoughts on the nature of prayer: Why do people pray? Why do I pray? What is prayer?

MORE IMPULSE THAN IDEA

Maria Flook, interviewed by Sarah Anne Johnson

I never use the word *idea* to describe my first attraction to a possible story. My first impulse is less an intellectual germ than a psychological or even an emotional tempest or affliction. No, I don't begin with an idea, but I guess I'm more comfortable calling it an impulse, or even a compulsion. I write about issues in human relationships, usually male-female. Sometimes it's a family dynamic that explodes into something sinister, or someone becomes vulnerable at a dangerous emotional price. There might be sexual tension, a romantic tether that becomes a monkey on their backs. They're troubled by one another. They *come* from trouble.

My fiction is hitched to real experiences and real persons. I've met, worked with, or even loved—people whose situations marked me somehow. Willis, in *Open Water*, was very like someone I once actually knew in Newport, Rhode Island. His mother, in fact, really was Miss Cuba, and his broken arm, that he breaks more than once in subsequent brawls, was a real detail. He was in a cast the whole time I knew him. Of course, fictional characters are transformed from their first origin or catalyst, and become a wholly new alchemy. I write about people in peril. I'm interested in seeing how people scramble to get out of a hole.

Ha Jin: I usually begin with a kind of feeling triggered by an event or something that will bother me. That's the best situation. If something bothers me, I have to write about it in order to let the feeling out. That usually produces the best outcome. But stories don't always come that way, especially with a novel. It may start with an event or a feeling, but down the road there will be a lot of labor and research depending on how much energy I have and how stubborn I am.

as interviewed by Sarah Anne Johnson

ALICE MATTISON
interviewed by Barbara Brooks

The very first poem in that collection [*Animals*], called "Secret Animals," has a set of twins who are joined at the spine, and who bear a child. That means the image of conjoined twins was with you some thirty years before you wrote your latest novel, *The Wedding of the Two-Headed Woman*, in which the image literally takes center stage, when some of the characters put on a play of that name.

I know. I keep returning to the image of conjoined twins. They are in my first novel, *Field of Stars*, too. In the poem and that novel, someone fears giving birth to conjoined twins. When I was pregnant with my third child I had that fear, and wrote the poem. Years later at a reading a woman in the audience asked if the conjoined twins could be an image of the connection of the pregnant mother and child, if my fear was that the child wouldn't ever be separate from me. I thought, Wow, I bet that's right. I had no idea what I was doing when I wrote that poem, but I do think the fear of conjoined twins is a fear of infringement on solitude. Of never being alone. As a writer, you have these images in your head and sometimes you have to go with them, or otherwise they'll go against you.

Does that mean that your material—your subject matter—has been with you, even if only subconsciously, from the beginning?

You don't know all your material, but you are who you are. Whatever your obsessions, or neuroses or fears, they probably are ones that you will continue to have. There is something about that image that is very powerful for me, and mysterious, and rather dreadful. I don't mean to use it again. I vow that I won't and then I do.

REVISITING CHILDHOOD FASCINATIONS

Andrea Barrett, interviewed by Sarah Anne Johnson

How did you get interested in the disappearance of British explorer Sir John Franklin and all of his crew on their voyage to discover the Northwest Passage?

I was a little girl when I first got interested in the Arctic. I don't know what it was that caught me then, but I gobbled up all these Arctic history books. I was really mad for this. I loved it. Then it all sank away in the emergency of puberty. When you're a teenager you're just thinking about being a teenager. The material surfaced again when I was writing *Ship Fever*. When I was doing the reading for the novella, I learned about one ship that came from Ireland with a load of immigrants and hit an iceberg off the coast of New-foundland. Everybody drowned. I wasn't able to use that terrible story in the novella, but it made me think about the coincidence in time between the immigrations from Ireland and the height of exploration in the Arctic, going on at exactly the same time. I thought I'd write a companion novella about someone exploring in the Arctic, but I turned out to be wrong about the size of it.

WALKING THE WALK

Barbara Scot, interviewed by Linda B. Swanson-Davies

When I was researching the Scotch Grove Presbyterian Church, I encountered a one-line reference to a communion cup. The early Scots, who'd been evicted from the Highlands, had, over twenty-three years, come to the Red River colony that became Winnipeg, and ultimately came down this ox-cart trail to eastern Iowa—a thousand miles—and they brought a communion cup with them the whole way. I didn't follow that up at that time, but I didn't forget that line, and all of a sudden one night, after I sold *Prairie Reunion,* I woke in the middle of the night, thinking about that cup: Where did I see that? Did I really see a line that said that? Is there really a cup? Is it still there?

So I went back to Scotch Grove, Iowa, and found the cup, and got permission to take it, and I am now recreating the journey of these Scots. And I feel like I am just a vehicle for finding this story which is so representative of migration of peoples, of exiles, of community. These were Highland Scots way, way up north, Southerlandshire, in this little parish of Kildonan. I've gone over there, and I went to the very church, which is now in a sheep pasture, and took the cup back to the very pulpit where the eviction notices were read. I found the exact people in a memoir. It's amazing. Now what I'm doing is that I'm carrying the cup on the whole journey. I'm starting in April. And at the end of this, I'm going to incorporate the people from that church and community with the elders that I still know.

WRITING ADVICE from Mary Gordon

One of the things that I do with my fiction students is to get them to try to consider that every family has a way of doing things. Then you bring your friend home from college and they say, "Why do you put the Kleenex in the piano bench?" You say, "Everybody puts the Kleenex in the piano bench." Your friend says, "No, they don't." So I think all families have odd ways of doing things that are considered very normal in the family or else are just puzzles that you can imagine have the inexplicability of the holy trinity. But I think that's an interesting way of looking at the family. You know how they inhabit oddly without realizing that it is odd. For example, in my grandmother's house, why did my uncle sleep on the porch? There were two spare bedrooms upstairs.

as interviewed by Charlotte Templin

Andrea Barrett: Sometimes I wake up in the middle of the night with an idea, but that doesn't happen often. Often they come to me through my reading. I see some little picture or some phrase that captures my fancy.

as interviewed by Sarah Anne Johnson

THE SEED OF THE NOVEL

Allen Morris Jones, interviewed by David Abrams

What was the inspiration behind *Last Year's River*?

The roots of the novel go deep. In the summer of 1996, I had an interview with a woman by the name of Dorothy who started the wheels turning. I didn't start writing seriously for another year or two after that, and I didn't start seriously working on the novel until after I'd quit my job at *Big Sky Journal*, in the summer of 2000. From the time I began writing full-time, it took me about nine months to finish writing the book. At that point, I had an outline sketched out and had taken lots of notes.

Going back to that interview with the woman, was she the inspiration for the character of Virginia? The novel is framed with reminiscences of an older Virginia, and I get the sense that your interview might have spilled over onto the page.

Here's the story. In the acknowledgment, I thank Dorothy. I would not have started writing about Wyoming at all had I not started to imagine, after a brief luncheon with this remarkable woman, what it was like to be her. She'd lived this incredible life—she'd owned a dude ranch, she'd hunted tigers from the backs of elephants in India, she and her husband had had the first fishing camp on Great Slave Lake. She was enjoying life to its fullest extent, even into her late eighties. I became very intrigued by her, and I went to interview her. She was a very small woman, petite, and very sensual in a non-sexual way. I became less interested in the details of her life, and I became more interested in her personality. This is a woman who, in her late eighties, was still managing to live such a vibrant life. She was an extraordinarily sophisticated, complicated woman. This, in a world, a culture, that tends to dismiss its elderly as irrelevant. So I began wondering what it would have been like to know this woman sixty years earlier, when she was just starting her life. That was the seed for the novel.

Were there any particular events in her life which led you to start thinking about what eventually became *Last Year's River*?

The only similarity was that Dorothy was a wealthy, privileged young woman who ended up traveling West. But that's about where the parallels between her and Virginia end.

....

SUSAN RICHARDS SHREVE
interviewed by Katherine Perry Harris
꠲꠲꠲

I was in Massachusetts, a little discouraged with my own work, as happens off and on in a long career, and one of my children had just dropped out of college. So I was feeling blue, thinking about this child, wondering what might be going on with her.

I started [*Glimmer*] with a sentence and an image of a girl, an unreliable narrator with a skewed sense of reality—locked in her dorm room believing a man just outside her door is trying to come in. Is he there? Is anything she tells us true? That the girl has a black father, which is true, and a dead mother who she describes as living came to me from nowhere, or perhaps somewhere. That's always the wonder and mystery of writing. I know the book had something to do with sadness for my own child who needed to come home, with alienation and otherness.

....

NOT A SIMPLE BEGINNING

Matthew Sharpe, interviewed by Sherry Ellis

⟹⟶⟸

Your first novel, *Nothing Is Terrible*, begins, "'That girl is not normal, and neither is the boy,' I overheard my uncle say to my aunt late one summer night a month after my parents had been killed in a car accident on the way home from a wedding. My twin brother Paul and I were ten years old at the time and were the children my childless uncle was talking about." With this beginning you juxtapose words and phrases that give the reader a preliminary sense of the uniqueness of Mary, a seeming hermaphrodite, who at age eleven runs off to New York with her thirty-seven-year-old teacher. At what point during your writing of this novel did you write and/or choose these sentences as the beginning?

I think I had the sentences pretty early on. In that case I was very consciously trying to write a late-twentieth-century version of the *bildungsroman*, the coming-of-age novel that had its beginning in the eighteenth century. It was a symbolic form, a way of dealing with a new class of person, the bourgeois subject, who is unheroic and in that sense normal. In my update of the form I wanted to deal with somebody who would be both normal and un-normal, depending on who is looking at her/him and defining her/him. In fact I wanted to deal with someone who is different from herself, and who will always be two contrary things at once, someone who is both normal and not normal, someone who is a girl and a boy, a criminal and a victim, a nice person and a not nice person. I wanted to at least signal some of that in the opening sentence.

AMY BLOOM

interviewed by Sarah Anne Johnson

What inspired you to write the title story in *A Blind Man Can See How Much I Love You?*

I had done all this research for a nonfiction piece on female-to-male transsexuals. It just stayed with me, particularly because I found myself thinking about how hard it would be for me if one of my daughters said to me that God made a mistake, and that she was supposed to be a man and she wanted to have the surgery. As devoted as I am to each one of them, and as fond as I am of them, I would support them in doing what they needed to do, but it would break my heart to lose my girls. And that's what I was thinking, and started developing this character Jane, the mother who wishes to do right in her own way. Her story is completely different for her than it is for the daughter/son. For him it's a story of liberation, and for Jane it's a story of loss.

RICHARD BAUSCH

interviewed by Jennifer Levasseur and Kevin Rabalais

Your stories "Aren't You Happy for Me?" and "Letter to the Lady of the House" both primarily involve dialogue. What is the preparation for writing these stories, the first written as a conversation between a father and daughter, the second, a long letter?

"Letter to the Lady of the House" was a song. I wrote it when I was twenty-three. It was called "Marie, I'd Do It Again." [Laughs.] I was twenty-three, and I didn't have any idea what that really sounds like. It was an old guy talking to his wife. The last verse is, "If it has come to this kind of thing/the silence shocked by the telephone's ring/then something's died within/but I know I loved you then/and, Marie, I'd do it again." I sang the song for years. One day I thought, I wonder if I can make a story out of that song. Since the song was in the form of an address to someone who wasn't answering, I just made it a letter. I never thought about having it as a conversation. When I finished it, I thought, "No. This doesn't work. He's straining; nothing really happens." So I left it off the end of *Spirits*. But it got resurrected later, essentially as it was, and *The New Yorker* published it, and I still get letters about it.

How do you find subjects for your work?

Well, most of the time, they find me. They occur to me in the flow of experience. "Aren't You Happy for Me?" came about when I was watching the movie *Father of the Bride* with my daughter and some folks—you know, the Steve Martin remake of that flick.

He's talking about a quarter of a million dollars for his daughter's wedding, and I said to my daughter Emily, "Did you do the math on this?" She said, "It's a lot of money." I said, "$250,000. That's $249,000 more than I'm going to spend on your wedding." We were joking around about it. I went upstairs, and I thought, What if there was something really hard? You know, in the movie, the kid is going to be a world-class geophysicist or something. He comes from a wonderful family. He's supposed to be a wonderful kid. But what if there is something really, really hard? What if she was calling her father to tell him she is marrying someone who is old enough to be his father? And then she's pregnant—the whole thing of adding trouble. What if the father's splitting up with her mother and he has news for her? It sort of wrote itself. One version ended with the wife saying, "Maybe they will be happy for a time. Weren't we? Weren't we?" I thought that's too Salingeresque. I decided to go on and say some more stuff. That took about three days to write from beginning to end.

....

ALL THAT WAS LEFT OF HIM
Annie Proulx, interviewed by Michael Upchurch

⟫⟩◆⟨⟪

As I was finishing up *Postcards*, the idea for *The Shipping News* came to me; all of it hung on a guy that I'd seen on the ferry. There was a man on the ferry who was coming back from the mainland, and he was drunk and he stayed up all night. Skinny guy with red hair and violet-colored plastic sandals: women's sandals. And he sang all night long while everyone around him was trying to go to sleep. He sang about not being able to find a job, and coming back, and what was the use, and so forth, in this very low voice.

I was seated right behind him. I could hear it fairly well, found it fascinating, wrote some of it down. So he was in mind to work into this story about shipping news. I wanted to write about the fact that there were no jobs and that the fishery was collapsing and unfolding and falling down. And, actually, he evaporated from the story. Only his plastic sandals stayed in, with the guy who sells Quoyle the boat. That was all that was left of him. But he more or less set the story going.

DAVID MALOUF
interviewed by Kevin Rabalais

How much do you know about the structure of a book when you begin writing?

I certainly have a sense of the book's dimensions when I begin. I know if it's long or short. That may mean only that I already know how the subject will unfold and that it will reveal further facets and depths of itself. When I start, I sometimes have nothing but the end. I'll begin somewhere inside the story and work to discover where the book should start. The book is something you walk around inside. As you go, you discover bits and pieces of it. Then you try to find a structure which works in terms of what the book reveals itself to be. In *An Imaginary Life*, for instance, I began with the poppy section, which is about four thousand words into the finished novel, and it was quite late that I went back and wrote the section that leads up to that point.

Frequently, I'll begin with a scene, sometimes involving one or two characters and their surroundings. I will then say to myself, Who are these people; what's this all about? Or I will say, What kind of world are these characters in; what's going to happen to them? I often have a feeling about something and will write the first paragraph in order to get it going. The first task is to strike the right tone. I often don't have much idea about what's going to happen as far as plot goes. I may have a strong sense of a life or of a person. Often, that comes from something I've heard. This could be as simple as somebody telling you a story and you think, Oh, what an interesting idea that is. And then you make up characters. But often I begin and don't have a clear idea of the character at all. Somebody, then, will suddenly pop into a paragraph, and she may even turn out to be the main character.

BASED ON A TRUE STORY

Beverly Lowry, interviewed by Stephanie Gordon

Your works are set in numerous locales, such as Mississippi, New York City, Houston, and the hill country of Texas, and are concerned with many different issues, such as sexuality, divorce, disruptions, losses, the passage of time, death, and the need to "only connect." Where do you get your ideas?

I get them from my life. Not as autobiography, but what I learn as I go: what I see or hear about, what I read about in the paper. *The Perfect Sonya* and eventually *The Track of Real Desires*, for example, started out with knowing women who had been single and raising sons, although I eventually discarded that idea for *The Perfect*

Sonya. Now I have a daughter-in-law who did just that. She and Brandon came into my life about ten or twelve years ago, and this enhanced my interest in the single mother raising a son. All of these things, and many others, feed into my writing. You read, you think, you stare out the window, things happen.

HA JIN

interviewed by Sarah Anne Johnson

Mr. Yang [in *The Crazed*], hospitalized after having a stroke, raves about events that could be from his life or not. His crazy behavior sets Jian Wan to trying to sort out what is real and what is not, both in what Mr. Yang is saying and in his own life. What drew you to the idea of juxtaposing an old man who's losing his mind with a young man at the beginning of his life, who up until now has behaved quite rationally?

I did nurse a professor two afternoons. He wasn't my professor, so I didn't look after him for long. He had a stroke, and he began speaking nonsense and truth at the same time. I was shocked and haunted by that. His own students who looked after him talked a lot about this with me. This is a kind of universal case in which a man has lost the lock on his heart. He can't keep his secrets anymore. What would happen if he didn't have any restraint? Then the truth could be disastrous to his family and others. That's how I was really bothered by this memory. I wanted to write a story that was both an old man's and a young man's.

Barbara Scot: I had returned after a long, long absence, and found a trunk of things that my mother had left for me, and in there was a box of letters—the letters were relatives' letters to her and first drafts of her letters, and they detailed the story of her brief, unhappy marriage—and this very mysterious note with three puzzling lines: "What do you think? You don't understand. You'll never know how much." They were all wrapped in her wedding dress. I waited ten years before I tackled it.

as interviewed by Linda B. Swanson-Davies

BEGINNING WITH AN IMAGE
Dan Chaon, interviewed by Misha Angrist

Let's talk about beginnings. In a couple of stories, you start by dropping the reader right into the scene by literally presenting him with an object or situation, almost as though you are holding them in your hands: "Here is a snake with a girl in his mouth." "This is a braid of human hair." It's very effective. Are those beginnings critical to how the stories subsequently unfold?

Most of the time they are. I began those two stories ["Passengers, Remain Calm," "Falling Backwards"] with those specific images in mind—they were the driving forces that got me to sit down and write the stories. Other times I start with a premise; for example, in the title story ["Among the Missing"] I began with the family drowning in the lake near the mother's cabin. But in the two stories you mentioned, I was beginning with an image and then trying to discover the story.

THE FINAL MINUTE AND A HALF

Robert Olen Butler
interviewed by Linda B. Swanson-Davies

You started writing *Severance* before the horrible beheadings began in Iraq. Is it weird for you, that you were writing them as they began?

Beheadings have always been with us, though they've become much more central recently. Yeah, it is odd how that has come forward. The book began when Elizabeth and I were in Saigon in early 1995, and we went to the war-crimes museum in Saigon and saw an old French guillotine. Standing in the presence of a guillotine, I began to meditate on that object and then did some reading about it and discovered quickly that there was a lot of thought, a lot of suspicion that, far from being a quick and painless and humane form of execution, that there was something going on inside those heads after the blade fell, and what more dramatic moment could there be than the last thoughts after beheading and before death. As a fiction writer I was intrigued by them.

I discovered a very strict form that made it even more interesting to me. There was honestly a lot of speculation, if this does happen, about how long the time period is. Some people think only a few seconds. There were some doctors who thought in terms of the way sugars are turned into proteins and so forth, that it could be six minutes. So the doctor quote is a kind of composite; a minute and a half seemed in a nice sort of moderate, in-between. A believable thing. And of course it is true that we speak at about 160 words per minute in a heightened state of emotion. It seemed to me an interesting notion. It's almost I guess a poetic impulse, isn't it? It's such chaos, the thought of those last wild musings after such an event, that I liked imposing this kind of strict form on it. Each story is exactly 240 words long. Some of the pieces are more or less full lives that are flashing, but in others there are seemingly trivial moments which were not, apparently, so trivial.

THE GOLDEN HOUR

George Makana Clark
interviewed by Linda B. Swanson-Davies

Remember that guy who had a rail spike driven through his head? I think this was at the turn of the century—it's in all the beginning psychology books—I think they were blasting a tunnel or something, and this spike went right through his head, and after that he turned mean. He could no longer complete a task without swearing at someone: His wife divorced him, his friends left him. For a while he traveled in a freak show. But if it were his soul—it's funny, I hear things like that and I wonder, Could I write a story about that? What if your soul was in between there and it was driven out and you were a soulless man? Last night there was a television show we were watching while we were getting the baby into bed, and it was a documentary on emergency medical technicians, and they spoke about a "golden hour," when a person would live or wouldn't live as they're trying to get them through the emergency. I thought that would be a wonderful time for a story to take place.

THE SINGLE IMAGE

Alberto Ríos, interviewed by Susan McInnis

I can start writing a story anywhere and as long as I write long enough, I will eventually tell a story. I don't think I necessarily have to impose plot, but plot I think is an organic thing much like getting on a boat and just going with it.

You've been doing this as writer and professor in a class you laughingly call Obsessions. But it's serious, yes?

It's very serious. I think it has transformed students. It has changed their way of thinking and of writing. It's an exciting notion. Each student comes up with one image. One student chose most recently "Two people drinking from the same glass." Very simple. Just a short phrase. Each student begins with a piece of writing based on their chosen image. A poem, perhaps. They stay with the image for the rest of the semester. That's all they write about. It would seem impossible to write for three or four months about a single image. But if you can do it, the result is magical: If you can draw the rabbit out of this top hat, you will be amazed by what's possible in the world, in all those things around you.

So, we begin with the image. We extend it first backward, rather than forward, because I don't think you should always go forward. So we go a little bit backward, to a sentence that is that image, and then to a word that is that image—not that describes the image, but is the thing. We are trying to get at what language represents. What is that image? And then we go to a letter, just as I was talking about earlier. We find a letter that is the image of two people drinking out of the same glass. It may be visual. It may have some meaning. It may be any number of things, but we find the letter that is it.

Then we go forward again. At this point it's like pulling a slingshot backward. When you let go of it, then you can go forward like crazy, and you've got so much farther to go if you've gone backward first. Suddenly that image has all sorts of potential. We then write it as a short story, as a prose scene, as epistolary writing, characters writing to each other. And after you've explored it, obviously you must add things, and that's what's fun. You start adding characters and setting, and it's just to accommodate the image. But in fact, you're doing all the right things you ought to do as a writer. By the end of the semester, we come back to the original form. If you wrote a poem at the beginning of the semester, then you write a poem again at the end. But the difference between those two poems, after millions of miles of exploration, is extraordinary, and it's what my students learn to call craft. That there's that much even in the single image.

WRITING ADVICE from Joyce Thompson

After you have the kernel of a book in mind, hold off starting to write it as long as you can, until you absolutely can't wait any longer. All the time you're not writing, your subconscious is writing anyway, so when you actually do start, you know a good deal more of the story than you imagined.

ANN PATCHETT

interviewed by Sarah Anne Johnson

⇒◈⇐

Your novels all have brilliant openings, my favorite being the opening sentence for *Taft*: "A girl walked into the bar."

I plagiarized that from Elizabeth McCracken. She has a line "a dog ran into a bar" and I loved that. Usually the first line comes to me a long time before I start the novel. This is true of *The Magician's Assistant*. I had the first line for a year before I started writing it. I think this is true of each novel, that I had the first line before I had anything else.

What do you think makes a great opening?

It's one of those things, you know it when you see it.

....

RECEIVING THE FIRST LINE

Patricia Henley, interviewed by Andrew Scott

⇒◈⇐

In the River Sweet began as a short story about a family in which the father and husband had been a POW in Vietnam. It was about the life the mother led while the father was a POW. I love doing the research for writing fiction, so I found myself lugging home library books about POWs. This was during the summer of 1998. *Hummingbird House* was accepted for publication in August of that year. Once it was accepted, my mind turned to another novel. I thought, I'm doing an awful lot of research for a short story and I began to build the idea for *In the River Sweet*. I did the library research and planned a trip to Vietnam. I was writing scenes, but I knew something was missing.

The strand of the story about the hate crime came late in the conceptualizing. I abandoned 150 pages and started over because the presence of the hate crime provided me with the first line and the stripped-down, close to the consciousness of the character's voice. Once I received that first line—"Jesus would not say fag, she knew that much"—I wrote the manuscript in ten months.

DRAWN INTO THE STORY

by Judith McClain

The birth of a story or novel always begins with an image for me, sometimes accompanied by the first several lines or, if I'm lucky, a whole paragraph. If the image sticks, I write the story. If it flees, I don't.

In his preface to *In the Heart of the Heart of the Country*, William Gass says, "From the outset, however, I was far too concerned with theme. I hadn't discovered yet what I would later find was an iron law of composition for me: the exasperatingly slow search among the words I had already written for the words which were to come…so that each work would seem simply the first paragraph rewritten, swollen with sometimes years of scrutiny around that initial verbal wound…."

It's true for me too: I begin—and end—with that initial verbal wound. I seem to forget this each time I enter a new story. I am ever hopeful that a story will take me someplace else, that the first paragraph is merely a launch into dark space, new territory.

Time and time again, however, the process proves to me that the entire story exists in the initial paragraph; that rather than moving away from that first image, my process is to enter inside of it somehow, by swelling each fragment and making a descent. I am not launched from the beginning so much as sucked inside a bunch of words with incredible force.

KRIK? KRAK!

Edwidge Danticat, interviewed by Sarah Anne Johnson

Krik? Krak! is named from a term that refers to the Haitian storytelling tradition. When an elder begins to tell a story, he calls out, "Krik?" and the audience responds, "Krak," before the storytelling begins. What can you say about how the tradition of storytelling in your life played into your desire to become a writer?

I don't think I would have been a writer if not for storytelling. It taught me to love stories and gave me a very strong introduction to stories. It put me in touch with that very special moment in Haitian culture when adults and children were together to exchange stories. The immediacy of it was wonderful, and I saw that a story told today is told one way and the same story told tomorrow is told a different way. It was a very vibrant moment of interchange, and each story was a gift. It's like listening to a person telling a joke, and another person learns it and passes it along. That's why I decided to call the story collection *Krik? Krak!* as a tribute to my first influences as a writer.

The story "A Wall of Fire Rising" starts with the line: "'Listen to what happened today,' Guy said, rattling through the door of his tiny shack." In that one line, by having the character say that, you invite the reader in to listen as well. You've also characterized Guy as living in an impoverished situation. All of this from one brief line. What do you try to accomplish with an opening?

Openings are the hardest part for me, because I subscribe to that school of opening in the middle, in media res. As a reader, I'm very impatient. Something has to grab me out of my life and pull me in. That's something you get from the storytelling tradition, because the audience is often restless kids. A good opening stops you in your tracks and makes you want to stop what you're doing and listen. There's a thread that takes you from the opening into the story. Sometimes it's just beautiful language, something that makes you want to trade your life for a minute for this other thing. I try to open in a way that creates curiosity or interest in the reader. A good opening makes whatever is going on around you seem irrelevant. That phrase *Krik? Krak!* is a call and response that takes you from this world into the world of the story. The opening is like the trap door that pulls you in, and every sentence, every step, is hopefully a better promise so that you don't regret that you were invited in.

....

Nomi Eve: I have had this picture in my head for three years now, this picture of Chasia just sitting in that carriage. This one image. That's what I write from. I write from these single images that get stuck in my head.

as interviewed by Linda B. Swanson-Davies

CHANG-RAE LEE
interviewed by Sarah Anne Johnson

Each novel opens with a memorable line, and a line that characterizes the narrator and the tone of the narrative to come. For example, Doc Hata, in *A Gesture Life*, finds security in his position in his town of Bedley Run. The book begins, "People know me here." What do you look for in an opening, and how do you arrive at your opening line?

I look for a line that institutes many things—such as a kind of metaphorical condition, voice, which is literally the sound and tone—then institutes a moment of story. Without that it's hard to start the story.

....

ELIZABETH MCCRACKEN
interviewed by Sarah Anne Johnson

Did you always have the opening line, "I do not love mankind"?

When Peggy was going to narrate the book [*The Giant's House*], that was always the first line. The only immortality I ask is that fifty years from now, in the back of literary magazines when they have quizzes where you match the first line of the book up with the book title—I want to be in those quizzes. I don't understand books that begin, "It was June." I don't understand why you would start your book that way. I don't object to the sentence when I am further into the book, but when I read books, I want to know something about the writer and the book from the first sentence.

....

THE IMPORTANCE OF WAITING

Melissa Pritchard, interviewed by Leslie A. Wootten

⟫⟨⟫

With "Revelations of Child Love for the Soul of Dame Mi Mah," a story in *The Instinct for Bliss*, I didn't initially wait long. Instead, I jumped into writing the story. After about five pages, I realized I wanted to be anywhere else—even grocery shopping, which I hate. Those pages got balled up and thrown away, and I did what I should have done to start with: I waited.

Describe the waiting process.

With "Revelations of Child Love," I waited in a state of tension for about two weeks, listening for the right voice. When I say voice, I mean point of view, but also narrative design—the story's architecture and organic form. The answer I needed came when I was at Mass. Good ideas have come to me when I've been in church. Instead of concentrating on the service, I was leafing through a hymnal. Suddenly, I knew the story would be in scriptural form. What evolved includes sixteen confessions—or revelations. It's about my mother. I wanted something that was sacred, but also funny. As with so many mothers and daughters, our relationship has been a mix of admiration and frustration, anger and joy, dislike and love. I wanted to strike a certain nerve on the page, but when I tried to write a conventional story, I couldn't get to the emotionally dangerous point I needed to get to. I had to wait for the right voice—the right form—that could carry the charge and danger this story needed.

Do you always know ahead of time what dangerous point you are aiming for?

No. Sometimes I have to write a draft or two to find it. I go by the same advice I give my students: If you aren't sure what the danger point is after finishing a draft, ask what secret you are keeping from yourself. My secret with "Revelations of Child Love" was I didn't want my mother to die—ever. She's still alive—eighty-four and practicing yoga—but I was full of anger and sorrow at the prospect of her eventual death. Once I understood what the story was about, I was able to anchor in and write fairly quickly.

....

ROY PARVIN
interviewed by Linda B. Swanson-Davies

I was wondering about what starts a story for you.

A lot of them are images and very vague feelings. And hopefully the images remain but the vagueness goes away and it becomes specific. I find that the journey that the writer goes through is that the vague becomes specific. I thought it'd be really interesting to write a book about snow, to have a metaphor that changes, the way metaphors should, and to have that over the course of three very long stories. And from there I kept thinking, you know, I wanted to write about people in their forties because that interests me because I'm in my forties. When you're in your forties, the idea of precociousness goes away. You can't really be precocious unless you *die* early, I suppose. Where we are is probably different from what we imagined when we were younger. And where we thought we were going is probably also different. There's a certain fork in the road that happens. It might be a slight fork, but nonetheless it's a fork.

Doesn't mean there aren't more forks waiting, but still.

Right. But it's sort of like the midterm exam. And I found it really very valuable. I found that things that had interested me in my twenties and thirties didn't anymore. I had written to a friend from college that I imagined my life being like a booster rocket. There's a booster rocket that went from twenty to forty, and that fell away. And there's another booster that takes you from forty to I don't know when. Maybe twenty-year increments are appropriate. Maybe it's ten years. And so I thought, Well, this would be a very interesting thing to write about.

WAITING FOR THE RIGHT TIME
Louis Begley, interviewed by Robert Birnbaum

I started working on a novel very seriously in late June, and I did quite well until the beginning of August. Then all of my children and all of my grandchildren came to visit in waves, and [since] the book that I was writing is a very unhappy book, somehow going on with it in this house full of happiness became really impossible. So I did some more or less journalistic things that I had to do. The birth of a book is extremely time consuming. September has been given over to various things, and half of October will be, and then much of November, as *Shipwreck* has also come out in Germany, and I have an extensive German book tour. So I get back to it in December.

Edwidge Danticat: The stories sometimes come in one line or one scene or, rarely, but it happens, fully formed. I've had many stories where I had ten pages and nothing was happening, and I put those away and pick them up much later. There's a deepening that comes with time that adds richness to a story. That's why some of the ideas stay story ideas and others become something else, novels, plays, even nonfiction.

as interviewed by Sarah Anne Johnson

MATTHEW SHARPE
interviewed by Sherry Ellis

The Sleeping Father begins with a description of circumstance. "Chris Schwartz's father's Prozac dosage must have been incorrect, because he awoke one morning to discover that the right side of his face had gone numb. This was the second discovery on a journey Chris's father sensed would carry him miles from the makeshift heaven of health." Do you believe that circumstance is a particularly effective means of enticing readers?

I don't think I have one particular way of beginning a book that I use repeatedly, or at least I hope I don't. I borrowed that opening from Kafka. *The Trial* and "Metamorphosis" have similar openings. I wanted that Kafkaesque sense that one's life is about to go out of control, in a terrifying and unknowable and absurd way. That's why I began in this particular story with circumstance. It is after all a kind of accident that causes the mechanics of the plot; that is, the accident of switching the pills.

DANIEL WALLACE

interviewed by Linda B. Swanson-Davies

You mentioned that you had this great technique that releases stories for you.

Self-deception.

Yes! That, I thought, was marvelous. What were the words again? "It happened…"

"It happened like this, it happens like this." This gives me the impression that I know what was happening.

So that you could know.

So that I could know eventually what was gonna happen. It's like taking something up on a dare. Kind of, Oh, sure, I can do that. You don't know if you can or can't do it until you attempt it, but you have to give yourself the illusion that you have some sort of power, some sort of control when you really don't have that much. I don't feel like I do. People can't really tell you how they do what they do. This is just one of the many tricks that keep you going. Or as they say in that movie that my son likes to watch, that *Toy Story*: I'm not flying, I'm falling with style. I just know if I couldn't have lied to myself and believed—that's the real interesting thing, believing your own lies. It's kind of like believing that you're good looking. If you believe it, you can get away with it. Other people start to believe it, too.

Sue Miller: Usually they come as a vague notion, an idea of what I want to be talking about. Then I begin to imagine situations which would convey that idea or contain it, and then I begin to people the situations with characters. It starts abstractly for me, but it happens closely together. I'm not pondering an abstraction for a long time. One comes on the heels of another, but it's the idea that interests me first.

as interviewed by Sarah Anne Johnson

WRITING BEYOND CONCEIT
Ron Carlson, interviewed by Susan McInnis

There's a story in *Plan B for the Middle Class* called "Sunny Billy Day." When I started writing, it was premise heavy. I said to myself, What if there was a baseball player with so much charisma that he could change an umpire's mind? I'd never seen it happen. I've seen it in hockey. I've seen it in football. But a baseball umpire, even when he's wrong, doesn't change his call. So that was the premise.

At the top, though—when you're just sitting down to write—most stories are a little more clever than is good for them. But if you stay close and careful, the people emerge with their human feet to carry the premise forward. It's like starting with an insupportable thesis, and then creating the evidence to support it. You do it carefully. If you don't do it carefully, you end up with an anecdote or a joke. The premise is a player in the story, but the story transcends that first good idea and grows beyond it.

AMY BLOOM

interviewed by Sarah Anne Johnson

Do you find that when you write your early drafts, the beginning you start with is what ends up on the page? For instance, in "Silver Water" we see Rose singing, so that we're introduced to her gift before we're introduced to her illness. Is that how you originally began, or did the beginning grow out of the story once it was written?

"Silver Water" had been in my head for about a year. Each scene was pretty clear to me. Some of the middle was muddled, as it often is, but I knew that it would begin with her singing, and end with her killing herself.

Do you typically get the beginning and ending like that?

Well, more than I get the beginning, ending, and middle. Sometimes you just get the beginning, and sometimes you just get the ending, and sometimes you get two lines of dialogue that you carry around for a year wondering, Who's going to say that?

. . . .

THE IMPORTANCE OF ENVIRONMENT
Beverly Lowry, interviewed by Stephanie Gordon

I started writing letters and keeping a journal that dealt with the things I saw and heard on the street or in the grocery store, which is a way of compiling information for future use. So you could say that by the time I moved to Houston in 1966, I had begun to write. And to think like a writer. To reflect on paper, make notes, jot down observations, not knowing why.

And Houston was very good to me. Houston was so wide open and classless; people didn't try to hold you back from accomplishing whatever you wanted. And that provided me with a lot of confidence, a sense that I would do whatever I wanted. It just didn't matter who my father or great-grandfather was, the way it had in the Delta. Whereas New York had been inhibiting, because New Yorkers seemed to know everything, Houston made me feel as if I could do anything.

While in Houston, I started writing *Lolly Ray*, which actually began as a short story. I was writing about this baton twirler, and then all these different characters started showing up in the narrative. I actually wrote those first two books as one, *Come Back, Lolly Ray* and *Emma Blue*. That's why they came out so close together.

··

A MAD DESIRE TO LAUGH

Lynn Freed, interviewed by Sarah Anne Johnson

⟶◆⟵

Do you start with a voice, a situation, an image?

I start precisely with those. Where do they come from? I suppose the desire, the need to create the life on the page, the world. And I always have a mad desire to be surprised, and, of course, to laugh. Not that one can intend these things; just that the expectation is there.

When you begin a novel do you have any idea of the shape or where it's going?

I may have an idea of where I think it will go, but usually in the writing it does not go there. Or it goes beyond. Intention can kill fiction, certainly for me. As soon as I find myself saying, I want this character to accomplish this, to go here, to go there, I know I've lost the piece. I should just shut down and go for a walk.

How about short stories?

They do indeed start from a character in a situation. How to find the way into that situation, how to begin the story—that is the labor. Some emerge from failed beginnings of novels. Some are just written. There are myriad paths to Buddha.

WRITING ADVICE from Kathleen Tyau

I try to write my stories from start to finish in one sitting. I call these my "beginnings." For the book I'm working on now, I've written many of these beginnings in longhand. I don't revise until I've found the heart of the story. And that's when I flesh a piece out and rework the language. Of course, it doesn't always happen this neatly because the stories come to me in different ways. Sometimes I have a character, sometimes just a phrase or title. There's no real logic to it. I freewrite until something gels and worry about the details later. Probably the images come to me first, because of freewriting.

as interviewed by Linda B. Swanson-Davies

Jayne Anne Phillips: Stories and novels often occur to me in their first lines or their first paragraphs. I've had the experience of writing a first paragraph that's very language oriented, but very cryptic in terms of the story or a narrative act. I'll hold on to that in a notebook for years before I find my way into the book that the paragraph describes.

as interviewed by Sarah Anne Johnson

MARY YUKARI WATERS
interviewed by Sherry Ellis

When you are writing a story, which usually comes first—plot or character?

There's no rule. Each story develops in a different way. Sometimes I'll just start with a feeling. Once I was talking with a poet, and I told her that one of my stories had started with a complex emotion that I had a real need to capture on paper. And then I created an entire story building up to that fleeting moment, so that the reader could experience the exact feeling I had. And the poet said, "Oh, that's exactly the way I write my poetry." That was a really nice bonding moment. Or sometimes a story might begin with a dilemma, and I keep writing to see how it's going to play out. For example, "Egg-Face" is a story that starts with the dilemma of a thirty-year-old woman who's never had a date or a job. I was interested in her predicament, and I wanted to see where it would take me. Or sometimes a story will start with an interesting little detail, one that often ends up being completely insignificant to the story.

But you have to start somewhere, and a curious fact or detail can get you into a story. For example, in "Since My House Burned Down," there's a brief section about a girl practicing her silverware skills so she can go to an omelet parlor. This detail came from a story my grandmother told me about her own youth. When she was growing up, the popular girls would be invited by their dates to eat at this tiny store that was open only for lunch. They sold a plain American omelet, served with ketchup from a bottle. It was such a status symbol to go there. I loved that story, because it was so funny and odd. I thought I'd start out with it and see what came of it. The story ended up taking off in a completely different direction, and the omelet never became a significant part. But at least it got me started. There are endless ways you can begin a story. Every time I start a new piece, I feel like I'm reinventing the wheel. And I always have this sense of panic, because I feel just as clueless as I did when I wrote my first story. I've never developed a pat system for these things. And I don't ever want to, because then it'll become like a factory, where I'm just cranking out stories from the same basic mold. I like it that each story poses challenges, that you can never rest on your laurels. That keeps it interesting, and rather scary.

Susan Richards Shreve: What I tend to do is imagine a story or a character or both and live with them in my head for a long time, as much as a year or two. Sometime in the course of imagining, I'll write a couple of sentences. Sort of like yeast. Eventually, I'll start to write.

as interviewed by Katherine Perry Harris

CHAPTER

10

ENDINGS

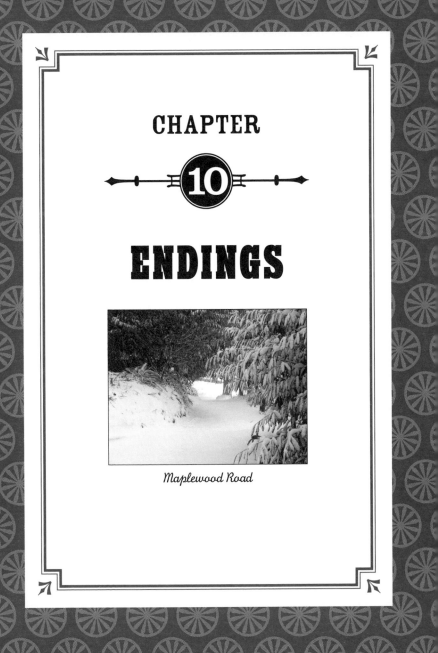

Maplewood Road

Elizabeth Cox: When I'm reading a story I look for some turn, some change, some event that gives a different perspective. In my own writing, I try to discover an ending, and I go a long while not knowing where the story is going. Sometimes the ending comes in the form of an image. In my first novel, *Familiar Ground*, the image was looking into the woods while driving somewhere and seeing a place that looked familiar—just a moment of imagining that you'd been there before. In *The Ragged Way People Fall Out of Love*, the image was people sitting around a table at dinner in Halloween costumes.... Sometimes an image offers a larger perspective.

as interviewed by Sarah Anne Johnson

CHITRA BANERJEE DIVAKARUNI
interviewed by Sarah Anne Johnson

Because stories are different, they resolve themselves differently. Some stories lend themselves to epiphany, while some end with a question. Other stories end with a flash-forward of something that may or may not happen. Some stories will end with an inner realization for the character, not necessarily an epiphany, but an understanding or a re-seeing of something that's been there all along. Sometimes a whole new image will come in that is only tangentially related, but thematically related. I'm always reading other writers and what they're doing. I came to writing fairly late after I'd finished all my formal education, so books have been my best teachers.

How is a short-story ending different from a novel ending?

The novel has a different pace. It's like a big wave that has been building up and up and up and now it has to crash, whereas the short story is more subtle. It's not that big dramatic crashing at the end, but more like a dancer's movement, subtle and artistic.

LEAVING IT THERE

Pam Durban, interviewed by Cheryl Reid

The last lines of your most recent stories, "Gravity" and "Soon," seem to open up and are reminiscent of Chekhov's movement toward a larger perspective.

Certainly, I have learned that from him and from Alice Munro. The stories in *All Set About with Fever Trees* are much more definite in their endings than these others. Those stories try to wrap up in a way that I am moving away from.

"Made to Last" sticks out in my mind that way. The last line is, "Did you see what we've done?"

It's interesting that you pick that one, because when I was rewriting the stories for the book, that ending nearly drove me crazy, because the story went on beyond that into a lot of explanation. That was probably the first story where I discovered how to leave it there. I wanted to find that last image or that last note or that last place for the story to come to rest without having to bring it to some kind of closure.

ANDRE DUBUS

interviewed by Jennifer Levasseur and Kevin Rabalais

Are there any stories you are most proud of?

They are mostly gone when I finish them. I remember the ones that were hardest to write. "Adultery" was hard, and I almost quit writing it a few times. "Dancing After Hours" was very hard, as well. I am fond of many of the stories in *The Last Worthless Evening.* I like "Molly" and "Deaths at Sea."

"Molly" was hard. It started from the point of view of a fishing captain who first sees the mother, Claire. It started on his fishing boat off the New Hampshire coast. Claire invites him over to her house for dinner. He's the first one who sees Molly. I didn't know how to finish it, and then a couple days later I realized it was finished, and that I just needed an epilogue. I wrote that epilogue with my daughter Cadence, who was three years old at the time, on my lap.

. . . .

MAKING THE PAINFUL CUT

Chris Offutt, interviewed by Rob Trucks

You mentioned having to cut the epilogue that you'd written for The Good Brother. *What did it cover?*

Shit, they go up to Alaska and live happily ever after and homestead.

Joe and Botree and the two kids?

And Johnny and his girlfriend and their daughter. Coop is dead of a heart attack. There were some lawsuits. The ACLU was involved and they got charged with criminal syndicalism. They dusted it off, like this old prosecution charge I discovered. And then I thought, What are you doing, Chris? You can't have this book and then have people go off to Alaska. It just was me trying to not let Virgil face the music, and that's what got me so tore up over it. When I cut it, I started crying, because I realized that Virgil couldn't just get off scot-free....

THE DREAM SOLUTION

Valerie Martin, interviewed by Janet Benton

Sometimes I have dreams that are solutions to problems I'm having, and they're inevitably stupid solutions. I had one not too long ago. I dreamed the solution for the end of this book that I had written six different endings for, *Italian Fever*. And I had this dream. I woke up and thought, That's it, this is wonderful, that's it. And I went back to sleep feeling happy. In the morning I woke up and examined my dream and it was just absurd. This couple goes off and starts pruning a rosebush. That's how it was going to end. It was really not satisfactory, but the dream brain thought, Oh, great solution. I get sleepy when I'm writing a lot, and a lot of times I go lie down and I think I'm going to go to sleep, but instead, before I go to sleep I start to think of what to do, and it solves the problem. I know a lot of people who do that. As soon as you lie down, all of a sudden it's clear.

Melissa Pritchard: "The Widow's Poet" was scary to write, especially toward the end when I had no idea what was going to happen. I actually had to force myself to continue because I was so afraid of what I would discover as I moved forward. Kind of like Bluebeard—don't open that door because you'll see corpses hanging in the closet. I'd open a door and there would be a smaller, darker door, then another and another. I really had to summon all my courage to make it to the end.

as interviewed by Leslie A. Wootten

HANDLING COINCIDENCE

Alice Mattison, interviewed by Barbara Brooks

In life, by some coincidence, we might both know the same Nathan, though in fiction, that could feel contrived. There is a major coincidence at the core of *The Book Borrower*, yet it feels quite natural.

We're all afraid of coincidence, but I think very often when we're caught up in a novel, we don't even notice it unless it's one of those thumping, thundering coincidences that come in at the end, and are just too neat and tidy, and make ending the story too easy. What's important is that it not seem as though the coincidence is in there to rescue the book or to rescue the characters. Then it's going to echo those nineteenth-century coincidences that almost depend on a universe organized by providence, in which the right thing always happens at the end. But if the coincidence starts the story going, or if the coincidence moves the story along, then it's much less noticeable and feels like coincidences in life, which of course happen all the time. And if the characters say, Look at that, what a coincidence, and then just move on, that's probably better than if the author tries to conceal it.

....

TIM O'BRIEN
interviewed by Jim Schumock

Your novel, *In the Lake of the Woods*, is kind of a mystery wrapped in an enigma, and I think it's probably your most technically difficult book.

I think so. It's an odd thing: On the surface, it's a very simple story. A man wakes up and his wife's gone. Where did she go? It's a traditional sort of search story, I suppose, on one level. On other levels, though, it's not: I offer a series of hypotheses as to what may have become of her. As I wrote each hypothesis—she drowned, she ran away from him, she left him for another man, she got lost, he killed her, they ran off together—as I wrote each of those hypotheses, I was convinced *that* was the answer. I ended up with a series of chapters that seemed to me equally credible. When I got to that point, I realized, My God, I can't put a traditional end on this book. Why hypothesize if you've solved the mystery? And I began then wrestling with hard dramatic and intellectual issues.

It occurred to me late one night, How can I submit this? What will people think when they read a story like this, with no answers at the end? And then other little challenges began popping up, and it occurred to me that, well, people are fascinated by the Kennedy assassination, for example, because we don't know. If Oswald had acted alone, and it was proven, there'd be no mystery. No JFK movie. I mean, you don't see many movies about the death of Truman, of old age. Custer's last stand remains with us—no survivors. Did Lizzie Borden take an axe? Amelia Earhart stays in the national mythology partly because we don't know what happened on that flight. There's a sense of not knowing that fascinates the human spirit, I think, and frustrates. The same for love: You know, you fall in love with someone and she seems to fall in love with you, and you ask her, "Do you love me?" and she says, "Yes." And then you ask, "How much?" And she answers, "With my whole heart," and then right away, you wonder how *whole* is her heart. We're all encased in our heads, and we can't read minds. There's a mystery about love because we can't enter that other person's mind. It's that mystery business that finally convinced me to continue this difficult book, knowing I'd be publishing a book with no traditional conclusion.

George Makana Clark: Where a story ends is where it ends—I've written on for four and five pages before I realize where the story really ends. It's difficult to delete those pages. That's why when I make changes to a story, I don't want the old versions of the story to be around, I don't want to see them—so when my computer says, "Replace file?" I always do. I think that's a strength of my writing.

as interviewed by Linda B. Swanson-Davies

THE ROLE OF ACCIDENT

David Long, interviewed by Linda B. Swanson-Davies

There are things that happen to you kind of out of the blue. In order to answer this, you have to talk about some of the fundamental rules of fiction. I remember having a conversation with Bill Kittredge years and years ago about the role of accident in stories. The notion is that you can't end a story with an accident because it's dishonoring the contract you have with the reader. In other words, in a story, things happen because of who people are. *Action determines character* is the most fundamental principle in fiction. Action equals character. Character equals action. You do what you do because of who you are. Sometimes it's a question of *reacting* to something that happens out of the blue, but you react according to who you are, and another person would react differently. You know, an accident ending a story would be like writing a murder mystery that takes place in a locked room, and on the last page you say, Well, it wasn't really locked. That's what I call dishonoring the contract.

But you could *start* a story with an accident. One of my early stories that I like still is called "Home Fires." A man survives an accident that should have killed him. The question becomes: What is he going to do with it? That's now information in his life. He drives over an embankment, and finds himself at the bottom of this long hill, unscathed except for having lost a tooth. He meets up with two women who are camping, running away from their homes together. They suggest to him that there's a possibility, since this occurs in the wilderness, that he could easily disappear.

He could be presumed drowned and the body never recovered. So he suddenly has the option of starting a new life. So he has A or B. A being: Go home. B being: Start a new life. And he chooses C, which is: Go home and start a new life.

....

TURNING AWAY FROM DEATH
Ann Patchett, interviewed by Sarah Anne Johnson

Early on in the narrative, you let it be known that all of the terrorists will die in the end. Why did you decide to reveal this up front?

Because I don't want to have the reader racing through the book [*Bel Canto*] wondering if they were going to live, if they were going to make it. They're not going to make it, and that's not the point. We're all going to die. We don't know how long we're going to live, and none of us will feel that it's long enough. It really isn't about quantity, it's about quality. These people have short and beautiful lives. I want the reader to focus on their life, rather than on their death. Also, it puts the reader in the same position that it puts the characters, which is, they know how it's going to end, and yet they put it out of their minds. So many readers have said to me, "I read that line, but I made myself forget it. I turned away from it." That's what the characters do. They know that it's not going to work. At the end everyone will say, "Of course this is where it was going. I didn't want to believe it."

That's how we are with our own death. We know that we're going to die, and yet we willfully turn away from it everyday to enjoy our beautiful life. There's something I refer to as the *Love Story* syndrome, in which Ryan O'Neal says, "This is about Jenny.

Jenny is dead." So you don't go into that movie wondering if she's going to beat the cancer. She's not going to beat the cancer, so you spend the movie looking at this beautiful girl in her average and charming life which is all so heightened by the knowledge of her imminent death. And even then you think Jenny's going to pull through.

SUSAN RICHARDS SHREVE
interviewed by Katherine Perry Harris

Your novels deal with understanding character, and how a person can make a life in a difficult world. Do you consider yourself an optimistic writer?

That's such a funny question for me because it goes to the heart of the matter. When I was a little girl, I was given a five-year diary. I wrote in it a few times, little entries full of angst and disaster, and at the end of each entry, I wrote, with no irony intended but in clear desperation, "We are all well and happy." Shortly after my first novel [*A Fortunate Madness*] was published, I met a salty old newspaperman who had read the book and said to me, "Nice, Susan, but you know there are no happy endings."

Like most writers, one of the things that draws me to this work is the desire to create order in a random world, which is, of course, an acknowledgement that there are no happy endings. However, in thinking of optimism—particularly of wrestling light from darkness—then ultimately, though certainly dark, I think of myself as an optimistic writer.

AN ABRUPT AND FINAL ENDING
Charles Baxter, interviewed by Stewart David Ikeda

You've said that ending your story "Saul and Patsy Are Getting Comfortable in Michigan" with an accident might have been a mistake. You bravely and miraculously amended this in its sequel, "Saul and Patsy Are Pregnant." Budding writers often struggle with the impulse to end a story by ending its lives, as you did there. But they are always impressed—and heartened—to hear that fiction can evoke such deeply felt responses, such as the rather violent encounter you had over these characters. Can you describe it, and how it made you feel?

I had come close to completing *Through the Safety Net* when my office mate at Wayne State University, named Dennis Turner, told me that he had liver cancer. Dennis had come from New York, from Queens, and when he first arrived here in Detroit, he thought that the Midwest was the end of the world. Then he discovered that he loved it and felt this was the right place for him to be. And when he was dying, I began to think about people who had relocated themselves, found themselves in some places which they found geographically unsympathetic, distasteful, and I began to think about a story like that. It's always been my impression that people on both the East and West Coasts consider the inhabitants of the Midwest to be lacking either intelligence or taste, or both—simply for living here.

I thought I'd get some of that off my chest in the story, and some of my anger from my friend's dying. And I thought, if circumstances can be that calamitous for him, I can write a story in which the reader is taken as much by surprise by the death of my characters as I was—I am—by the death of my friend. I intended to make a couple as lovable as I could, and then send them through the windshield of a car at the end.

No magazine wanted to take the story, so it appeared in the book without a previous publication. When the book came out, though, that story received quite a bit of attention. Contemptuous attention by *Publishers Weekly*, if I remember correctly, which found that the accident at the end was not convincing. But it convinced some people—particularly people who became fond of these two.

It was in a literary setting, at a poetry resource-center meeting in Detroit's Book Cadillac Hotel, a place that's now out of business. A group of Michigan poets used to meet every year for readings, workshops, things of that kind. And I remember *Through the Safety Net* was on display there and, at one point, a woman came up to me and grabbed me by the lapels and said, "You have the nerve to kill off that nice pair of lovable people!"

But I did have the nerve. It was exactly my point.

Ha Jin: I always know the main direction of the story. Otherwise, I will waste a lot of time. Without an ending, I can't start a story. Sometimes I plan an ending; it needs to be revised later on. But from the very beginning I need a sense of the direction, or I'll be groping around without knowing where I'm going.

as interviewed by Sarah Anne Johnson

ENDING IN THE RIGHT PLACE

Chang-rae Lee, interviewed by Sarah Anne Johnson

⟹⬦⟸

Your endings are distinctive, and each gathers up the threads of the story and spins a wonderfully resonant image that carries the narrative into some unknown future. *Native Speaker* ends with Henry helping his wife dismiss her speech class. She pronounces each student's name as they leave. "Now, she calls out each one as best as she can, taking care of every last pitch and accent, and I hear her speaking a dozen lovely and native languages, calling all the difficult names of who we are." What does a great ending accomplish, and how do you arrive at your endings?

It's more like a feeling than anything intellectual. When you're toward the end of a book, a lot of things are building up. There's pressure that keeps accruing in terms of all the ideas that you're talking about and all the language and all the emotion. It points you toward a certain kind of feeling at the end, whether it's explosive or quiet. In that book it was going to have to do at least emotionally with what Henry's left with, after all that language. With each book I felt that the person was in the right place in the world he's in and he's thinking about the right things in terms of what's gone on. Jerry Battle's off by himself, but still close by. He's with the family but without them too. He's not at the center anymore. That felt right to me. It's a question of where the story wants to place the character. With Henry, he's in a mask but he's still there at ground zero for these young kids learning the language. That seems to me the right place for him. The word *difficult* was something I made sure to think about and put in. The difficult part speaks to the turmoil and frustration that he's seen and experienced, and saying that it's not easy to have all this difference and variation, though still embracing it.

THISBE NISSEN

interviewed by Linda B. Swanson-Davies

There's a bit of a cryptic message that I didn't entirely notice until I closed the book [*The Good People of New York*]. A bit of a secret, sweet and romantic. How did you decide to put that in there? Did you have it from the beginning?

The chapter about going to Zinnia, the psychic, was taken from a kernel of a story about a widowed woman who had gone to a psychic, and that psychic somehow was only seeing the letter *D*. It was just that weird. So sometime after that reading, she was sitting at a bar, and there was a man who was very attractive to her sitting down the bar—they had this very intense chemistry going on. When he finally came over to introduce himself, his name was Dennis Dee. And they wound up together. It was so bizarre, but I loved that story and wanted to use it.

The last chapter was based around that anecdote, and another friend's story of someone standing up and doing this incongruous toast in the middle of a meal, and everyone thinking, Oh God, okay, here we go. I'm not really positive how I came to put them together. Maybe I started just by choosing a name that started with an *S*, and then thought to myself, Oh my God, what if he's the one? Wanting to plant that in there. Maybe my wanting to take care of her, or wanting at the end to feel like Roz was on a right track. She's such a strong person; she had gotten thrown by things that had happened in her life that she never expected to happen, and I think there was a little bit of me wanting to give something back to Roz. It seemed okay to have that—it was okay to have that romantic notion that maybe he was the boat she wanted, that it was all right, and you weren't stupid to think it, and you weren't silly or flighty or romantic to think it. Like maybe if you keep your faith a little longer, maybe that'll come.

WRITING ADVICE from Edwidge Danticat

The biggest obstacle in terms of the writing itself is finding something that keeps you writing and allows you to finish pieces. I was always struggling with that self-doubt about what I was doing, sometimes with the material and sometimes just with the process itself. Someone gave me the best advice I'd ever had. I couldn't finish anything I had started because they never lived up to what I had in my mind, and this friend said that my writing never matched my vision because the mind is infinite and there are only so many words in any language. Once I settled with that, I could continue to write.

as interviewed by Sarah Anne Johnson

Elizabeth Cox: I love the moment when something turns in an unexpected way. I love wandering into a place, then having something happen that wasn't expected to happen. This process is part of the discovery, and keeps me from manipulating or creating an agenda. I have a note to myself on my desk lamp: Offer a life, not a text. I think this is a quote from a theologian—Niebuhr, I believe. Anyway, it sounded like a good one to remember.

as interviewed by Sarah Anne Johnson

ENDS SHOULD REFLECT THE CHARACTERS
Kevin Canty, interviewed by Linda B. Swanson-Davies

When people talk about tragedy, they talk about somebody who was walking down the street and a cinderblock fell down off a building and killed them. That, to me, isn't a tragedy. It's just one of those random things in the world. It just comes along and squishes you like a bug. It has nothing to do with what you want or what you're after.

For me, tragedy involves the will. It involves trying, striving. A tragic hero is someone who's trying for something and, usually through their own fault, falling short. That's one of the things I'm always dealing with when I'm trying to teach writing. Students will be cooking along with: Are they going to break up or are they not going to break up—and then they get into a car accident. It all comes back to the whole idea that actions in the story should somehow reflect the characters, the people that are in them. The outcome of those actions should have something to do with them.

DAVID LONG
interviewed by Linda B. Swanson-Davies

Endings of stories are magical. It's real hard to find that little click that transforms everything in the ending. John Updike is a master at it. That last little snap, I call it cranking it over one more crank. A lot of times it happens just in words, something's embodied in a word. There's a story, also in *The Flood of '64*, about a Wobbly organizer who is hanged: "The Last Photograph of Lyle Pettibone." A young boy takes a photograph, the first important photograph he's ever taken. So he's developing the film in the basement of his father's hotel, and he sees the pictures of a wedding party he'd taken earlier, the official guests, "Everyone dignified before the camera … and there at the end of the roll, Lyle Pettibone, uninvited, hanging from a trestle just west of town." It's the idea of being *uninvited*—that one word unlocked all the energy of the whole story for me.

Another example from an earlier story, called "Morning Practice." One time my mother, who's a cellist, was about to put her cello in the car when somebody called her back to pick up some music, and then she just backed over the cello. In my story, a young woman has come home to be with her father after the mother has died and they realize the cello is missing. Then they realize that it had been taken to be repaired, and so they have to find it. It becomes a mission for this girl to find her mother's cello. They finally find it, and she has this revelation: It hasn't been fixed yet. It's just a pile of wood. It means nothing after all of that. But she then walks down these long stairs, back to the street, with her father, "unaccompanied."

Again, that word—*unaccompanied*—unlocked the whole energy of the story. It was a pun in the sense that it was a musical term, but it meant that they were together, the two of them.

And that was the end.

Yes. In those cases, some aspect of the story was unlocked by using a critical word right at the end. Often there's something more dramatic than that, but there should be something right at the end that turns it.

BRAD WATSON

interviewed by Robert Birnbaum

I was surprised but pleased by the way *The Heaven of Mercury* ends. Something echoes and reverberates at the end.

When I was writing it I realized I had this chapter with Birdie's spirit wandering around and hovering before this boy on a beach-house deck—I had that around for two or three years and didn't know how it was going to work into the book. When I was writing these last drafts, I began to realize there was some echo in the sense there is this boy on the deck, there is Finas's grief over the loss of his own boy, the sense of Finas being a boy when he first loved Birdie, and the vision of the butterflies which had resonance for me in connection with Birdie wandering around as a spirit. It was one of those things that began to feel more and more right, the more I got there. I wasn't at all certain that this ending would work, even though I had it as an ending, those lines, actually for a couple of years. The book made its way after a little back wash, made its way back, feeling done and right. If I kept at it and waited long enough this book would kind of form itself, almost like a planet forming out of the particles. I just had to be patient and let gravity do its work.

LET ME REMEMBER THIS

Mark Salzman, interviewed by Linda B. Swanson-Davies

I was so moved near the end of *Lying Awake*, when she looked around the room and tried to etch the scene in memory, praying that whatever her own future might be, God would reward her sisters for their generosity of spirit. I'm very conscious of trying to etch things in my memory. And I wonder if there are things like that for you?

Oh, yeah. There are moments where I can hear myself saying, Let me remember this. Let me make this a deeper picture so it doesn't fade, because you know that it's so precious. It's so ephemeral and it's going to disappear. If only I could have this preserved so I could taste it again later. It's such deep yearning. Yeah, it was a great joy to be able to use that image, finally, because that's a feeling that comes up a lot.

Amy Bloom: I think a good ending hangs in the air like a musical note. It's just done. I don't think my endings are bound to ambiguity. I do think there's an avoidance of tying things up with a bow. But it's not the same thing.

as interviewed by Sarah Anne Johnson

CHAPTER

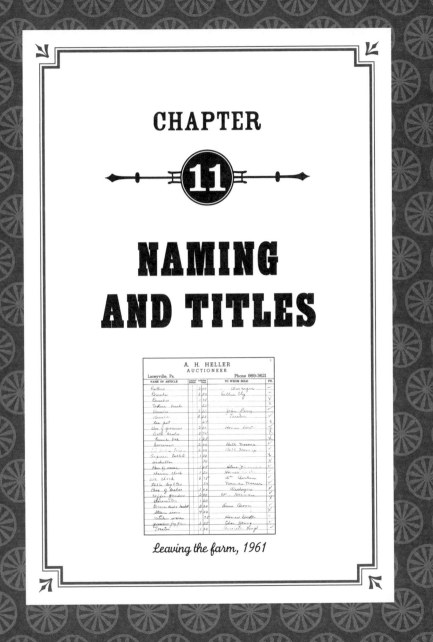

11

NAMING
AND TITLES

Leaving the farm, 1961

LORRIE MOORE
interviewed by Jim Schumock

Where does the title of your novel *Who Will Run the Frog Hospital?* come from?

It comes from the title of a painting by Nancy Mladenoff. I saw the painting after I had begun the novel, and I was still at the beginning, at a fairly vulnerable place, where many things could fall into it. There's always that place in a manuscript, when you're working on it, where things can just fall in and become part of the batter, so to speak. And then there's a place later on where the manuscript has closed up and you're just working within the narrative. I came upon this painting in a gallery in Madison, at one of these vulnerable, open moments in my manuscript, and to me the painting was just so perfect and so funny and so great that I bought it and turned it into a fictional painting in the book—one of the characters paints—and I actually used the title of the painting for the title of the novel. Of course, I got permission from Nancy to do all that. She was really great: not only a great sport but also very interested to see this happen to her painting. It was all very curious and intriguing for her.

The title and the painting refer to a couple of different things metaphorically. It's a picture of two girls who are whispering, and there are frogs in the foreground in front of them, frogs who are injured. One is in a splint. One has a bandage around its head. And it looks, when you first see this image, as if the girls had been kissing the frogs, roughly, and had injured them, and the frogs had still somehow failed to turn into princes. So in that way, it seemed like a feminist witticism to me. I was very interested in that image, and that idea is in the book. The idea that these frogs are injured by boys and that the girls are there to rescue them is also part of the painting *and* the book. It is also something the two girls in the novel do as children: They go to the swamp and try to save the frogs who have been shot with BBs by boys in the neighborhood. And of course there's a reference to a medical institution in Paris as well, and some argumentation about who will actually supervise and manage the place. So the book's title refers to several different things.

NAMING AND CLAIMING

Jamaica Kincaid
interviewed by Linda B. Swanson-Davies

Now I've become very interested in names, and I came to it through the garden, through the naming of things. The invention of plant nomenclature came about through a man named Carolus Linnaeus inventing that system. He first applied it to plants from the New World. The names they were called by the people who knew them were not honored, and that was how that system came into being. They would not have agreed to that system being used on the plants with names that they, the Europeans, knew among themselves, but they agreed to it starting with these captured things, renaming them. It's no accident, no coincidence, that, for instance, names are such a controversy with Africans in this part of the world. They can't decide whether they're Black, Negroes, African-Americans, whatever, and they're often rechanging their names, because naming is a part of possessing. You make a claim and you name it. It's deep. So in that sense I started, unknowingly, this inquiry on myself because I'm very interested in naming.

....

CHOOSING A CHARACTER'S NAME
Annie Proulx, interviewed by Michael Upchurch

What about the characters' names? I read that you find them in the phone book. Do you find them all in the phone book? Diddy Shovel? Biscuit Paragon? Aren't some of them inventions?

Yes. No. Phone books are part of the writer's arsenal. I keep notebooks of names and, when I'm working on a book, I want the names to fit the place. If there's one thing I hate, it's a name that's instantly forgettable, and that's because I'm a reader. I spend a lot of time reading and I don't like to lose track of the characters, and if the characters have good names, I remember them.

I will get the names from phone books, bulletin boards, from tourist information, from bibliographies, lists of fishing guides, park attendants. Anybody! Newspaper advertisements. Stories. Not the whole names, mind you, just first or last. If you're ever looking for names, by the way, Chinese historians have the most amazing names of anybody anywhere.

So, what I'll do is take literally hundreds of first names and hundreds of last names, and make lists of them on opposing pages. And then when it comes time and I've got my character from my other notebook—my character's physical description—I go to my name notebook and poke around until I find a first and a last that fit together okay for that character. And there we are.

....

PAM DURBAN

interviewed by Cheryl Reid

The title of your novel-in-progress is Big Buckra. Could you explain the title?

Buckra was a black term sometimes used to describe white people. I kept coming across it in the slave narratives gathered by the WPA Federal Writers Project. I've read all of the South Carolina narratives and most of the Georgia narratives.

These were oral histories passed down and recorded by the WPA workers?

In the thirties, the Federal Works Project sent out writers to interview people who had been born into slavery. That's the historical record we have of the voices of people who were born into and lived in slavery. It's a tremendous archive of interviews. And most of them still exist in typescript, and that's how you read them in the books. In several of the South Carolina narratives, people would say, "Our white folks was all big buckra." Big important white people. But there is always an irony, of course, in how they were using it.

ELIZABETH COX

interviewed by Sarah Anne Johnson

What importance do you place on the names of characters? What do you consider when choosing names? [In *Saved*] Warner James, or Warn, the preacher who seduces Evie, is particularly interesting, as are Josie Wire and Beckett.

Those names came quickly, without thinking. I laughed when the man said his name was Samuel Beckett. I like when names come in from the side like that, as if I were overhearing them, just learning them myself. I mean, I don't plan anything ironic or subtle, I just want the name that fits the character.

....

Alice Mattison: In real life you can know somebody quite well and not know his or her name, or not use it. Many people live with somebody and hardly ever speak the person's name aloud. But in fiction, names stand for bodies. As you move through a room, it's your body that other people look at. But as you move down a page, it's your name that keeps turning up. So names have much more importance in fiction than they do in real life, and if a name gives off the wrong feel then it's really going to matter.

as interviewed by Barbara Brooks

Amy Hempel: "Tumble Home" is an epistolary novella comprised of a single letter. The narrator is writing to the painter, and the painter is never named. It doesn't really matter, in a way. I shied away from naming him because I have a horror of the "made-up" thing. The writer Sam Michel has a devastating phrase—when his own work isn't going well, he says, "It's just another made-up thing." I didn't want a made-up thing in the middle of this long narrative. I rarely name anything.

as interviewed by Debra Levy and Carol Turner

MINING OBITUARIES
Paul Theroux, interviewed by Michael Upchurch

You have some awfully unusual names in your books—Parker Jagoda in *Chicago Loop*, Orlo Fedewa and Mister Phyllis in *Millroy*, and many others. Do you keep a names notebook?

Every so often I do, or a name occurs to me. I have been known to make long lists of names. In all the notebooks, the working notebooks for novels, I have pages of names. I read obituaries just for the names. I was very glad and felt vindicated when I saw that Henry James did that—and I'm no Henry James, we know that. But Henry James's notebooks push on for a couple of pages, then you see long lists of very funny names, always terrific names, and he got them from the *Times* obituaries.

Nothing's worse than having a character and thinking: "I had a name—I just can't think of it."

CHOOSING A TITLE
by Scott Allie

If a title doesn't come to me as soon as I have the idea for the piece, I try not to worry about it, and try to find the title in the prose somewhere, pull a phrase out that stands alone. I had a book I was editing that needed a title, and in one of the stories there was something about dusk, and the phrase "the remaining sunlight," which I thought would make a good title. So I'm always holding out for one of those to show up.

But in a story I was working on last year, there was no title presenting itself. And there was something about the characters that I had no place to spell out in the prose. It is a father-and-son story, a pretty ugly one about personal disappointment, and both characters happen to be magicians. It's suggested in the text, but there's nowhere that it's spelled out. I thought of a song by Lou Reed, called "Halloween Parade (AIDS)." He said that when he played the song for friends, initially just "Halloween Parade," no one understood that it had to do with AIDS. What that song is really about is the wonderful people in the Village's Halloween Parade, and how many of them are gone now. But he never says in the song why they're gone—the song's in praise of them, not agonizing over what got them. So he put the disease in the title, to pull it together. When I read that he'd done that, I thought it was really strange, but then fifteen years later I'm doing it myself: "The Magicians." The title became a way to say something that had no place in the prose. It might seem a little precious, but it solved a problem.

WHAT'S IN A NAME?

Roy Parvin, interviewed by Linda B. Swanson-Davies

I thought it was odd that the word *May* comes up so often in this book [*In the Snow Forest*].

Is that true?

Yes. Both in terms of the name and just the month.

Oh, that's funny, because "May" was the first story, my first good story. I don't like it very much now....Richard Ford wrote a wonderful essay where he talks about how books are provisional. You write them over time. I'm not as eloquent perhaps as Richard Ford, but I would say that I try to think of them as snapshots, and hopefully they're snapshots of yourself. Even if the writing was not about yourself, it's about you at a certain point in your life, and what interests you at that point. And yet you have to hope that you're not wearing a Nehru jacket. Or platforms, or something particularly foolish.

I think it might have been an unconscious thing. "May" was a story that I had written—I was writing full-time at that point, and I hadn't sent anything out—and my wife, Janet, said to go to this writers' conference. They have these things called writers' conferences. And I said, Well, you know, what are they? She described them to me, and I said, That sounds good, and she said, There's one in Napa, California. I think this woman, Pam Houston, will fall in love with your work. So I said okay, and Janet knew that I wouldn't do anything until she sent away for the application. I filled it out, and I sent "May." Pam was extremely effusive about the work. It was a wonderful thing. She took me under her wing and I think, subconsciously, there must be some of that coming out in there, that the word *may* was on my lips. Also, May is typically the first month that we can get into the cabin up in Trinities. There's still snow in May. We hiked, just recently, in June and came across snow.

So it's an opening point.

It's certainly an opening point. It's when winter is holding on by its barest, but it is still there, and spring is just exploding. It's among my—I always say "this" is my favorite time of year up here in the mountains—but there's something very, very special about May. And it's usually the earliest we can get into our cabin without snowshoeing.

So May represents access.

Exactly. It's permission and it's access in other ways.

RESPECTFUL APPROPRIATION
Amy Bloom, interviewed by Sarah Anne Johnson

How do you come up with the titles for your stories?

I read a lot of poetry, so periodically I steal from poets. I do give them credit. There are a lot of Dylan Thomas titles in that first collection. For instance, "Light Breaks Where No Sun Shines" is from a Dylan Thomas poem. In the latest collection, the title "Stars at Elbow and Foot" is from the Dylan Thomas poem "And

Death Shall Have No Dominion." Sometimes they come from my imagination, or sometimes from things I've heard people say, like "A Blind Man Can See How Much I Love You." Usually I don't have to struggle a lot, though sometimes I do.

How did you decide to use hymns for the chapter titles in *Love Invents Us*?

I listen to a lot of gospel music, so that was just a labor of love.

BRAD WATSON
interviewed by Robert Birnbaum

When did you decide on the title for *The Heaven of Mercury*?

Just last year, when I thought the book had something in common with *The Divine Comedy*. Because of Finas being guided by Birdie's presence in his own mind through some of the things that had happened in the past. So I thought there was something of a parallel there. I was looking through a new translation of *Inferno*, and then I picked up my old translation of *The Divine Comedy*, and when I looked through *Paradiso*, I saw *The Heaven of Mercury*. The town was already Mercury, by that point. I turned to that chapter and it turned out to be about betrayal, and I thought that fit. Also, a heaven on earth, not necessarily paradise, but one in which there was communion with the dead, seemed to fit. I don't pretend to be a Dante scholar.

CHARLES BAXTER
interviewed by Stewart David Ikeda

Why did you change the novel's title from *Leavings* to *Shadow Play*?

I was asked to. Virtually everyone to whom I showed an early draft said that *Leavings* was an inadequate title, or it was distasteful, or it would incur the irony and sarcasm of reviewers. One of the meanings of *leavings* is "leftovers." One of the other connotations is of waste, offal or *ordure*, as the French would say, shit. It's just asking for trouble. I changed it, but it seemed that by changing it I lost something: a thematically announced focus for readers. Because that book really is about leavings—about leaving other people, about the things they leave behind. And, to some degree, it is about *ordure*; it's about waste. I could see the logic of what they were saying, but a number of writers have told me it was a shame the novel shed that title.

. . . .

NAME AS CLUE TO CHARACTER
Melissa Pritchard, interviewed by Leslie A. Wootten

Eleanor's variety of names reflects the many transformations and incarnations she goes through in her various decades of life. As a girl, nicknames are often dropped on her, and she rolls right along with them. Jaz, for example, is what her father calls her, and she never knows why. Moo, Mooser, Nors, and Noser are nicknames friends give her. The various married names—Eleanor Luther, Nora Bettinger—are representative of how women—particularly of my generation—were trained to trade in their own last names for their husbands'. If you divorced and remarried, you simply traded names again, kind of like trading baseball cards. Pearl Marvel is a nom de plume from Eleanor's brief stint as a romance writer. The name Nora materializes as she gains maturity and a greater sense of self.

THE SIGNIFICANCE OF TITLES

Charles Baxter, interviewed by Linda B. Swanson-Davies

Titles. Do they come to you, or do you think them up? What purpose do you think they serve?

Sometimes a story can do perfectly well without any specific title. You don't remember the title for very long and it doesn't matter. But with some stories, the title is extremely important.... With my book, *Believers*, the title is quite important because all of the stories in that book are about moments in which a character either chooses to believe or not to believe in something that he or she has been told or that seems to have happened. I've had titles changed on me. My first novel had a different title, but my agent and editor said you can't use this title. And my second novel had a different title than the one it eventually had. My newest one, *The Feast of Love*, is a title that I've always had for that book. Just always had it right from the start. I knew where I was going with it. I didn't know how I was going to get there, but I always knew that the book thematically was going to be about love.

Daniel Mason: That's one of the problems with the Burmese words. I know that most readers wouldn't be able to pronounce them. It's a problem with a name like Khin Myo, the character in the book. Her name is very difficult to pronounce. Almost everyone who I talk to about the book will say, The woman, what's her name, how do you say her name? or, How do you say that town? I thought of using a Burmese name that would be easier to pronounce. The boy has an easy name to pronounce—Nok Lek; anyone can say that. And yet Khin Myo is such a typical and beautiful-sounding name there that I couldn't stay away from it.

as interviewed by Linda B. Swanson-Davies

ON SECOND THOUGHT

Daniel Mason, interviewed by Linda B. Swanson-Davies

The name of the book—because we've just gone through naming with *Mother Knows*, I know how hard names can be to come by. How was it for you, with this? *The Piano Tuner* is a lovely name.

I like the name a lot now. It was *Salween River Fugue* when I sent it to the publisher, which I liked because I thought it captured both the musical and the Burmese sides of the book. But every time I mentioned this name to anyone, they all said, What? Because who would know the Salween River? And the word *fugue* is not a word people use on a day-to-day basis either. So I had this feeling that they were going to want the name to be changed, and they asked if I had any ideas for another name for the book. *The Piano Tuner* had always been one possibility. I knew that there were some other books called *The Piano Tuner*, and so I didn't think I was allowed to use the name. Then I learned that names aren't copyrighted.

I can see why you'd want to use the original name, but I can also see why it would have been difficult.

I think *The Piano Tuner* is wonderful. I had thought of it, and my agent had recommended it, picked it as a name that he had liked. So I started thinking about it again—maybe this is a good name. I liked it because the book really is about him, the piano tuner.

USING THE NAMES WE HAVE
Ernest Gaines, interviewed by Michael Upchurch

I changed the names of all these places, but I use my family names. For example, the parish, Pointe Coupee, where I come from, I call it St. Raphael Parish because my stepfather, who raised me, his name was Raphael. The town I call Bayonne, it's based on the town of New Roads, Louisiana. But Bayonne was the maternal name of my grandfather's people: his mother's people. And the river there is called the False River, but I have a brother named Charles, so I name it the Charles River. So not only do I use the names and the characters indigenous to the area I come from, but I also use my folks' names. *In My Father's House*, I used St. Adrienne, the town where Philip Martin is a minister. My mother's name is Adrienne.

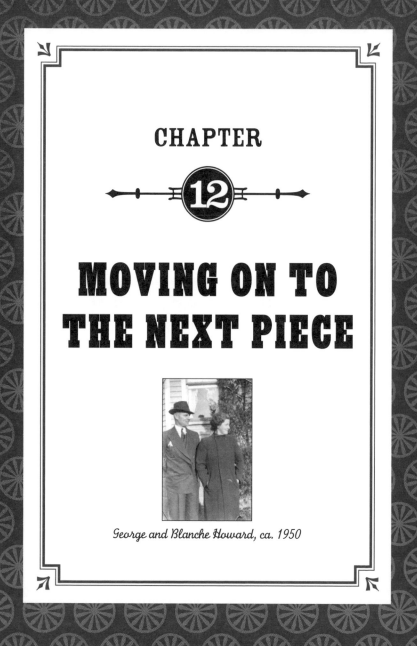

CHAPTER

12

MOVING ON TO THE NEXT PIECE

George and Blanche Howard, ca. 1950

Kathleen Tyau: After I sent the manuscript to my editor I felt some … postpartum loss, but recovered once I started writing the next story. Always there is the next, whether you have a publisher or not.

as interviewed by Linda B. Swanson-Davies

DON'T LOOK BACK

Stephen Dixon, interviewed by Linda B. Swanson-Davies

You seem extremely modest in your opinion of your own work.

Why not be modest? Try being cocky in what you're doing and you lose it. You think you've done it so don't need to do it, perhaps. I haven't got time for being anything but modest. Meaning: Finish one thing, on to the next thing. I like what I'm doing at the time I'm doing it, but that's as far as my feeling toward my work goes. Once it's done, it's done. I don't look back and think I did something good there; nah, I go on and on and on, for I'm much too obsessed a writer to look back and take gratification in what I've done. I want to forget what I've done and write as if I've never done anything. It keeps things surprising; it makes the writing exciting.

I don't know if I'm widely read. I don't get much feedback and I'm glad I don't. I write, I send out, I accept the rejections as gratifyingly as I accept the acceptances; in time, everything seems to get placed. What is there to be cocky about? The number of stories written and published, the number of books published. They are nothing to me. What is important to me is what I'm doing now, and if I've finished something new, and what I've done is old. The second I finish it, it's old, it's done, it's gone, and it's on to the next.

ANNIE PROULX

interviewed by Michael Upchurch

I'm piling up stuff I know that I'll need on the book that I do after the one I'm working on now. I've been compiling the materials for a couple of years now: books and papers and photographs and odds and ends.

This is for the book that will follow Accordion Crimes?

Yes. So, in a sense, I'm working on that now in a low-key kind of way. But usually the ideas for the stories come in a great, mad rush when I'm finishing something, finishing a piece of writing, on the final pages of the last draft, after you're working on it and working on it, and you're sick unto death of it, and it's just the last little bit. At that time, you're so damned fed up with the thing, you'll do anything. Your mind is racing around madly, thinking anything would be better to write than this. Anything at all! A grocery list would be better to write. And then, of course, all kinds of marvelous ideas for books unwritten come into mind.

Do they come and go?

No, they come to be selected—or rejected. That's how *The Shipping News* came, and definitely how *Accordion Crimes* came: just in a quick click.

Antonya Nelson: Even when a story's done, the same material revisits me. It's not as if the material goes away or is tamed just because a story's written or published. It crops up, comes back in other forms. If I go back through my books, I can find an image, a motif, an idea, a character coming back in a new incarnation, because I'm still compelled by it. Nothing fully disappears, which makes the revision process ongoing, even into new material. I'm always rethinking what I thought I had figured out.

as interviewed by Susan McInnis

THE TRIUMPH, THE LETDOWN
Brad Watson, interviewed by Robert Birnbaum

You are moving down to Florida to teach and then you are scheduled for a publicity tour. How long, two or three months?

I hope two months intensively and then maybe some scattered readings. It's a distraction when you are trying to start another book and you have to continue to think about the one you just finished. I had a hard time with that with the first book.

Is there a sense of being finished when the final draft is done?

Yeah, I want to move on. I want to get to the next thing. I don't want to get caught up in talking about this book to the degree that I can't continue to work. I think, all too easily, that lands you in a kind of a stasis. You are talking about something that is over and when all the talk about that is done and there is quiet again, you realize you are nowhere. You are not in the middle of anything, anything new. It's a letdown. I've tried to get started on this book so I have momentum and I don't have to overcome the inertia that inevitably follows this kind of activity.

....

BACK TO THE BOOKS

Lynne Sharon Schwartz, interviewed by Nancy Middleton

⇒◆◆⇐

I thoroughly enjoyed Ruined by Reading, *as a compulsive reader myself. Did you have the idea for this book in you for a long time?*

Well, it came about in a funny way. Actually, I wrote it out of a kind of desperation. Right around when *Leaving Brooklyn* was published—1989—I didn't know what to write next. I thought I'd written myself out, that I didn't have a subject. So I pondered, Well, what do I know? And the only thing I came up with was reading. And I decided, Well, I'll write something about reading, just out of the blue, and see what happens.

And it became this long, meandering piece that just went here and there—and I let it, because I didn't have anything else to do. It became an essay, which was published in *Salmagundi*, a literary magazine that comes out of Skidmore College. And that was that. Then, years later—last year or a year or so ago—an editor at Beacon Press wrote and asked whether I would consider expanding the essay into a book. My initial reaction was, "No, I've said all I can say about it." But I thought it over and—to make a long story short—I did it.

BACK TO THE WELL

Kent Haruf, interviewed by Jim Nashold

When you finish a book, do you get postpartum depression?

I guess it's something like that. There's a kind of letdown. Somehow it has to do with the fact that you've been intensely involved with something for a number of years. Now that's over. So you're out of sorts, and you're not sure what do to with yourself.

Do you immediately start preparing for the next book or give yourself a break?

No, I feel I have to fill up again. There's a song a friend wrote called "Getting Back to the Well." I have to fill up again. I have to feel some emotional compulsion to write the next book, so I wait for that. I begin to make some notes about the next book, but I don't actively start writing for a while.

....

ROBERT OLEN BUTLER

interviewed by Linda B. Swanson-Davies

The Deep Green Sea is maybe the last Vietnam book I ever write in the sense that once you finally recognize all that on a deeply personal level as a Greek tragedy, then, you know, that's pretty much the final word.

NOMI EVE

interviewed by Linda B. Swanson-Davies

Now what's going to happen when you're done with this story?

I'm not a person who thinks, Oh, I have to write ten books, fifteen books. I might. I have to write this one. In the back of my mind, I have a thought that I need to write a book about literature. I'd love to write about other books. Maybe that will be my next calling.

Last month was the first time I was ever able to imagine a fiction beyond this one. It's been so all-consuming to me that I couldn't imagine.

....

BACK OUT INTO THE WORLD

Amy Hempel, interviewed by Debra Levy and Carol Turner

Do you see yourself moving in this new direction, meaning longer works, or was it a temporary deviation, or do you have no idea?

I don't have any idea, because I feel like I've put everything I know, everything I've been thinking of, into the book. I feel emptied out—in a good way. I don't have a thought in my head about what's next, fiction-wise. So, as before, I'll do some magazine work, get out into the world, see some different things. Hopefully spark something.

Stephen Dixon: The feeling that drives me to my typewriter—and it is a typewriter, a manual, and it's always been a manual—once I'm working on a story, it's easy to answer what the feeling's like. It's to complete the story. But once a story's completed, the feeling's different. It's to start a new one, or to continue a novel. I am a driven writer; I don't feel good when I don't have something to write. So I write every day and after I finish a story or novel, I start another story or novel the next day. The feeling that drives me is a sweaty, anxiety-ridden feeling; it insists I start something, try something, try many things, till I have something to write the next day. Writing is a wonderful torment; it's banging your fists against the wall until … you have something you've written.

as interviewed by Linda B. Swanson-Davies

PATRICIA HENLEY

interviewed by Andrew Scott

What most surprised you about *Hummingbird House*'s success?

The surprise came when the book was accepted. After that, I wasn't surprised. I think that's partly because I was at work on the next novel, *In the River Sweet*. And I have always tried to be at work on something new when a book comes out, so that I don't worry too much about how the published book is received.

David Long: It's very satisfying to have written a book, but, unfortunately, by the time it's published and you're out hawking it, you're on to the next book and you're deeply troubled by the complexities of that work. So the moments of satisfaction are kind of glancing blows.

as interviewed by Linda B. Swanson-Davies

IT'S NOT WHAT YOU THINK

Amy Hempel
interviewed by Janice Levy and Carol Turner

You finished *Tumble Home* at Yaddo in the fall of 1995. At the time, you said you thought you'd feel elated and relieved. But in fact you were having nightmares and losing things.

Well, you know things aren't what you think they're going to be. I did expect to feel great and relieved, and I felt a great deal of anxiety. Clearly, it's twofold. It's, Well, what now? And it's, What of this? What of this thing? Here's a reckoning, now you have to judge this thing or appraise the thing you've just spent all this time on. And what if it doesn't hold? And it took all that time and effort. So it was an anxious time.

You once mentioned that you usually take a year off after the publication of a book.

Not intentionally, it's just worked out that way. It took about a year with the two previous books. I just didn't think of writing any fiction, nothing occurred to me, I had no ideas. I didn't mind that; I did other things, other kinds of writing.

KEEP GOING

Ernest Gaines, interviewed by Michael Upchurch

Along with the Bayonne setting, some of the books share minor characters (Sheriff Sam Guidry is one) and recurring names—Pichot, Hebert. And all the books seem to share certain types of characters: strong-willed aunts and desperate young men on a crusade. Do you see these as separate books or one big book?

It's, I think, one big book. Well, they're like chapters, I suppose, in what you'd like to do. And that's one of the reasons why you keep writing. If you can put everything in one book, there's no point in writing another book. Because you fail! You fail in every book. And so you keep going, keep going, keep going. I see each one as a finished piece of work, yes, but what I would like to say in writing I have not said well enough. So I go to another book to try to get it better the next time—and you won't say it the next time, either. As Faulkner once said, "And once you've done it, you might as well cut your throat, because there's nothing else to do." And you never will do it. You never will do it.

....

Jayne Anne Phillips: I don't think that any of the novels know that you've written any of the other novels. It's always like work without the net. It doesn't get easier. I think it's actually easier in the beginning because you don't know what you're wading into.

as interviewed by Sarah Anne Johnson

CHAPTER

13

RESEARCH

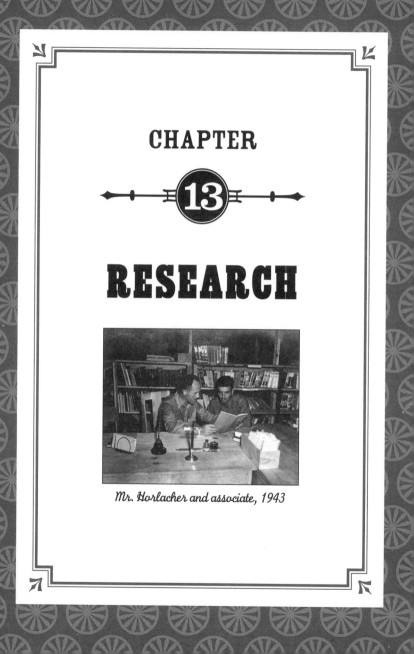

Mr. Horlacher and associate, 1943

Siri Hustvedt: The book I'm writing now [*What I Loved*] is narrated in first person by a sixty-eight-year-old man who was born in Berlin. I've been reading about the Jewish community in Berlin in the twenties and thirties. Most of this will never appear in the novel. It's just background for the story to take place in New York many years later. But I want to know; I want to have it right even if it's never mentioned. I think sometimes hiding behind the curtains of a book is that knowledge. I know I'm not going to get it wrong. I even found an apartment in Berlin; I went there and have it in my mind.

as interviewed by Jennifer Levasseur and Kevin Rabalais

ANDREA BARRETT
interviewed by Sarah Anne Johnson

How were you able to create the setting of the Arctic region with such clarity and specificity? How were you able to conjure this place in your mind and in your senses?

Most of it was from reading. In those Arctic expeditions, everyone was keeping diaries: the ship's doctor, the ship's naturalist, sometimes several of the officers, almost always the captain, sometimes the crew. So there's a lot of material available from a lot of expeditions, and a lot of specificity in those materials, and also in the letters—descriptions of the weather, of the cold. Those were a huge help. I was actually able to go to the Arctic and see it for myself when I got a Guggenheim fellowship between the second-to-last and last drafts. I went up to the north coast of Baffin Island for a couple of weeks and looked at the sky and the plants. It did help. The book was the better for that.

....

COINCIDENCE AND GOODWILL

Mark Salzman, interviewed by Linda B. Swanson-Davies

Before you really got into the writing of *Lying Awake*, you did a year of research, reading up on the cloistered life, and then you decided that you had to meet some of these people. What did it feel like when you first decided that you needed to do that? Were you excited or thinking, Shoot, what was I thinking? Why would they talk to me? And then, after that, what was it like to meet them?

Well, absolutely, the idea seemed daunting. For one thing, I figured here are these people who don't—obviously don't—want to be disturbed. How am I going to get an introduction without being intrusive? And then I would have to be right upfront about the fact that I'm not Catholic. And here I'm writing about a woman who has a neurologic disorder and perhaps mistakes what she experiences...

It might seem disrespectful.

Yeah, it just seemed to me that they would have every reason in the world to just pass on the opportunity to take their time to help me out. It was daunting. So I went about it the long way. I sent out my feelers as far as I could and finally got an introduction to an abbot, a male contemplate who is the head of a monastery in

Santa Fe. He has an email address, so we started emailing back and forth, and, because of this person who introduced me to him, he was willing to hear me out. Well, he was very welcoming. He said, Listen, why don't you come out, visit our monastery for a while. First of all, we have a guest house; you're welcome to that. That'll give you a sense of the day-to-day life. It applies, male or female doesn't matter. Then let me do my best to try and help get one of the nuns to come and talk to you. So I flew out there, rented a car, stayed at a little motel, drove out there, and there at the end of a seventeen-mile dirt road—well, it had rained the day before and I started on this dirt road, and before a mile passed the car sank in the mud. It was real panic because I was in the middle of nowhere.

Waiting for the dirt to dry.

Yeah, so I dug the car out and knew I wasn't going to try to drive another sixteen miles through that. So I backed out and decided to wait till the next day. Next day, same thing. Three days in a row, got washed out. And they don't have a phone, so I couldn't tell them, and here they were expecting me. I felt really bad. And angry—what a waste. So on the last day I decided to go out walking, and I just wandered around from near where I was staying. All of a sudden I looked up and there's a sign that says Mt. Carmel Rd. And I thought, Well, what a coincidence. Under it was another sign that said Carmel Light Monastery. Now, I knew that there was a Carmel Light Monastery in Santa Fe. I'd heard about it, but I didn't know it was there. I had no intention of just walking up and knocking on their door. But that is exactly what I did, because at that point I was so frustrated, and it seemed so wild that that would happen that I figured, Well, I'll tell them. So I went up and buzzed this little buzzer near this round metal thing that you can't see through, and a few seconds later a little voice said, "Praise be Jesus Christ, may I help you?"

Wow.

I told my story to this voice. Then she said, Wait a moment, I'll speak to our prioress. Then another voice came, and after she heard me out she said, Step through the door to your right. So I did, and there was a little parlor and a curtain. A few minutes later, the curtain opened—the little finger pulled it across. She looked at me. She said, I thought a novelist would be older. So that was her first impression of me. That I was too young. But anyway, she was fabulous. From the first minute I looked at her and talked with her, I felt comfortable with this woman. From the start she seemed to think that there was a reason that I had come up that road, and she was convinced that she should do everything that she could to help. She could not have been more helpful, more enthusiastic. She let me borrow so many reading materials and answered all my questions. It was so fruitful that I ended up going back several times more and spending time with her. And then going early in the morning and sitting in the chapel on the other side of the screen from them, listening to them do the chanting. That's what got things going in the right way. Not only getting an authentic feel for what's going on, but also having that personal connection with a woman who impressed me so deeply, that really raised the bar on how respectfully to treat this whole world. Once I met her, I wanted these characters to be sympathetic. I wanted them to be warm. I wanted them to be interesting.

You wanted them to be real.

Yeah. Because she was so deeply kind and generous and she was extremely revealing and trusting. It was just great. It was a deep satisfaction to be able to send her the book, and to get a letter, right away, back. She really enjoyed it, and that's satisfying. She seemed to have unshakeable confidence that the book was not going to be exploitative. And I thought so, too, but how could I tell her that? You can't just say, Well, it won't be.

NO SUBSTITUTE FOR EXPERIENCE
Allen Morris Jones, interviewed by David Abrams

Did you have to do a lot of research for *Last Year's River*?

I read a bunch of books, mainly in three different areas: New York in the 1920s, France during World War I, and Wyoming in the '20s. New York and France were both very, very easy to research—certain areas of the library, you'd turn around twice and knock over a half a dozen books on the subject. But Wyoming in the '20s was much harder. I ended up going through a lot of old newspapers and spent a lot of time at the local libraries going through microfilm.

And then I spent time walking around in the hills, taking photos. I bought bird and plant identification books. I'd hike around next to the river and see what kind of flora was growing there. So research is really all a kind of melange of resources—some of it's experiential and some of it's traditional library stuff.

Did you feel like you needed to put yourself in Henry's environment—walking around where he would have walked—to get a better feel for it?

There's no question about that. I can't imagine writing about a place without having seen it or physically experienced it.

HA JIN

interviewed by Sarah Anne Johnson

How much research do you typically have to do?

It depends. For instance, my next book [*War Trash*] is set in Korea. The whole book is told by a prisoner in the American prison camps, so I had to do a lot of research about everything from clothing to food in order to create the material sensations. Once I wrote a draft of this story, I realized there were things that I had to understand better, so I read a lot of books and looked at pictures to find the right details. It's a very laborious process, but it helps me understand the characters and find the small details of the world they inhabit. Whenever I come across a good detail, I feel pleased.

. . . .

COVERING THE UNDOCUMENTED
Valerie Martin, interviewed by Janet Benton

What was your experience in writing the St. Francis biography?

Oh, that was torture. The torture never stops. It's like his life.

I've heard you describe how he stayed up all night praying.

Yeah, he stayed up all his life praying. Oh, you mean when he was with his friend, and his friend woke up, and St. Francis was beside the other bed, kneeling on the floor weeping and saying,

"My God, my all." He did it all night long, and in the morning his friend said, "Francesco, I've made up my mind. I am going to do what you're doing, I'm going to give everything away, and you can tell me what to do from now on." That was his first brother. Yeah, that was a real research and sort of chutzpah project—it's a biography, but it's not written like a biography, it's presented in scenes. It does have some footnotes, lots of notes, about things that can be documented. Some things really can't be documented. He's a character who is too fascinating not to want to look into a lot, so I did, and I wrote this book.

What sorts of research did you do in Italy?

Every time I could find a place he went, I went, and I usually drove a car up the mountains he walked up barefoot, and I was still exhausted. I walked from the parking lot to the grotto or rock or the crummy little cave that he slept in. So one thing we know about him is that he had enormous calf muscles. [Laughs.] He walked all the way to Egypt, so he was an amazing walker.

The book is called *Salvation: Scenes from the Life of St. Francis.* Are the scenes based on the paintings you saw?

Some are, and some of them come from old accounts, some of which may or may not have happened. For a few I was able to put him in a certain place and another person at a certain place at a certain time; whether they ever saw each other is up for grabs. This is not original to me. Peter Ackroyd does it, lots of people do it. And I've tried not to make wild guesses, and, really, I only do that once, I think. I tried as much as I could to document the scenes. Of course, it was the thirteenth century, so there's a whole lot of stuff that's basically guesswork. But the story is told in succinct scenes, as if you were looking at paintings—that's the idea—which is how his life has often been told. Of course St. Francis turned out to be really pretty complex, much more complex than I'd originally thought.

....

CHANG-RAE LEE
interviewed by Sarah Anne Johnson

Each of your novels seems to have required research of some kind. For example, *Native Speaker* must have required research about spying and speech therapy and inner-city politics; *A Gesture Life* required research about the Japanese comfort women, as well as research about the details of life as a soldier and medic; and *Aloft* required research about flying, non-Hodgkin's lymphoma, and pregnancy, among other things. At what point do you conduct your research, and how do you go about finding what you're looking for?

A Gesture Life took the most research and in that case the research happened first. In the other books, I backed into it. With Jerry Battle I researched the plane. Both *Aloft* and the *Native Speaker* feature landscapes I knew quite well. With Henry Park, once I discovered who he was, I had to go back and learn more about industrial spies, or speech therapy. Research is important, but it's not terribly important. Except for in *A Gesture Life*, which partly focuses on a historical period. I wanted to make sure that I had that period right so that it would be as accurate and authentic as possible.

THOMAS E. KENNEDY

interviewed by Linda B. Swanson-Davies

⟨⟩⟨⟩⟨⟩

Prior to doing The Book of Angels, *you did some research on black magic. How did you decide to do that? What did you gain from that?*

Well, I guess what I gained was an insight into another aspect of the imagination. I have always tended to think of the imagination in purely positive terms, but in fact the imagination is a land of many spirits. I think the way in which the imagination is used by magicians, insofar as I understand it—I don't pretend to be a real expert—is not really a positive way. Magicians, particularly black magicians, will try to use the powers of the imagination to conceal, to deceive, to trick, to create illusions that will in some way foster the private intentions of their will. Whereas, hopefully, a creative artist is using the same power, but using it to try to reveal, to create illusions that will foster a greater enlightenment. So I think that research was helpful in that way, in seeing that there are two sides to this, a yin and a yang to the imaginative faculty.

Did you find that research affected you—did you become more personally wary? Because that book is scary as the dickens.

Well, I found it a little scary, too, but I don't think I became more frightened. What I think I did was come to terms with my fear by writing that book, because I was frightened by the fact that there are people actually doing this kind of thing. For example, someone might put an ad in a personals column to try to attract a person in a vulnerable position and take advantage of that person, using every manner of vile tactic to do so. It's such a horrifying thought, and it made me feel personally vulnerable also. But somehow writing the book gave me a sense of, not mastery, but coming to terms with it, and recognizing that we have other powers that are equally strong, and perhaps stronger than such evil intentions. I talked last night about the four tenets of the magician—to know, to dare, to will, to keep silence. And the person who keeps silence is a person who has cut himself off from something very natural, because I think it's a natural human quality to want to break silence—to want to reach out, to want to touch others, and not just to be manipulative. The person who's manipulative, and the person who is psychopathic in that way, I think in the end will always wind up alone, and that is a personal hell. They say hell is other people, but I think hell is one's self, one's self all alone. Like the famous ancient mariner, "Alone, alone, all, all alone, alone on a wide wide sea." That's a lot of alone.

WHEN TRUTH IS STRANGER
Sandra Cisneros, interviewed by Robert Birnbaum

In weaving this story [*Caramelo*] you include what seems to be factual information about Mexican history, Mexican-American history. Some seems not quite believable. For example, you describe conquistador Hernando Cortez, when asked by the king about the topography of a particular part of Mexico, crumpling up a piece of paper and tossing it on a table. That was a wonderful description, but when I thought about it I was skeptical about whether that was a real event. It seemed too dramatic.

He did. [Laughs.] According to the story, to my source, that's what he did to describe the landscape of Oaxaca. I was so startled. I found it in one of these old travel books, these guides to Mexico from the thirties, forties, and fifties. It was a footnote.

What I am speaking to is how you discern, in a novel, what is fictitious and what is factual. Did Elvis Presley really...

See, there is another one. Elvis Presley really allegedly said that.

Presley was quoted, when he was making a movie in Mexico, as saying he wouldn't kiss a Mexican?

Yes, the newspapers reported that he said that. Whether he really said that is subject to debate. But was there a big national boycott? Yes! Did everyone get up and get pissed? Yes! That is true.

....

BEVERLY LOWRY
interviewed by Stephanie Gordon

Regarding your book on Madam Walker, *Her Dream of Dreams*, how much research did you have to do, and how long did it take for you to pull it all together?

I worked on it about seven years, beginning by doing historical research. I was woefully behind in my knowledge of American history, so I started a timeline that began with the arrival of the first black people in America in 1619. I needed a good grounding in how the history of her people might have affected Madam Walker and who she was. And since "might have" was what I had, I had to go for it, all out. End to end, the timeline went on for about five hundred pages. I went to Indianapolis a number of times, to Vicksburg, Pittsburgh, St. Louis, Denver, all the places she lived. I'd done research for *Crossed Over*, but nothing I'd done before came close to the work I did for the Madam Walker book. My friend and colleague Steve Goodwin said I'd become a regular "library girl." [Laughs.] It's true that I spent a lot of time in libraries, in archives and with microfilm machines, tracking down the elusive, fugitive fact about my characters. It was very absorbing. Research can be grueling but very rewarding. In fact, you have to watch it or you'll get hooked, do research forever and never write anything.

Can you tell me more about this book?

It's from the point of view of a white woman who grew up in the South, in an area where whites were in the minority, and which was racially segregated, and in which African-American culture was sort of mixed with white culture. Also, I had to deal with a lot of stories created about her in order to sell products, so it became a matter of trying to figure out what was true, or not, and what we might not ever really know the truth about. So the book involves some speculation. Madam Walker was a drummer—a fantastic saleswoman, whose marketing techniques challenge those of today. My father was a salesman without peer as well, so I have an understanding what it was to make up stories but to sell something as if you believed in it.

Madam Walker was born free, two years after the end of the Civil War, but the book covers the time from before her birth, because I wanted to be able to discuss her background, too. I did a lot of research on the family who had owned her parents, the Burneys. They were very interesting, but I ended up not using much of it.

During the final weeks I was working on this book, I put a sign over my computer that said, "If the information applies only to white people, cut it." At that point the book was about nine hundred pages long, so it became necessary to trim back huge amounts. But that is the nature of research. I had a great time writing that book. No complaints.

But there's no set way to do research. You go here, you go there. You write and write, and then you cut out what doesn't work. There's also a lot of speculation in the book, which I noted in the opening chapter. So where does a writer draw the line? For instance, Madam Walker had three husbands, although husband number two was left out in all the official accounts. But her first husband, Moses McWilliams, who had fathered her child, had disappeared; maybe he was lynched, maybe not. But we don't know much about him at all past him giving Madam Walker a daughter. So I created a death for him, based on what was going on around Vicksburg at that time. The book kind of rides a line, like all biography. I back up whatever I can with a lot of hard factual information, and then in order to keep the pact I have made with the reader, I say when I'm speculating.

Andre Dubus: For this Western, for instance, the next thing I have to do is call a music store and find out what would be a nice waltz to play on the gramophone in 1891. There's not a lot of necessary research in my work, but if I have to, I do it. There's always somebody to ask, and people like to tell you about their work.

as interviewed by Jennifer Levasseur and Kevin Rabalais

EXPLORING CULTURAL ARTIFACTS

Andrea Barrett, interviewed by Sarah Anne Johnson

⟹◈⟸

How do you go about conducting your research? What types of resources do you consult and where do you find them?

I go to the library, nothing esoteric. I do read an enormous amount, but I'm not a great rummager in archives and lost papers and crumbling things, although I have friends who do that and I admire them enormously. I'm a reader of books, and of memoirs, and of diaries, and of collections of letters. I also look at a lot of visual material. If it's from a period when photography existed, I look at old photographs, which I find enormously helpful. I look at paintings. I look both at things about the time, and things made at the time. It's interesting in one way to look at an etching made in 1857 of the things on Charles Darwin's desk, and it's interesting in another way to look at a painting or an etching made in 1930 about the things someone thought were on Charles Darwin's desk. They say two different things. Some of the things are about 1857 and some are about 1930, but it's all interesting. If there's music that I know from the period, I listen to the music. If I can, if the languages are available to me, I also look at novels and poems written in the period. Even though they may not be about what I'm researching, they tell me something about the tonality of the culture then, about what people are thinking, what things seemed important to them.

How concerned were you with getting the historical facts accurate?

I am pretty concerned. There are people who purposely bend historical fact in their fiction, but while that can make for interesting fiction, I'm not one of them. Because I spent a brief time formally studying history, it makes me nervous to bend what seems to be a known fact. There are people who would argue that there are no known facts, but again, I'm not one of them. If there's a historical person passing through a story or a novel, I won't have had him or her grow up in a place where they didn't grow up. I won't send a person to the Arctic when I know he went to the Antarctic. I won't have a woman living in Philadelphia when I know that during those years she was living in France. Those very basic things I will stick to.

BALANCING RESEARCH AND WRITING
Andrea Barrett, interviewed by Sarah Anne Johnson

At what point do you stop your research and start writing?

Usually after the initial subject matter has suggested itself, I'll have to read pretty hard for a while just to get my feet under me. It's hard to write something about Gregor Mendel if you don't know what decades he lived in and you don't know what city his monastery was in. You have to get a sense of the period and the place in the most general way. But often I can start when I have only that general sense, because the research is very specific for the story or the sections of the novel. When I get to a part in *The Voyage of the Narwhal* where the men sail off on a ship, suddenly I realize that I don't know anything about how ships are built or where the stove is. I have to stop everything, and go learn about ships. As the ship comes up past Newfoundland to the edge of Greenland, I realize I don't know anything about Greenland. I don't know when the Danes went there or who administered what or what the Inuit peoples were doing or what the weather was like or what the coastline was like. The research lurches along stepwise.

It takes you on a journey of your own.

So much so. There's a hidden map of each story and each novel which exists beneath the story and which is the map of my own path through all these different areas of inquiry and exploration and learning.

How do you manage all of this historical information in a narrative, and what is the effect you want the history to achieve in the narrative?

I want the history to be correct insofar as it can be, but I also, ultimately, want it to be subordinate in the sense that I am writing a novel and not writing history. After the first draft or two, a lot of my efforts in further drafts and revisions are to take out much of the factual material I earlier worked so hard to learn and put in. I always put in too much. There are always long digressions and long ponderous passages and things that no person would actually say to another person.

Do you hate cutting them?

I do initially. I'm always glad in the end that I did. I always get used to it. I tend not to miss them soon after I've cut them, even though, each time, I think, Oh, that was so interesting. I wish I didn't have to take that out.

But you asked how I managed all the information, and maybe you meant that in a more literal sense. It's evolved over time, and it's still evolving, and I don't have a perfect system. I keep thinking I'll find one and I never do. For various books and sets of stories I've used various cumbersome, not very well-organized combinations of three-ring binders full of notes, index cards, hanging files, smaller files, larger files, boxes, tubs, tins, maps on the wall. There's always a ton of paper around. It's hard sometimes to remember what's where and be able to get my hands on the stuff I need about, say, a ship's berth. I used to take notes on yellow pads, so there would be heaps and heaps and heaps of yellow sheets piled in folders all over. I'm trying to do some of this on the computer now, but I'm just learning to do that.

ELIZABETH MCCRACKEN
interviewed by Sarah Anne Johnson

How much research did you have to do about giants in order to write accurately about James in The Giant's House?

I did a lot. I love research. I have to be careful, because I sometimes use research as a way of procrastinating. I did most of the research after I'd written the book. This was something that was useful about writing the book in Provincetown—I couldn't do much research. I didn't have a car. I couldn't find the nearest library on the Outer Cape. I hadn't done that research in advance because I didn't know I was going to need it—James was going to be dead. I made a lot of it up, and when I returned to Boston, I did the research. I looked at medical journals. I looked up an actual world's tallest man's appearances and read a book by a family friend of his. I did research specifically on him and on giantism, and put that into the book afterwards. But on the first draft, I just concentrated on the characters without trying to bend them to the facts.

MARIA FLOOK

interviewed by Sarah Anne Johnson

How much research do you do before you write?

I research things as I write. When I'm working, I'm already immersed in characterization and in the story map, and I sort of know where I'm headed, but I often stop to work on some fact checking, finding the technical word or identification for something. For instance, today I called the Harvard Map Library to find out the correct name for those raised, three-dimensional maps. They're called *tactile relief maps*, with the molded topography.

Other times I might do more complex research that will actually steer my narrative into a new and exciting bend. In my first novel, I contacted the Chrysler Historical Archives to get the specs on the maiden Plymouth Duster. They sent me 8x10 glossies and their ad campaign from that year; their slogan was "Plymouth Makes It!" I've visited many spots—coast-guard stations for *Open Water*, a plastic-flower warehouse, a motorboat show room, the Arrow Shirt Company's corporate offices on Madison Avenue, and for the memoir, I was in touch with Naval Base Norfolk. I had to find out what ships were in port when my sister lived there. I had to know more about the carrier, the *Independence*, that she went on, and I researched what was happening in Vietnam at that time. I read about the dishonorable discharge her boyfriend got for "fragging" an officer, and learned why he wasn't convicted for the crime.

In my research about the *Andrea Doria*, it was very compelling to learn more about the two girls who were in the disaster that my sister and I survived. If I hadn't retrieved every tidbit about the actual shipwreck, I couldn't have *felt* all the layers of my reaction to it, as I have now. In this way, research can help direct impulse, but usually it enriches and deepens your levels of information.

Was it true that you had had tickets for that ill-fated crossing on the *Andrea Doria*, but instead took an earlier ship, and one of the two girls who were moved into your cabin was killed when it would have been you and your sister?

Yes, there were two other sisters. One was swept away in the collision and lost at sea, but her older sister was plucked from the Italian liner by the prow of the *Stockholm*. She was found two days later in its crumpled bow when the Swedish liner was docked in New York. I learned that the surviving sister, Linda Morgan, is now a nurse. I think about her and her little sister who was swept away. Fate dealt a random blow that touched the four of us, but touched us so differently.

....

RESEARCH TO UNDERSTAND

Barbara Scot, interviewed by Linda B. Swanson-Davies

You did a great deal of research. There is a lot of history in *Prairie Reunion*.

As a historian, it saddens me that more of it couldn't have been included. I could have filled my first draft with footnotes; I found out so much about the area. I was trying to understand my mother, and then I had to understand my father, the man she'd loved, and to understand them, I had to understand the Scotch Grove Presbyterian Church that was the basis of the community for all of us. That turned out to be such an experience. Their thoroughly intact records go back to 1887, which is not that unusual. I highly recommend anyone, whether they're interested in their own family history or the history of place, to check into their little church records. It's just amazing what is there. Now you would have to raid psychiatrists' offices to get what I found out in that church.

ELIZABETH COX

interviewed by Sarah Anne Johnson

When someone suggested that I write a novel, I knew that I would not read a book on the novel, at least not at first. First I took a course in the sonata and symphony at Duke University. I studied the way a sonata develops the statement, development, and reiteration of that form, and how reminding phrases come back all the way through. I wrote my first novel, *Familiar Ground*, listening to symphonies and sonatas—Beethoven, Dvorak mostly. With my second novel, I took a course in astronomy and physics, and incorporated some of the astronomy into the book. At first I incorporated too much. When I showed it to a friend of mine she said that she "just skipped over those parts." So I took most of it out.

Did you find that the bigger idea of it gave you a lens through which you could look at what was happening in your story?

Yes. Exactly. I find that I understand complexities by looking at something larger. For my third novel, I read nature writing and biology, and I used much of my research in *Night Talk*. In this next novel, I'm reading about string theory in physics. Difficult reading, but Brian Greene, an expert on string theory, makes the ideas more accessible. Basically I love the idea that particles are divided into electrons, protons, and neutrons, which are made up of quarks, then upquarks, downquarks, neutrinos, then, finally, strings. Everything in us and around us is vibrating. Isn't that a beautiful thought?

It goes back to the symphony idea that you started with.

Right. It goes back to music. I can't imagine how I will use any of my reading this time, but I'm learning something.

WHAT THE READER SKIPS
Andre Dubus III, interviewed by John McNally

I do find myself doing a lot of research. It's a tricky area for writers: How do you incorporate all you've learned without bogging down or killing the story? When do you do it? Should you do it?

For me, I tend to research as I go along and only once I've written myself into a corner of life about which I'm completely ignorant. After *House of Sand and Fog* came out, I wrote what I thought was a new novel. My imagination, for whatever weird reasons of its own, brought me a character who had been raised on a dairy farm. Well, I don't know jack about dairy farms, and don't even drink milk! So I called dairy farms, visited one, visited a feed-and-grain store, learned a lot. Research material tends to give us a lot to work with and can even send the story down a much truer and deeper path. I got pumped up and wrote and wrote and wrote. After two years, I had over two-hundred handwritten pages and was feeling a bit lost, a normal feeling, like I'd stumbled off the trail and would never find it again. Whenever that happens, I stop writing and just read the whole thing from the beginning, telling myself I've never seen one word of this thing before, reading it like a reader and not the writer. What I found was eighty straight pages of the dullest prose ever about dairy farming! Elmore Leonard said once, "Try to leave out the parts the reader skips over." All that dairy-farm life I needed to know, but the reader didn't. I cut it all, except one page, and ended up with a forty-seven-page story called "The Bartender" [published in the Spring 1999 issue of *Glimmer Train Stories*].

So that's one of the dangers, but I do believe strongly it's something writers need to do. If I read of an East Coast birch tree in an Arizona desert, it's going to stop me and kill that dream the writer's working so hard to cast. I also think taking the time to find the real tree, if there is one, will help the writer go more deeply into the story in a way he or she could never have foreseen. I've just finished the draft of a new novel, and, for the first time, am spending weeks researching the next one because I know next to nothing about that world I'm about to step into. I'm getting all pumped up again, which means I'll probably make the same mistake as before and put in all this stuff I'm going to have to cut!

Jayne Anne Phillips: The only research I do with my books is to immerse myself in the music of the time, to look at the popular culture of the time, to look at the icons.

as interviewed by Sarah Anne Johnson

BECOMING THE CHARACTER
Chris Offutt, interviewed by Rob Trucks

Tell me about your research for *The Good Brother*. How far did you take it?

How far did I take it? I went to Kentucky. I flew my family to Montana. I started in Kentucky and made this drive, took notes all the way, stayed in the hotels I thought Virgil would stay in. During the course of writing I acquired a variety of false identification including three birth certificates, a passport to British Honduras, a pilot's license, a military European driver's license, a private-investigator's license, various library cards wherever I could, as many as I could, in order to sort of become him.

Virgil Caudill started out being based on my brother. He was the good brother in my family. All the memories that Virgil has of childhood and his brother are about my brother and me. But during the course of writing—it was a three-and-a-half-year project—it shifted over into much more being my perceptions instead of my brother's—and then, of course, Virgil became his own person to a certain extent.

In Montana we rented a house in town and I rented a fishing cabin out in the woods up Rock Creek to write in, because that's where Joe was going to live. Virgil changes his name to Joe Tiller in the novel. I grew my hair long. I grew a big beard, as Joe did, played cards where he played cards, acted like he acted. I didn't talk much for a year and a half until we went broke, then I had to talk. I lived in that cabin for three or four days a week, then I'd go to live with my wife and kids three or four days a week.

When I was at the cabin I tried to be Joe Tiller. I tried to be my brother who had become Virgil Caudill who then became Joe Tiller. It was very hard. It was hardest on my wife. I was gone a lot and she never knew who was going to walk in the door, Chris Offutt, Joe Tiller, or Virgil Caudill.

My motivation for the book, really, had to do with identity. In two years, my identity changed. I went from a guy who had held fifty jobs, an unemployed graduate student in debt, and a guy who couldn't hold on to a relationship, to a husband, a father, and a writer. In two years. And it was overwhelming for me in every way. Utterly overwhelming. My behavior was very erratic. How I perceived myself was different. My roles were very different, how other people perceived me was very different, and I wanted to write about identity. That, to me, is what the whole book's all about.

....

SUSAN RICHARDS SHREVE
interviewed by Katherine Perry Harris

One of the things I like best about writing fiction is the chance to live another life without suffering the consequences or taking on the responsibility for it. In terms of time and place and characters, I like to take on a world that is not my own. It is a way of learning while you are writing. It is also a way of surprising yourself, revealing something you didn't think you knew, discovering through invention a part of your sleeping self.

Presently I'm writing about a biologist. I wanted to do this because my youngest child is interested in biology and I know very little about it, so this research will give me a chance to understand her work better. The book, which is called *A Student of Living Things*, has about a hundred pages now. The biologist, a young woman with deep passions and a dangerous innocence, is living out her "story," and I'm leaving spaces—mental ones—to fill in with research to make her work credible. But for my purposes, especially metaphorically, it's important that she's a biologist. The book is about devotion to life. So in the process of writing, research for me is a matter of discovering what I need to know and pursuing it.

ANN PATCHETT
interviewed by Sarah Anne Johnson

What drew you to write about a magician's assistant? How did The Magician's Assistant unfold in your imagination?

The book is so not about magic or a magician's assistant. I wanted to have a profession in which you have a primary and secondary member of a relationship in which the secondary person believes that they couldn't possibly do what the primary person does. In other words, it could have been a story about a surgical nurse and her surgeon who worked together every day, and then the surgeon died and the surgical nurse realizes that in fact, just by having been there and watching all those years, she can perform the surgery as well. But she never knows that about herself until the surgeon dies. This is basically the relationship of a lot of marriages. In those long relationships, everyone picks up different roles, and they believe that there are things that are their responsibility that they know how to do, and they believe they couldn't possibly do the other things, because their partner does them. Then if the partner leaves or dies, the person has to come to terms with the fact that they can do all sorts of things. That's a really interesting transition to me. The magician and the assistant were the flashiest, most metaphorical jobs that I could give them and put them in the best-looking outfits.

What was funny about that, though, was that when I was about halfway through the book, I sent it to my friend Elizabeth, who said that it was appalling, that I knew nothing about magic. She wanted me to do some research, so I did. I had never really given it much thought, but what I discovered when I started doing my research with half the book written, was that I hated magic. I had literally given no thought outside of the pretty costumes, the doves, the stage, the pink lights. When I started going to magic shows and reading books about magicians, I saw that it's so sleazy. It's carnival sleazy. I never would've written that book if I'd done my research ahead of time.

Did you get anything useful out of the research?

Nothing. Of course, anything you want to know about magic, you can't find out in a book about magic. What I discovered was that magic was all about authority. I read one book by Harry Blackstone Jr., in which he said—and not in any condescending way—that the reason there are virtually no female magicians is that a woman cannot command the authority in a room. There are always going to be men and women who won't give their total suspension of disbelief to a woman the way that men and women will give it to a man. Magic is about dominance in a way. Unless you have complete authority over the room, and every person believes you—because they're fighting it, everyone is looking for the trick—unless the magician can dominate the whole room, the magician can't succeed. And women can't do that because there are both men and women who will never take women seriously.

That was such as fascinating thing to me. I realized that writing is a lot like magic. It's about dominating your audience, and making them believe what you say is true. What I ended up having to do was write the scenes in which Sabine is performing the acts with such confidence that it would be reasonable to the reader that she was not saying to herself in her narrative, "And now I'm doing this. Now I'm doing that." When you're reading it, you're thinking that she just totally knows what she's doing. That's the way writing is. You have to command the reader's belief, which I completely believe that women can do in books. It makes a perverse kind of sense to me that they can't do it on stage as magicians.

. . . .

EDWIDGE DANTICAT

interviewed by Sarah Anne Johnson

The Farming of Bones is a love story amidst the 1937 massacre of thousands of Haitians living in the Dominican Republic, on orders from the Dominican dictator Rafael Trujillo. How did you go about conducting the research for this book?

I visited the places where the story takes place. Even though it was many years later, I went to read testimonies and talk to people. I read a lot, even unrelated things that were written in the same year so that I could get a sense of the period and imagine myself there. I needed physical details about what kinds of cars they were driving, what kinds of clothes they were wearing. I did research like that for about a year and a half before I started writing. A story in *Krik? Krak!* began to visit that time, but in a very different way. I didn't have the novel until I had the main character, Amabelle. I was reading an old issue of *Collier's* magazine with a story of the massacre. It was about a Dominican colonel who killed his maid at the dinner table to prove his loyalty to Trujillo, the president of the Dominican Republic. I realized the maid was Amabelle, but she lives. Once I had that, and all the research, I could enter the story.

SUE MILLER

interviewed by Sarah Anne Johnson

I did do research for *While I Was Gone*, but not for the minister's life, because that was something very familiar to me from my family background. But I leaned on others for different kinds of information. My brother, for instance, is a vet, and he was enormously helpful to me. We had a prolonged correspondence about certain episodes in the book, which was really enjoyable. He's my youngest brother, and I didn't know a lot about his work or his feelings about it. It was great to have him be able to help me and tell me what he knew. He told me what it felt like to be a vet. He could talk openly about things like euthanasia in a way that I think someone who didn't know me might not have been able to.

The police were wonderful, too. I went down to the Cambridge Police Station, in part because I wanted to see it—I have a few little scenes set in it. Three detectives sat down and talked to me. I asked them about my hypothetical situation, and they were very concrete in telling me what would happen. They were willing to discuss differences, too, between police procedures when the crime in my book happened, and what they are like now. I also asked about what the procedures would be around an unresolved case that got opened up again, about how much evidence is left around, and that sort of thing. They were tremendously helpful to me.

There's always been some level of research in every book that I've done. For *The Good Mother*, I did a lot of research about contested divorce cases, which I didn't know anything about, and the civil institutions that deal with custody issues. I read a lot of trial transcripts, and went and sat in on some civil cases—you can't sit in on custody cases—just to get a sense of the courtroom. There are usually things that I have to learn. It gets me out into the world, asking questions about characters' lives.

....

KEEPING IT IN CONTEXT
Chang-rae Lee, interviewed by Sarah Anne Johnson

What were the challenges in writing sections set in a historical time and place?

Those were hard at the beginning because I'm not a historical writer and I didn't want it to seem at all inauthentic or false. Once you start writing it, it's like anything else. There are particular features of that time and place, and certain language, but in the end, people are people. Once you get into it, the story moves along. The only thing that I tried to remember was to try not to make it seem so historical. In the end, acknowledge the context, but realize that these people were just people and they'd do what they had to do.

....

THEN FORGET IT ALL AND WRITE
Elizabeth McCracken
interviewed by Sarah Anne Johnson

⟴

Who is the narrator of the new book?

A man named Mose Sharp. He's a straight man in a comedy team. He goes into vaudeville after the death of his favorite sister and he teams up with a comic named Rocky Carter. They're the comedy team of Carter and Sharp, and they become quite successful in vaudeville and movies for a short period of time. The book follows their career.

Did you conduct a lot of research about vaudeville before you could write the novel, or did you wait until you'd already written the draft, like with *The Giant's House*?

I did more research before I wrote. There was a real temptation to stay in the basement at the Boston Public Library and read back issues of *Variety* for days on end. I love that kind of research, but in the end I wind up tossing much of it aside. Frequently I do research to get an idea of that I'm writing about, then I try to forget it all and write.

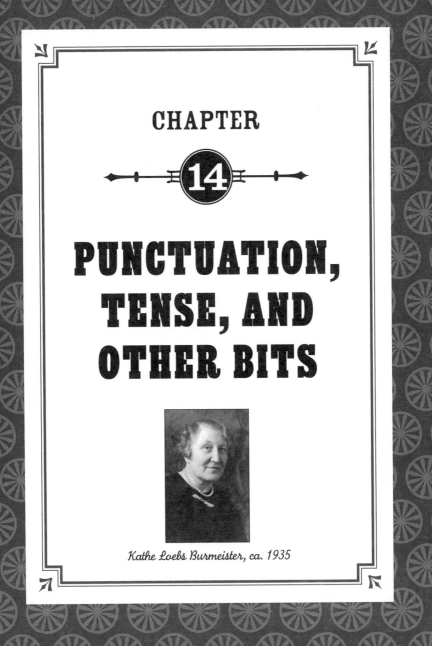

CHAPTER

14

PUNCTUATION, TENSE, AND OTHER BITS

Kathe Loebs Burmeister, ca. 1935

PAUL THEROUX

interviewed by Michael Upchurch

In punctuation, generally, I don't use a lot of semicolons. I tend to use colons rather than semicolons. Dashes—I've exploited the dash quite a lot. The exclamation mark I've used, I hope, to good advantage. All of these are things that it's very easy to overdo. A question in the middle of a paragraph is something I've found is a way of sending or turning a paragraph or an issue around. A question mark in expository prose is often a wonderful thing. Too many questions, and you're done for. Too many exclamation marks, and you're done for. It's all a matter of balance and proportion, I guess.

When I wrote *The Mosquito Coast*, I was trying to write not so much the way a thirteen-year-old would speak—because we all know thirteen-year-olds may or may not have that vocabulary—but to have a thirteen-year-old's rhythm. When that book went to the copy editor, they took out almost every dash and turned it into a semicolon. I started to rub them out, and then I gave it back and said, "Please, put all my punctuation back. It was all done deliberately." The same thing with *Millroy*. So I think it's more the dash than the exclamation mark. But I find judicious use of punctuation to be very effective. I hate prose that's over-punctuated. And I've always tried to write with the utmost clarity of expression, but without simplifying.

In writing, excessive use of italics can be very off-putting—or too many narrators, stories within stories, eccentric paragraphing, or absence of punctuation. All of those things. So what do we do about *Finnegans Wake*? I don't know *what* we do about *Finnegans*

Wake! Except just stand four paces away and admire it—but don't imitate it. *Ulysses* is a masterpiece, no question. It has excessive technique, but it actually works. It sounds a bit pompous that I should be approving of Joyce, giving Joyce the nod. But that's an example of lots of technique. You have to be a genius to get away with that, and there aren't enough geniuses around to do it. The rest of us have to depend on something much simpler: being ourselves, rather than assuming elaborate techniques that we haven't mastered.

PUNCTUATION AND PACING
Colum McCann, interviewed by Robert Birnbaum

One of the things I was struck by in *Dancer* was this monologue by the character Victor, in which I don't think there were any periods.

Right, there are none.

The intense focus was like a tight head shot of the character. You get that close to Rudolph in that way. Why Victor?

Victor is almost like the shadow image of Rudy. Victor was everything.... I could go through Victor and deal with all the issues of sex. All of the things, if you make him the main character of the book and you put him through all of that directly, people would pull away and say, "Oh no, don't do that." In some ways it was a way to glance off and come at Rudy by glancing off. But in other ways I began to fall in love with him. It was like, God, who is this character and where the hell is he coming from? From me.

Yes, thirty-five pages without a full stop. I knew that I wanted to do that because I wanted to capture the energy of the seventies and I wanted it to feel like you had gotten a couple of blasts of coke up your nose and you were like, Whoa, okay. And where am I going to go next?

So it shifts and turns and shifts and turns. But also to embrace how wonderful it was for people, it seems. I talked to a lot of people who were around in the early seventies, and they are a little bit tired of all the moralizing now that goes on about it. At the time they were having great fun. It was like taking a Coca-Cola. The way we take a cola was just like having a line of coke. People didn't see that it was going to damage you. People didn't see that ultimately all of this stuff is going to collapse and we are going to get this dreadful disease that's going to plough us under. None of that was there. There was just this, "Hah," that we embraced the world. I loved doing that character of Victor.

CAROLYN CHUTE

interviewed by Barbara Stevens

You write in both past and present tenses. How do you decide which to use?

Past tense seems to give the reader the notice that the voice already knows something that is about to happen, and this builds a tension. Present tense means the voice doesn't know what's going on either, but there's an immediacy, which seems to bring the reader closer to the voice and the experience, but might sacrifice the tension which would have to be developed in other ways, such as a constant hammering, a rhythm of events, so that the reader expects something to happen again and again.

Your punctuation is distinctive—lots of ellipses and capitalized words. Was this something you deliberately developed?

Ellipses give me the feel of poetic space, a pause which I prefer at times to just a comma. I want a more visual pause, so that words or groups of words float on little islands, like in poetry. I still use words in caps sometimes but not as much. That's one of the things I would change in *The Beans of Egypt, Maine.*

....

FREE SENTENCES, FREE THOUGHTS
A.J. Verdelle, interviewed by Nancy Middleton

I had 181 pages with no punctuation. So I had to go back and put it in. That was my first step. But I think that the lack of punctuation enabled me to make fresher sentences, because there's no propensity for a lot of "the girl, the boy, the work, the school." There's no stopping all the time. There's no stop/start motion, so a lot of my sentences start in places that I never would have thought of without my punctuation step. The one I remember the most is "Disbelief is an emotion, you know." I never would have gotten that sentence if I'd sat down and written it straight out. It doesn't start the way a sentence normally does.

We have certain tendencies in writing, and one of our tendencies is to take big concepts like disbelief and try to lead up to them, so that disbelief is much more likely to be at the end of the sentence than at the beginning....

You want to let things fly in writing as much as possible. That's why I've come up with strategies to make it happen.

WRITING ADVICE from Monica Wood

There is a writing phenomenon that I call "the black hole of the past perfect." A flashback requires the past perfect to establish a switch in time: "He had built the parade float back in August, when his wife was still alive. She had helped him make flowers out of Kleenex. His daughter had also put in her two cents...." Once in the past perfect, many writers don't find their way back out. The past-perfect tense kills the story's momentum, reminding the reader at every verb that the events being described are already over.

What I do is drop the auxiliary (had) as soon as possible, usually in the second or third sentence, and revert to the simple past tense. Sometimes you establish time in the first sentence and then immediately switch to the simple past tense. "He had built the float back in August. His wife helped him make flowers out of Kleenex. His daughter also put in her two cents...." It's that simple.

SLAP YOUR PARAGRAPHS
by George Makana Clark

Unfortunately, many of us have been brainwashed for a dozen or so formative years to believe that each paragraph consists of a topic sentence followed by several supporting sentences. The idea that all writing should be composed of standard paragraphs is base propaganda put out by the same dullards who made you sit in the front of the classroom for habitually sleeping during their lectures. These grammar fascists would have you mold your ideas into uniform cinder blocks of paragraphs to be piled, one upon the other, until you have built a dreary monolith to bad writing.

A paragraph break simply represents a division of ideas. Don't shape your ideas to fit some arbitrary construct of what a paragraph should look like. Rather, allow your ideas to determine the shape of the paragraph.

The implications of abandoning the standard paragraph can be staggering. Paragraphs can be broken mid-sentence or even mid-word. A paragraph can encompass an entire novel (this can be quite fatiguing for the reader), or contain only a scrap of punctuation:

!

With freedom comes responsibility, though. Don't abuse your readers by placing paragraph breaks willy-nilly. Instead, combine or separate your ideas according to the message you're trying to communicate.

The shape of a paragraph can have a subtle effect on the reader. The smaller the paragraph, the more weight is given to the words contained therein. A succession of small paragraphs creates a sense of urgency for the reader. Paragraphs of varying length help keep the reader off-balance and interested. Even bland, standard paragraphs, such as the one you are presently reading, sometimes have their place.

The next time you start struggling to organize your ideas into neat packages, ask yourself, Just who's in control here, me or the paragraph? Slap that paragraph around a little bit, and show it who's boss. Break it!

....

WRITING IS RHYTHM

Daniel Wallace, interviewed by Linda B. Swanson-Davies

When I started writing—I'm not exaggerating—I didn't know how to write a paragraph. I didn't know how to paragraph. I would just type and I wouldn't know where to stop. I wouldn't know how to do that pause that moves to the next thing, and I had to learn all that.

How'd you do that?

By doing it. Just by writing it. I read, obviously, looked at other books, and read my own stuff. I did this before computers were that prevalent, and I remember the first stories that I wrote. I knew they didn't look right. They were just blocks of text. So then I would retype them, and paragraph them so they *looked* right, but they didn't sound right, because the paragraphs didn't make any sense. It was just indenting one little sentence. And I had to figure out, So what makes a paragraph? What makes you stop? These are just blocks of words.

And what did you conclude?

That just like music, writing is rhythm. I think that there's a rhythm to a piece of work. You could time it out, almost. And once you get to that point where there's the rest, it's a sense that you develop through the doing of it. It's not magical or inborn or anything like that, but it's the sense, it's sort of a sixth sense that you can learn. I really do believe that you can learn how to write, if you're interested in learning how to write. Just over time I've learned how to hear the rhythm of a story and the rhythm of a sentence.

One interesting exercise I did that actually helped in that regard was what I did with one of my favorite stories ever, called "The Deaths of Distant Friends," by John Updike. It's very short. I set it up by my typewriter and typed it as though I were actually writing it. I copied it. Word for word. And looking at it, in that form, in a way demythologized it, brought it down to earth. I realized, This is how he did it. The same way that I do it.

When you see somebody like John Updike, who's a beautiful writer, you don't think he writes with the same instruments that you do. You think he has something different, something special. You think they bring in a special typewriter for John Updike. Or he doesn't really have to type. He just has to look at it and do whatever, but when you type his story, it brings it down to your level. Because everybody's on the same level. Everybody's doing the same thing.

CONTRIBUTOR BIOGRAPHIES

Scott Allie (1969–) writes and edits for Dark Horse Comics and Glimmer Train Press. His writing includes *The Devil's Footprints*, set in his hometown of Ipswich, Massachusetts. He lives in Portland, Oregon, with his wife and child. scottallie.com

Born in New York and raised until age ten in the Dominican Republic, **Julia Alvarez** (1950–) is a writer-in-residence at Middlebury College in Vermont. Her most recent novel is *Saving the World*. The novel *How the García Girls Lost Their Accents* was a *New York Times Book Review* Notable Book, and *In the Time of the Butterflies* was made into a movie. She also has published poetry and books for young readers. juliaalvarez.com

Russell Banks (1940–) is the author of many novels, two of which, *Continental Drift* and *Cloudsplitter*, were finalists for the Pulitzer Prize. Two novels, *Affliction* and *The Sweet Hereafter*, were adapted into feature films. *The Angel on the Roof* is a collection of thirty years of his short fiction.

Andrea Barrett (1954–) is the author of five novels, most recently *The Voyage of the Narwhal*, and two collections of short fiction, *Ship Fever*, which received the National Book Award, and *Servants of the Map*, a finalist for the Pulitzer Prize. A MacArthur Fellow, she's also been a Fellow at the Center for Scholars and

Writers at the New York Public Library, and has received Guggenheim and NEA Fellowships. She lives in western Massachusetts and teaches at Williams College and Warren Wilson College.

Richard Bausch's (1945–) novels include *Hello to the Cannibals*; *Good Evening Mr. & Mrs. America, and All the Ships at Sea*; *Rebel Powers*; *Violence*; and *The Last Good Time*. *The Selected Stories of Richard Bausch* was published in 1996. He is the recipient of the Lila Wallace–*Reader's Digest* Writer's Award and the Award in Literature from the American Academy of Arts and Letters. He lives in rural Virginia.

Charles Baxter's (1947–) work includes four novels, most recently *Saul and Patsy* and *The Feast of Love*, which was a National Book Award finalist and is being made into a motion picture; four story collections, most recently *Believers*; a book of poetry, *Imaginary Paintings;* and two books of essays about writing, *Burning Down the House* and *Beyond Plot*, which will come out in 2007. His stories have appeared in *The New Yorker*, *The Atlantic Monthly*, *Glimmer Train Stories*, and *Harper's*, among other journals and magazines. His fiction has been widely anthologized and translated into ten languages. He is the Edelstein-Keller Professor of Creative Writing at the University of Minnesota.

Louis Begley (1933–) is a writer and retired lawyer. His novel *Wartime Lies* won the PEN Hemingway Award and other awards; *About Schmidt* was a National Book Critics' Circle Award finalist and was made into a feature film. His latest novel, *Matters of Honor*, will be published in 2007.

Melanie Bishop (1956–) teaches writing and literature at Prescott College in Prescott, Arizona, where she is also founder and editor of the literary magazine *Alligator Juniper*. She received an MFA from the University of Arizona. She's published fiction and nonfiction in *Glimmer Train Stories, Georgetown Review, Greensboro Review, Florida Review, Valley Guide, Hospice Magazine, Puerto del Sol, Family Circle*, and *UnderWire*, and has received the Chesterfield Screenwriting Fellowship sponsored by Steven Spielberg. She is currently at work on a memoir and a screenplay.

Amy Bloom (1953–) is the author of a novel, *Love Invents Us*, and two collections of stories: *Come to Me*, nominated for a National Book Award, and *A Blind Man Can See How Much I Love You*, nominated for the National Book Critics' Circle Award. Her stories have appeared in *Best American Short Stories, Prize Stories: The O. Henry Awards*, and numerous anthologies. Her book *Normal: Transsexual CEOs, Crossdressing Cops, and Hermaphrodites with Attitude,* is an exploration of the varieties of gender. Her new novel, *Away*, will come out in 2007. A practicing psychotherapist, she lives in Connecticut and teaches at Yale University.

Sir Robert Olen Butler (1945–) has published ten novels, most recently *Fair Warning* and *Mr. Spaceman*; three volumes of short stories, including *Had a Good Time* and *A Good Scent from a Strange Mountain*, which won the 1993 Pulitzer Prize for Fiction; and *From Where You Dream: The Process of Writing Fiction*, edited by Janet Burroway. Butler, whose work has been widely published and won numerous awards, teaches creative writing at Florida State University in Tallahassee, where he lives with his wife, the novelist Elizabeth Dewberry.

Ethan Canin (1960–) is a member of the Iowa Writers' Workshop faculty, which he joined after eight years of mixing writing with the practice of medicine. Author of two collections of stories—*Emperor of the Air* and *The Palace Thief* (made into a movie, *The Emperor's Club*)—and three novels—*Blue River, For Kings and Planets*, and *Carry Me Across the Water*—he is also director of the Sun Valley Writers' Conference.

Kevin Canty (1954–) is the author of the novels *Into the Great Wide Open, Nine Below Zero*, and *Winslow in Love*, as well as the short-story collections *Honeymoon* and *A Stranger in This World*. His work has been published in *The New Yorker, Esquire, GQ, Details, Story*, the *New York Times Magazine*, and *Glimmer Train Stories*. He lives in Missoula, Montana.

The latest of Australian-born **Peter Carey**'s (1943–) novels is *Theft: A Love Story*. Two of his novels have been awarded the Booker Prize: *True History of the Kelly Gang* and *Oscar and Lucinda*, which was made into a film. His *Collected Stories* appeared in 1994. He lives in New York City.

Ron Carlson (1947–) is the author of seven books of fiction, including *At the Jim Bridger* and *The Hotel Eden,* a *New York Times* Notable Book and *Los Angeles Times* Best Book of the Year. In 2003 Norton published *A Kind of Flying: Selected Stories*. He is a professor of English at Arizona State University.

Born in New Delhi, **Vikram Chandra** (1961–) teaches at the University of California in Berkeley. Both his novel *Red Earth and Pouring Rain* and his story collection *Love and Longing in Bombay* received the Commonwealth Writers' Prize. His new novel, *Sacred Games*, will be published in 2007.

Dan Chaon (1964–) has published two story collections, *Fitting Ends* and *Among the Missing*, a finalist for the National Book

Award. His novel *You Remind Me of Me* was published in 2004. His fiction has appeared in numerous journals and anthologies, and won both Pushcart and O. Henry awards. He teaches at Oberlin College in Ohio.

Carolyn Chute's (1947–) novel *The Beans of Egypt, Maine* was adapted for a motion picture in 1994. Her subsequent books include *Letourneau's Used Auto Parts*, *Merry Men*, and *Snow Man*. She lives in Parsonsfield, Maine.

Sandra Cisneros's (1954–) novel *The House on Mango Street* won the American Book Award from the Before Columbus Foundation. Her other books include a novel, *Caramelo*; a story collection, *Woman Hollering Creek*; and several books of poetry. She lives in San Antonio, Texas.

George Makana Clark's (1957–) story "The Center of the World" was included in the 2006 *O. Henry Prize Stories*. The collection *The Small Bees' Honey* appeared in 1997. His short stories, plays, and poetry have appeared in *Chelsea*, *The Georgia Review*, *Glimmer Train Stories*, *Massachusetts Review*, *The Southern Review*, *Transition Magazine*, *Zoetrope: All Story*, and elsewhere. He has just completed his first novel, *The Raw Man*.

Elizabeth Cox's (1942–) most recent book is the novel *The Slow Moon*. Her other books are the novels *Night Talk*, *The Ragged Way People Fall Out of Love*, and *Familiar Ground*, and the story collection *Bargains in the Real World*. Her poetry has been widely published, most recently in *The Southern Review* and *The Atlantic Monthly*. She is an instructor at the Bennington Graduate Writing Seminars and teaches at Wofford College in South Carolina. She lives in Spartanburg, South Carolina.

Haitian-born **Edwidge Danticat** (1969–) grew up in that nation's capital, Port-au-Prince, and moved to Brooklyn when she was twelve years old. Her most recent book is *The Dew Breaker*, which was preceded by the story collection *Krik? Krak!* and the novels *The Farming of Bones* and *Breath, Eyes, Memory*. She has published two young-adult novels, *Anacaona: Golden Flower* and *Behind the Mountains*, as well as a travel narrative, *After the Dance: A Walk Through Carnival in Jacmel, Haiti*. She is also the editor of *The Butterfly's Way: Voices from the Haitian Dyaspora in the United States* and *The Beacon Best of 2000: Great Writing by Men and Women of All Colors and Cultures*. Her writings have been anthologized and translated into many languages and won numerous awards and honors.

Toi Derricotte's (1941–) books of poetry include *Tender*, which won the 1998 Paterson Poetry Prize, *Captivity*, *Natural Birth*, and *The Empress of the Death House*. *The Black Notebooks*, a literary memoir, was published in 1997 and won the Annisfield-Wolf Book Award for Nonfiction. She teaches at the University of Pittsburgh.

Chitra Banerjee Divakaruni (1956–) is an Indian-born author and poet whose work has been published in over fifty magazines, including the *Atlantic Monthly* and the *New Yorker*. Her latest novel is *Queen of Dreams*. Her other novels are *The Vine of Desire*, *Sister of My Heart*, and *The Mistress of Spices*. Her collections of stories are *The Unknown Errors of Our Lives* and *Arranged Marriage*. She teaches at the University of Houston and divides her time between Houston and Northern California.

Stephen Dixon (1936–) is the author of thirteen novels, most recently *Phone Rings* and *End of I*. His novels *Interstate* and *Frog* were both finalists for the National Book Award. Dixon has written over 450 short stories, which have appeared in *Harper's, Glimmer Train Stories, Playboy, Esquire, The Paris Review, Triquarterly,* and *Boulevard.* He has received many awards, including the O. Henry, two NEA Fellowships, and the Pushcart Prize. He is a professor of fiction at Johns Hopkins University.

Andre Dubus (1936–1999) served five years in the Marine Corps before becoming a full-time writer of short stories. His last story collection was *Dancing After Hours,* preceded by *Selected Stories, The Last Worthless Evening,* and others. In 1998 he published a volume of essays, *Meditations from a Moveable Chair.* Dubus received the PEN/Malamud Award, the Rea Award for excellence in short fiction, the Jean Stein Award from the American Academy of Arts and Letters, and the *Boston Globe*'s Lawrence L. Winship Award.

The second novel by **Andre Dubus III** (1959–   ), *House of Sand and Fog,* was a finalist for the 1999 National Book Award and was made into a movie in 2003. His other books are *The Cage Keeper and Other Stories,* and his first novel, *Bluesman.* Andre Dubus III is the son of Andre Dubus. He teaches at the University of Massachusetts at Lowell.

Pam Durban (1947–   ) is the author of two novels, *So Far Back* and *The Laughing Place,* as well as a collection of short fiction, *All Set About with Fever Trees.* Her stories have been anthologized in *The Best American Short Stories of the Century, The Best American Short Stories, 1997,* and *New Stories from the South 2006, The Year's Best.* She teaches at the University of North Carolina at Chapel Hill.

Stuart Dybek (1942–   ) is the author of three collections of short fiction, *I Sailed with Magellan, The Coast of Chicago,* and

Childhood and Other Neighborhoods, as well as a volume of poetry, *Brass Knuckles*. A professor of English at Western Michigan University, he lives in Kalamazoo.

Nomi Eve (1968–) has an MFA in fiction writing from Brown University and has worked as a freelance book reviewer for the *Village Voice* and *New York Newsday*. *The Family Orchard*, her first novel, was based on her own family's history. Her stories have appeared in the *Village Voice Literary Supplement*, *Glimmer Train Stories*, and *International Quarterly*. She now lives outside of Philadelphia.

Maria Flook (1952–) is the author of the novels *Lux*, *Open Water*, and *Family Night* (which received a PEN/Ernest Hemingway Foundation Special Citation and was a *New York Times* Notable Book), and the nonfiction books *Invisible Eden* and *My Sister Life: The Story of My Sister's Disappearance*. She has also published a collection of short stories and two books of poems. She teaches in Boston, where she is writer-in-residence at Emerson College. mariaflook.com

Lynn Freed's (1945–) latest book is *Reading, Writing, and Leaving Home: Life on the Page*. She has published five novels, most recently *House of Women* and *The Mirror*, and a collection of short stories, *The Curse of the Appropriate Man*. Her work has been published in *Harper's*, the *New Yorker*, and the *Atlantic Monthly*, among others, and is widely anthologized and translated. She is the recipient of the inaugural Katherine Anne Porter prize for fiction from the American Academy of Arts and Letters. lynnfreed.com

Ernest Gaines (1933–) has published eight books of fiction, including *Catherine Carmier*, *Bloodline*, *The Autobiography of Miss Jane Pittman*, *In My Father's House*, and *A Gathering of Old Men*.

A Lesson Before Dying, his most recent novel, won the 1993 National Book Critics' Circle Award. *Mozart and Leadbelly: Stories and Essays* appeared in 2005. He has been awarded a MacArthur Foundation grant for writings of "rare historical resonance."

Dagoberto Gilb (1950–) is the author of the story collections *Woodcuts of Women*, *The Magic of Blood*, and *The Last Known Residence of Mickey Acuña*, as well as the essay collection *Gritos*. His essays have appeared in the *New Yorker*, *Harper's*, and *The Best American Essays*. He is on the faculty of Texas State University, San Marcos.

Mary Gordon (1949–) is the author of the novels *Pearl*, *Spending*, *The Company of Women*, *The Other Side*, and *Final Payments*; a collection of novellas entitled *The Rest of Life*; two books of essays; and a biography of Joan of Arc. She has also written a memoir, *The Shadow Man*. Winner of the Lila Wallace–*Reader's Digest* Writer's Award, a Guggenheim Fellowship, and the 1997 O. Henry Award for best short story, Gordon teaches at Barnard College and lives in New York City.

Jim Grimsley (1955–) is the author of five novels: *Boulevard*; *Winter Birds*, a finalist for the PEN/Hemingway Award; *Dream Boy*; *My Drowning*, a Lila Wallace–*Reader's Digest* Writer's Award winner, and *Kirith Kirin*. He lives in Atlanta and teaches at Emory University.

Patricia Hampl (1946–) has published two memoirs, *A Romantic Education* and *Virgin Time*. She has contributed stories to *American Poetry Review*, *The New Yorker*, *The Paris Review*, and *Iowa Review*. She also is the author of two volumes of poetry and an essay collection, *I Could Tell You Stories*. She teaches at the University of Minnesota and lives in St. Paul.

Kent Haruf's (1943–) honors include a Whiting Foundation Award and a special citation from the PEN/Hemingway Foundation. His latest novel is *Eventide*; a previous novel, *Plainsong*, won the Mountains & Plains Booksellers Award and was a finalist for the National Book Award, the *Los Angeles Times* Book Prize, and the *New Yorker* Book Award. He lives in his native Colorado.

After publishing four collections of stories, **Amy Hempel** (1951–) published her complete *Collected Stories* in 2006. She has a keen interest in guide dogs for the blind, and this theme found its way into her 2005 collection *The Dog of the Marriage*. She teaches and lectures in libraries, hospitals, and universities including Bennington and Columbia, while remaining involved in writing workshops such as Bread Loaf.

Patricia Henley's (1947–) forthcoming novel is entitled *Home Plate*. Her first novel, *Hummingbird House*, was a finalist for the 1999 National Book Award and the *New Yorker* Best Fiction Book Award. She has also written two books of poetry and three story collections: *Friday Night at Silver Star*, which won the 1985 Montana Arts Council First Book Award; *The Secret of Cartwheels*; and *Worship of the Common Heart: New and Selected Stories*. Henley has taught in Purdue University's MFA program for nineteen years and also teaches in the low-residency MFA program at the University of Nebraska at Omaha. patriciahenley.com

David Huddle's (1942–) most recent works of fiction are *Not: A Trio*, *The Story of a Million Years*, and *La Tour Dreams of the Wolf Girl*. Among his other books of short fiction are *Tenorman*, *Intimates*, and *Only the Little Bone*. His most recent poetry collections are *Grayscale* and *Summer Lake: New and Selected Poems*. His work has appeared in *Esquire*, *Harper's*, *Story*, *The Best American Short Stories*, *Glimmer Train Stories*, and many others. He teaches at the University of Vermont and the Bread Loaf School of English.

Siri Hustvedt's (1955–) latest novel, *What I Loved*, was nominated for the Prix Étranger Femina. She has published two other novels, *The Blindfold* and *The Enchantment of Lily Dahl*, as well as collections of essays, most recently *A Plea for Eros*. She lives in Brooklyn.

War Trash, the most recent novel by **Ha Jin** (1956–), was a Pulitzer Prize finalist and winner of the PEN/Faulkner Award; his novel *Waiting* won the National Book Award. He was born in Liaoning Province in China and began publishing in English in 1990. His most recent story collection is *The Bridegroom*.

Charles Johnson (1948–) is the S. Wilson and Grace M. Pollock Endowed Professor of English at the University of Washington in Seattle. His fiction includes *Faith and the Good Thing*, *Dreamer*, and *Middle Passage*, for which he won the National Book Award. His most recent story collection is *Dr. King's Refrigerator and Other Bedtime Stories*. His nonfiction books include *Turning the Wheel: Essays on Buddhism and Writing*, *King: The Photobiography of Martin Luther King Jr.* (co-authored with Bob Adelman), and *Being & Race: Black Writing Since 1970*. He has received the Lifetime Achievement in the Arts Award from the Corporate Council for the Arts, as well as many other awards. oxherdingtale.com

Allen Morris Jones (1970–) co-edited *The Big Sky Reader* and is the former editor of the *Big Sky Journal*. He has published a novel, *Last Year's River*, and a book about hunting, *A Quiet Place of Violence*. He has lived and worked in Montana most of his life.

Thomas E. Kennedy's (1944–   ) most recent books include the novels of The Copenhagen Quartet, four novels about his adopted city: *Kerrigan's Copenhagen, A Love Story*; *Bluett's Blue Hours*; *Greene's Summer*; and *Danish Fall*. Also recently published are *The Literary Traveler*, a book of travel pieces co-authored with Walter Cummins, and a collection of essays on the craft of fiction, *Realism & Other Illusions*. His stories, poems, essays, and translations from the Danish appear regularly in the U.S. and Europe. A resident of Denmark, he teaches in the low-residency MFA program at Fairleigh Dickinson University.

Jamaica Kincaid (1949–   ) is the author of several works of fiction, including *Annie John, The Autobiography of My Mother, Lucy*, and *At the Bottom of the River*. The most recent of her nonfiction books is *Among Flowers: A Walk in the Himalaya*.

Carolyn Kizer's (1925–   ) volumes of poetry include *Yin*, which won a Pulitzer Prize, *Mermaids in the Basement, The Nearness of You*, and *Harping On: Poems 1985–1995*. In 2000 she brought out *Cool, Calm & Collected: Poems 1960–2000*. She has also published a collection of essays, *Proses: On Poems & Poets* (1993), and edited *100 Great Poems by Women*.

David Koon (1974–   ) has published stories in *Crazyhorse, Glimmer Train Stories*, and *New Stories from the South*, among others.

Chang-rae Lee (1965–   ) is the author of the novels *Aloft, A Gesture Life*, and *Native Speaker*, which won the Hemingway Foundation/PEN Award for first fiction and other honors. Selected by *The New Yorker* as one of the twenty best writers under forty, he teaches writing at Princeton University.

Doris Lessing (1919–   ) is one of the most celebrated writers of the twentieth century. Her most recent books include the novels *Ben, In the World* and *Walking in the Shade.* A Companion of Honour and a Companion of Literature, she was awarded the David Cohen Memorial Prize for British Literature in 2001. She lives in North London.

Banishing Verona is the most recent novel by **Margot Livesey** (1953–   ). Her stories were collected in *Learning by Heart*, and her other novels include *Eva Moves the Furniture*, *The Missing World*, *Criminals*, and *Homework*. Born in Scotland, she currently lives in the Boston area, where she is a writer-in-residence at Emerson College.

David Long's (1948–   ) short stories appear in the *New Yorker*, *GQ*, *Story*, and many anthologies, including the O. Henrys. His third collection of stories, *Blue Spruce* (1997), was given the Lowenthal Award from the American Academy of Arts and Letters. His novels are *The Falling Boy*, *The Daughters of Simon Lamoreaux*, and, most recently, *The Inhabited World*. He has written a book on writing, *Dangerous Sentences*, and is at work on a new novel. davidlonglit.com

Beverly Lowry (1938–   ) is the author of six novels, including *The Track of Real Desires* and *Breaking Gentle*. She has published two nonfiction titles: *Her Dream of Dreams*, about Madam C.J. Walker, and *Crossed Over*, about her friendship with Karla Faye Tucker. She directs the creative-nonfiction program at George Mason University and lives in Washington, D.C.

Novelist and poet **David Malouf** (1934–   ) was born in Brisbane, Australia, and has lived in England and Italy. *Johnno*, his first novel, is considered an Australian classic. He is the author of five other novels, including *The Conversations at Curlow Creek* and *An Imaginary Life*, as well as several books of poetry and two novellas, "Child's Play" and "The Bread of Time to Come."

Lee Martin's (1955–   ) most recent book, *The Bright Forever*, was a finalist for the 2006 Pulitzer Prize in Fiction. In 2003 he published *Turning Bones*, part of the American Lives Series at the University of Nebraska Press. He is also the author of *Quakertown*, *From Our House*, and *The Least You Need to Know*. He directs the MFA program in creative writing at Ohio State University.

The latest novel by **Valerie Martin** (1948–   ) is *Property*. Other novels include *Mary Reilly*, *The Great Divorce*, and *Italian Fever*. Her most recent nonfiction title is *Salvation*, a reconsideration of St. Francis's life. A native of New Orleans, she now lives in upstate New York.

Daniel Mason (1976–   ) published his novel *The Piano Tuner* while attending medical school. His story "A Registry of My Passage Upon Earth" was published in *Harper's*, and his second novel, *A Far Country*, is due in 2007.

Alice Mattison teaches fiction in the Bennington Writing Seminars. The most recent of her story collections are *In Case We're Separated* and *Men Giving Money, Women Yelling*. Her novels are *The Wedding of the Two-Headed Woman*, *The Book Borrower*, and *Hilda and Pearl*.

Colum McCann (1965–   ) is the author of the novels *Dancer*, *This Side of Brightness*, and *Songdogs*, and the story collections *Everything in This Country Must* and *Fishing the Sloe-Black River*.

He has received the Pushcart Prize, the Hennessy Award, and the Princess Grace Memorial Literary Award. He lives in New York City.

Judith McClain has published stories in *KQ/AR*, *Glimmer Train Stories*, *Iowa Woman*, and *American Short Fiction*. She won the Heekin Award for nonfiction and the Rhode Island State Council on the Arts Award in literature.

Elizabeth McCracken (1966–   ), author of the novels *Niagara Falls All Over Again* and *The Giant's House*, was honored as one of *Granta's* 20 Best American Writers Under 40. She also is the author of *Here's Your Hat What's Your Hurry*, a short-story collection.

John McNally (1965–   ) is the author of two novels, *America's Report Card* and *The Book of Ralph*; and a story collection, *Troublemakers*; and he has edited four fiction anthologies. A National Magazine Award finalist for fiction, he teaches at Wake Forest University in Winston-Salem, North Carolina.

Most recently, best-selling novelist **Sue Miller** (1943–) has written *Lost in the Forest*. Among her other novels are *The Good Mother*, *For Love*, *While I Was Gone*, and *Family Pictures*. She has published a memoir, *The Story of My Father*. The title story of her collection *Inventing the Abbotts* was made into a movie for which she co-wrote the screenplay.

Lorrie Moore (1957–   ) is known for her short stories, published in the collections *Birds of America*, *Like Life*, and *Self-Help*, as well her her novels, *Who Will Run the Frog Hospital?* and *Anagrams*. Her stories have been included in *The Best American Short Stories of the Century* and the O. Henry and Best American Short Stories anthologies. She teaches at the University of Wisconsin at Madison.

Mary McGarry Morris (1943–   ) is the author of *Vanished*, which was a finalist for the National Book Award and the PEN/Faulkner Award; *A Dangerous Woman*, which was chosen by *Time* as one of the five best novels of 1991; *Songs in Ordinary Time*, an Oprah Book Club selection; and three other novels. She lives in Andover, Massachusetts.

Mary Morrissy (1958–   ), a native of Dublin, is the author of a collection of short stories, *A Lazy Eye*, and two novels, *Mother of Pearl* and *The Pretender*. She has won a Hennessy Award, a Lannan Literary Prize, and was shortlisted for the Whitbread Prize.

Jordanian-born **Abdelrahman Munif** (1933–2004), in his Cities of Salt trilogy of novels, chose as his subject the effects of Western oil interests on traditional Arab societies in the last century. His books, widely read in the Middle East, have been banned in Saudi Arabia.

Antonya Nelson's (1961–   ) latest offering is *Some Fun*, a story collection. Previous collections were *The Expendables*, *Female Trouble*, *Family Terrorists*, and *In the Land of Men*. She has published three novels, most recently *Living to Tell*. In addition to writing, Nelson also teaches, dividing her time between New Mexico State University and the University of Houston.

Thisbe Nissen (1972–   ) is the author of two novels, *Osprey Island* and *The Good People of New York*, and a story collection, *Out of the Girls' Room and Into the Night*. She also co-authored *The Ex-Boyfriend Cookbook*. Her work has appeared in *Story*, *Seventeen*, *Vogue*, *Glamour*, *StoryQuarterly*, and the *Virginia Quarterly Review*, among others. A native New Yorker and a graduate of Oberlin College and the Iowa Writers' Workshop, where she was a teaching-writing fellow and a James Michener Fellow, she lives, teaches, gardens, and collages in Iowa City.

Sigrid Nunez (1951–) has published five novels, including *A Feather on the Breath of God*, *For Rouenna*, and, most recently, *The Last of Her Kind*. Her work has also been included in several anthologies, including two Pushcart Prize volumes. Among her other awards are a Whiting Writer's Award, the Rome Prize in Literature, a Berlin Prize Fellowship, and a Fellowship from the New York Foundation for the Arts. sigridnunez.com

Tim O'Brien (1946–) received the National Book Award in fiction for *Going After Cacciato*. His novel *The Things They Carried*, which reflected his tour of duty in Vietnam, was excerpted for *The Best American Short Stories of the Century*. *In the Lake of the Woods* was named best novel of 1994 by *Time* magazine. His most recent novel is *July, July*.

Chris Offutt (1958–) is author of the story collections *Kentucky Straight* and *Out of the Woods*, the novel *The Good Brother*, and the memoirs *The Same River Twice* and *No Heroes*. He lives in Iowa City, Iowa. He recently made his comics-writing debut with "Another Man's Escape" in an issue of *Michael Chabon Presents: The Amazing Adventures of the Escapist*.

The title story of **Roy Parvin**'s (1957–) collection *In the Snow Forest* originally appeared in *Glimmer Train Stories*. A previous collection was entitled *The Loneliest Road in America*, and his essays have appeared in *Northern Lights*. Parvin has won the Katherine Anne Porter Prize and has been nominated for a Pushcart. He lives in the woods of Northern California.

Ann Patchett (1963–   ) is the author of *Bel Canto*, which won the PEN/Faulkner Award. Her other novels are *The Magician's Assistant*, *Taft*, and *The Patron Saint of Liars*. Her memoir, *Truth & Beauty: A Friendship*, appeared in 2004.

Jayne Anne Phillips (1952–   ) is the author of three novels, *Machine Dreams*, *Shelter*, and *MotherKind*, and two books of widely anthologized short stories, *Black Tickets* and *Fast Lanes*. Excerpts of her forthcoming novel, *Termite*, have appeared in *Granta*, *The Southern Review*, and *Ploughshares*, and on narrativemagazine.com.

Melissa Pritchard (1948–   ) is a professor at Arizona State University. She is the author of two story collections, *The Instinct for Bliss* and *Spirit Seizures*, and two novels, *Phoenix* and *Selene of the Spirits*. Pritchard has been awarded a Pushcart Prize and has been included in the O. Henry Awards anthology. She lives in Tempe, Arizona.

Annie Proulx's (1935–   ) *The Shipping News* won the Pulitzer Prize for Fiction, the National Book Award for Fiction, and the *Irish Times* International Fiction Prize. She is the author of two other novels: *Postcards*, winner of the PEN/Faulkner Award, and *Accordion Crimes*, and two collections of short stories, *Heart Songs* and *Close Range*. *The Shipping News* and her story "Brokeback Mountain" have been made into movies. She lives in Wyoming and Newfoundland.

Frederick Reiken (1966–   ) has published two novels, *The Lost Legends of New Jersey* and *The Odd Sea*, which was chosen by *Booklist* as one of the twenty Best First Novels of the Year and won the Hackney Literary Award. He lives in Boston and teaches at Emerson College.

Alberto Ríos (1952–   ) was born in Nogales, Arizona, on the Mexican border, the son of a Guatemalan father and an English mother. His short-story collections include *The Iguana Killer*, which won the Western States Book Award, and, most recently, *The Curtain of Trees*. His memoir is *Capirotada: A Nogales Memoir*. He has won the Walt Whitman Award from the National Academy of American Poets, and the Pushcart Prize. He is a professor of English at Arizona State University.

Carol Roh-Spaulding's (1962–   ) fiction and poetry have appeared in numerous journals and anthologies. She is the author of the chapbook "The Brides of Valencia," which won the A. E. Longman Prize for Long Fiction, and is completing *Navelencia*, a thematic collection of stories based on her mixed-race Asian-American background. Her fiction has won several awards, including the Heathcote Award from the National Society of Arts and Letters, a Cohen Award for best story of the year in *Ploughshares*, and a Pushcart Prize.

Mark Salzman (1959–   ) taught English in Hunan Province, China, and drew upon his experiences there to write the memoir *Iron & Silk*, which was made into a film of the same title. He has published another memoir, *Lost in Place*, and three novels: *Lying Awake*, *The Soloist*, and *The Laughing Sutra*. *True Notebooks* is an account of his work teaching writing to juvenile delinquents. He is the happy father of two girls, Ava and Esme.

Lynne Sharon Schwartz's (1939–   ) most recent story collection is *Referred Pain* (2004); her poetry collection *In Solitary* appeared in 2003. Among her other works of fiction are the novels *Disturbances in the Field*, *Leaving Brooklyn*, *Rough Strife*, and *In the*

Family Way: An Urban Comedy. Her works of nonfiction include *Ruined by Reading* and *Face to Face: A Reader in the World*. She has received awards from the Guggenheim Foundation, the NEA, and the New York Foundation for the Arts.

Barbara Scot (1942–) is a former high-school teacher who now lives in a houseboat moored near Portland, Oregon. Her first book was *The Violet Shyness of Their Eyes: Notes from Nepal*; her second, *Prairie Reunion*, was a *New York Times* Notable Book for 1995. Most recently she published a memoir, *The Stations of Still Creek*.

Bob Shacochis (1951–) is writer-in-residence at Florida State University. His first collection of stories, *Easy in the Islands*, won the National Book Award for First Fiction, and his second collection, *The Next New World*, was awarded the Prix de Rome from the American Academy of Arts and Letters. He has published a novel, *Swimming in the Volcano*, and the nonfiction works *Domesticity: A Gastronomic Interpretation of Love* and *The Immaculate Invasion*.

Matthew Sharpe (1962–) is the author of the novels *The Sleeping Father* and *Nothing Is Terrible*, as well as the story collection *Stories from the Tube*. He is the writer-in-residence at Bronx Academy of Letters, a writing-themed public high school. His stories and articles have appeared in *Harper's*, *Zoetrope*, *BOMB*, *American Letters & Commentary*, *Southwest Review*, and *Teachers & Writers* magazine.

Carol Shields (1935–2003) was born in Chicago and lived in Canada for most of her life. She is the author of three short-story collections and eight novels, including the Pulitzer Prize-winning *The Stone Diaries* and *Larry's Party*, winner of the Orange Prize. Her *Collected Stories* appeared in 2005.

Susan Richards Shreve (1939–) has published twelve novels (most recently *A Student of Living Things* and *Plum & Jaggers*) and twenty-six books for children, and has co-edited five anthologies. An original board member of the PEN/Faulkner Foundation in Washington, D.C., she served as its president from 1985 to 1990. She is a professor at George Mason University.

Robert Stone (1937–) is the author of seven novels, among them *Bay of Souls*, *Damascus Gate*, *Outerbridge Reach*, and *Dog Soldiers*, which won a National Book Award for fiction. His story collection, *Bear and His Daughter*, was a finalist for the Pulitzer Prize. He wrote the screenplays for the films *WUSA* and *Who'll Stop the Rain*, both based on his books.

William Styron (1925–) published his first novel, *Lie Down in Darkness*, in 1951. He is best known for two controversial novels: the Pulitzer Prize-winning *The Confessions of Nat Turner* and *Sophie's Choice*, which was made into an Oscar-winning film. *Darkness Visible* is a memoir; his other works include a play, *In the Clap Shack*, and a collection of his nonfiction pieces, *This Quiet Dust*.

Karen Swenson (1936–) is the author of several books, including *An Attic of Ideals*, *East-West*, *A Sense of Direction*, and *The Landlady in Bangkok*, which won a National Poetry Series prize. She has been nominated for the Pushcart Prize three times, and her work has appeared in *The New Yorker*, *The Nation*, *The Paris Review*, *American Poetry Review*, and other periodicals.

Paul Theroux's (1941–) novels include *The Family Arsenal*, *Millroy the Magician*, *My Secret History*, *My Other Life*, and *Kowloon*

Tong. His travel books include *Riding the Iron Rooster*, *The Great Railway Bazaar*, *The Old Patagonian Express*, and *Fresh Air Fiend*. His novels *The Mosquito Coast* and *Doctor Slaughter* have both been made into films. He divides his time between Cape Cod and the Hawaiian Islands, where he is a professional beekeeper.

Joyce Thompson (1948–) is the author of five novels, including *Bones*, *Merry-Go-Round*, and *Conscience Place*, and the story collection *East Is West of Here*. She has been a writing teacher and an editor and now lives in Oakland, California.

Kathleen Tyau is the author of two novels that draw upon her Hawaiian-Chinese heritage: *A Little Too Much Is Enough* and *Makai*. A winner of the Pacific Northwest Booksellers Award, her work has appeared in *American Short Fiction*, *Story*, *Glimmer Train Stories*, and *Boulevard* and has been anthologized in *Intersecting Circles*, *Growing Up Local*, *Fishing for Chickens*, *The Writers' Journal*, and *The Stories That Shape Us*.

A.J. Verdelle's (1960-) novel, *The Good Negress*, was awarded four national prizes: a PEN/Faulkner Finalist Award, an award from the American Academy of Arts and Letters, a Bunting Fellowship at Harvard University, and a Whiting Writers' Award. She also writes creative nonfiction, primarily essays on photography. She has taught writing at Princeton University and the Fine Arts Work Center in Provincetown, Massachusetts.

Daniel Wallace (1959–) is the author of the novels *The Watermelon King*, *Ray in Reverse*, and *Big Fish*, which was made into a film directed by Tim Burton. His stories have been published widely in magazines and anthologies, including the *Yale Review*, *The Massachusetts Review*, *Shenandoah*, and *Glimmer Train Stories*, and his illustrated work has appeared in the *L.A. Times* and Italian *Vanity Fair*. He recently finished writing and illustrating a novel called *Oh Great Rosenfeld!* He lives in Chapel Hill, North Carolina. danielwallace.org

Mary Yukari Waters (1965–) was born in Kyoto, Japan, and moved to the U.S. at the age of nine. She has published a story collection, *The Laws of Evening*, and her work has been included in *The Best American Short Stories*, *The Best Stories from a Quarter-Century of the Pushcart Prize*, and *Zoetrope: All-Story.* She is the recipient of an O. Henry Award and a Pushcart Prize.

Brad Watson is the author of a story collection, *Last Days of the Dog-Men*, and a novel, *The Heaven of Mercury*, a finalist for the National Book Award. His most recent story appeared in the Amazon Shorts series. Now working on a collection of stories and a collection of novellas, he teaches at the University of Wyoming in Laramie.

Mark Winegardner (1961–) published two novels, *Crooked River Burning* and *The Veracruz Blues*, and a story collection, *That's True of Everybody*, before he wrote the best-selling sequel, *The Godfather Returns.* Another sequel, *The Godfather's Revenge*, appeared in 2006. His stories have been published in *The Best American Short Stories*, *American Short Fiction*, and other periodicals. He teaches and directs the creative-writing program at Florida State University in Tallahassee, Florida.

Tobias Wolff (1945–) is the author of several story collections and two memoirs: *This Boy's Life* (which became a movie in 1993) and *In Pharoah's Army*, a finalist for the National Book Award. His novel *The Barracks Thief* won the 1985 PEN/Faulkner Award for Fiction.

Monica Wood (1953–) is the author of three novels, *Any Bitter Thing*, *My Only Story*, and *Secret Language*; and a book of linked stories, *Ernie's Ark*. She is also the author of three books for writers: *The Pocket Muse*, its forthcoming sequel *Pocket Muse: Endless Inspiration*, and *Description*. Her short stories have been read on Public Radio International, awarded a Pushcart Prize, and published in numerous magazines and anthologies. Born and raised in the mill town of Mexico, Maine, she now lives in Portland. monicawood.com

Robert Wrigley (1951–) teaches at the University of Idaho in Moscow. His most recent book of poetry is *Lives of the Animals*. A former Guggenheim and NEA Fellow, his collection *Reign of Snakes* won the Kingsley Tufts Award.

INTERVIEWER BIOGRAPHIES

David Abrams interviewed Allen Morris Jones. David Abrams's stories, essays, and reviews have appeared in *Esquire*, the *Readerville Journal*, *The Missouri Review*, *Greensboro Review*, *The North Dakota Review*, *Fish Stories*, and other literary quarterlies. He regularly contributes book reviews to the *San Francisco Chronicle*, *January Magazine*, and the *Long Island Press*. Abrams lives with his wife and three children in Richmond Hill, Georgia, where he is currently at work on a novel about the Iraq War.

Misha Angrist interviewed Dan Chaon. Misha Angrist's fiction has appeared in the *Michigan Quarterly Review*, the *Best New American Voices* anthology, *Elysian Fields Quarterly*, and elsewhere. He works as a science editor in Durham, North Carolina.

Kevin Bacon interviewed Peter Carey, with Bill Davis.

Janet Benton interviewed Valerie Martin. Janet Benton, who works as a writer and editor, has an MFA in fiction writing from the University of Massachusetts, Amherst. Along with teaching a fiction workshop, she has taught courses in creative writing, editing, grammar, and composition at several universities, and works with authors on work in progress, including *The Mozart Effect* and *Ticket to Ride: Inside the Beatles' 1964 and 1965 Tours That Changed the World*. She received three fiction fellowswhips and two awards and is currently at work on a historical novel set in nineteenth-century Philadelphia.

Robert Birnbaum interviewed Charles Baxter, Louis Begley, Sandra Cisneros, Colum McCann, Brad Watson, and Mark Winegardner. Robert Birnbaum is editor-at-large of the literary and cultural website IdentityTheory.com, where he has published hundreds of interviews.

Barbara Brooks interviewed Alice Mattison. Barbara Brooks's fiction and interviews have appeared in *Glimmer Train Stories*, *Writer's Digest*, *The Writer's Chronicle*, *Inkwell*, *The Ledge*, *Jabberwock Review*, and elsewhere. She lives in Cazenovia, New York.

Ana Callan interviewed Mary Morrissy. Ana Callan is a poet and novelist, originally from Ireland, now resident in Oregon, where she conducts writing workshop intensives on such subjects as mystic poetry and spiritual memoir. She has published a novel for young people, *Taf*, and a poetry collection, *The Back Door*. anacallan.com.

Mike Chasar interviewed Julia Alvarez, with Constance Pierce. Mike Chasar's poems are in *Poetry*, *Alaska Quarterly Review*, *Antioch Review*, and the *Black Warrior Review*. He is guest editing (with Dee Morris and Heidi Bean) an issue of the *Iowa Journal of Cultural Studies* with the special theme "Poetries," and is otherwise writing about American poetry and literary culture at the University of Iowa.

Bill Davis interviewed Peter Carey, with Kevin Bacon.

Sherry Ellis interviewed Matthew Sharpe and Mary Yukari Waters. Sherry Ellis is the editor of *Now Write!* an anthology of fiction-writing exercises. She is at work on *Illuminating Fiction*, an anthology of author interviews, a novel tentatively called *The*

Goode Books, and a second anthology of writing exercises. She teaches writing in Concord, Massachusetts, and provides private coaching to writers.

Stephanie Gordon interviewed Beverly Lowry. Stephanie Gordon received her PhD in creative writing and American literature from the University of Georgia in 2003. She currently teaches writing at Auburn University. Her work has been published in *The Writer's Chronicle*, *Studies in American Indian Literature*, *Southern Poetry Review*, *Studies in the Humanities*, *GSU Review*, and others.

Katherine Perry Harris interviewed Susan Richards Shreve. Katherine Perry Harris holds an MFA in fiction from George Mason University. Her work has appeared in *So to Speak*, *The Writer's Chronicle*, and *The Writer Magazine*, among other publications. She is currently a communications coordinator for the University of Missouri.

Stewart David Ikeda interviewed Charles Baxter. Stewart David Ikeda is the author of the novel *What the Scarecrow Said* and vice president for the publishing company, IMDiversity, Inc. His work has been published in *Story*, *Ploughshares*, *Pacific Citizen*, the *Mineta Review*, *Glimmer Train Stories*, and the anthologies *Voices of the Xiled*, *Yellow Light*, and *Last Witnesses*. sdikeda.com

Sarah Anne Johnson interviewed Andrea Barrett, Amy Bloom, Elizabeth Cox, Edwidge Danticat, Chitra Banerjee Divakaruni, Maria Flook, Lynn Freed, Ha Jin, Chang-rae Lee, Elizabeth McCracken, Sue Miller, Ann Patchett, and Jayne Anne Phillips. Sarah Anne Johnson is the editor of *Conversations with American Women Writers* and *The Art of the Author Interview*. She is program coordinator of the YMCA National Writer's Voice program.

Ellen Kanner interviewed Margot Livesey. Ellen Kanner's fiction has appeared in the anthology *The Luxury of Tears* and in *Florida Living* magazine. She is contributing editor of *Pages* and the *Edgy Veggie*, and a syndicated columnist featured in the *Miami Herald* and in five hundred newspapers weekly. She is a contributor to *Bon Appetit*, *Eating Well*, *Vegetarian Times*, and others.

Stephanie Kuehnert interviewed John McNally. Stephanie Kuehnert's fiction has been published in *Hair Trigger*, *fó* magazine, and on inkstains.org. Her interviews and essays have appeared on *Virginia Quarterly Review*'s website and on freshyard.com. Her zine was featured in *Zine Scene* by Francesca Lia Block and Hillary Carlip. Stephanie received her MFA in creative writing from Columbia College Chicago. She has recently completed her first novel, *All Roads Lead to Rock 'n Roll*, and is working on a second novel.

Jennifer Levasseur interviewed Richard Bausch, Vikram Chandra, Andre Dubus, Stuart Dybek, and Siri Hustvedt, with Kevin Rabalais. Jennifer Levasseur and Kevin Rabalais, editors of *Novel Voices: 17 Award-Winning Novelists on How to Write, Edit, and Get Published*, have appeared in numerous international publications, including *Brick*, *Glimmer Train Stories*, the *Kenyon Review*, *Tin House*, *Missouri Review*, *World Literature Today*, and *Five Points*. Louisiana natives, they live in Melbourne, Australia.

Debra Levy interviewed Amy Hempel with Carol Turner. Debra Levy's work has appeared in *Columbia*, *Alaska Quarterly Review*, *Glimmer Train Stories*, *Carolina Quarterly*, and elsewhere. She lives in Indiana.

Melissa Lowver interviewed William Styron. Melissa Lowver is a marketing director for Ascent Media, which provides services to electronic-media content providers. She has written for trade magazines including *Millimeter* and *Broadcast Engineering*.

Susan McInnis interviewed Ron Carlson, Toi Derricotte, Patricia Hampl, Antonya Nelson, Alberto Ríos, and Karen Swenson. Susan McInnis writes and teaches writing for the Center for Distance Education in Fairbanks, Alaska.

John McNally interviewed Andre Dubus III. John McNally is the author of two novels, *America's Report Card* and *The Book of Ralph*; and a story collection, *Troublemakers*; and he has edited four fiction anthologies. A National Magazine Award finalist for fiction, he teaches at Wake Forest University in Winston-Salem, North Carolina.

Nancy Middleton interviewed Lynne Sharon Schwartz, and A.J. Verdelle. Nancy Middleton's short stories, author interviews, and books reviews have appeared in the *South Carolina Review*, *Glimmer Train Stories*, *Belles Lettres*, and other literary magazines. A native of upstate New York, she now lives in Pennsylvania and is currently at work on her first novel.

Jim Nashold interviewed Kent Haruf. Jim Nashold is co-author of the biography *The Death of Dylan Thomas*. He lives with his wife in Durham, North Carolina.

Constance Pierce interviewed Julia Alvarez, with Mike Chasar. Constance Pierce recently retired from the English Department at Miami University and now lives in St. Augustine, Florida. Her work includes a novel, *Hope Mills*, and a story collection, *When Things Get Back to Normal*.

Kevin Rabalais interviewed Richard Bausch, Vikram Chandra, Andre Dubus, Stuart Dybek, and Siri Hustvedt, with Jennifer Levasseur; and David Malouf. Kevin Rabalais and Jennifer Levasseur, editors of *Novel Voices: 17 Award-Winning Novelists on How to Write, Edit, and Get Published*, have appeared in numerous international publications, including *Brick*, *Glimmer Train Stories*, *The Kenyon Review*, *Tin House*, *Missouri Review*, *World Literature Today*, and *Five Points*. Louisiana natives, they live in Melbourne, Australia.

Cheryl Reid interviewed Pam Durban. Cheryl Reid completed her MFA in creative writing at Georgia State University in 2004. She is raising her children, Reid and Grant, and working to complete a novel, *My Banishment*, in Atlanta.

Jim Schumock interviewed Robert Olen Butler, Ethan Canin, Stephen Dixon, Dagoberto Gilb, Jim Grimsley, Carolyn Kizer, Thomas McGuane, Lorrie Moore, Tim O'Brien, Carol Shields, William Styron, Paul Theroux, Robert Stone, Tobias Wolff, and Robert Wrigley. Jim Schumock is the main host of *Between the Covers*, a weekly literary radio program on KBOO in Portland, Oregon. His book of interviews is *Story Story Story: Conversations with American Authors*. He is currently working on a novella, a memoir, and a second collection of interviews.

Andrew Scott interviewed Patricia Henley. Andrew Scott lives in Indianapolis. His latest project is *Welcome to the Moon*, a screenplay based on one of his short stories. He teaches at Ball State University.

Barbara Lucy Stevens interviewed Carolyn Chute. Barbara Lucy Stevens is a writer and artist. She lives in Providence, Rhode Island, with her husband and four children.

Linda B. Swanson-Davies interviewed Charles Baxter, Ana Callan, Kevin Canty, George Makana Clark, Stephen Dixon, Nomi

Eve, Charles Johnson, Thomas E. Kennedy, Jamaica Kincaid, David Long, Daniel Mason, Mary McGarry Morris, Thisbe Nissen, Sigrid Nunez, Roy Parvin, Carol Roh-Spaulding, Mark Salzman, Barbara J. Scot, Bob Shacochis, Joyce Thompson, Kathleen Tyau, and Daniel Wallace. Linda B. Swanson-Davies is co-editor, with Susan Burmeister-Brown, of *Glimmer Train Stories* and *Writers Ask*.

Charlotte Templin interviewed Mary Gordon. Charlotte Templin is professor emeritus of English at the University of Indianapolis. She is the author of *Feminism and the Politics of Literary Reputation* and editor of *Conversations with Erica Jong*. Her articles and interviews with contemporary women writers have appeared in *American Studies*, the *Missouri Review*, the *Boston Review*, and other publications.

Rob Trucks interviewed Russell Banks and Chris Offutt. Rob Trucks is the author of five books, including *Cup of Coffee: The Very Short Careers of Eighteen Major League Pitchers* and *The Pleasure of Influence: Conversations with American Male Fiction Writers*, as well as countless essays, reviews, and features. His work has been published in *Spin*, *BookForum*, *NoDepression*, *Philadelphia Weekly*, *Glimmer Train Stories*, *Black Warrior Review*, *New Orleans Review*, *The Distillery*, and *River City*. He lives in Long Island City, New York.

Carol Turner interviewed Amy Hempel, with Debra Levy. Carol Turner has a BA in English from Sonoma State University and an MFA in creative writing and literature from Bennington College. Her work has appeared in *Byline*, *Cottonwood Review*, *First Intensity*, *Flyway*, *Love's Shadow: Writings by Women* (anthology), *Many Mountains Moving*, *Owen Wister*, the *Portland Review*, *Primavera*, *Rag Mag*, *Strictly Fiction*, *Sulphur River Literary*

Review, Glimmer Train Stories, and others. She is also the author of *Economics for the Impatient*.

Michael Upchurch interviewed Ernest Gaines, Doris Lessing, Abdelrahman Munif, Annie Proulx, Jonathan Raban, and Paul Theroux. Novelist Michael Upchurch is the author of *Passive Intruder* and *The Flame Forest*, and his short fiction has appeared in *Christopher Street, Carolina Quarterly*, and *Glimmer Train Stories*. His reviews and essays have appeared in the *New York Times Book Review, American Scholar, Washington Post, Chicago Tribune*, and other publications. Since 1998, he has been the book critic for the *Seattle Times*.

Eric Wasserman interviewed Frederick Reiken. Eric Wasserman is the author of a collection of short stories, *The Temporary Life*. He is currently writing the screenplay adaptation for his book and is completing a novel set during the height of McCarthyism. He lives in Los Angeles where he teaches at Santa Monica College, West L.A. College, and Compton College. ericwasserman.com

Leslie A. Wootten interviewed Melissa Pritchard. Leslie A. Wootten lives and writes on a farm in Casa Grande, Arizona. Her author interviews have appeared in *Bloomsbury Review, Glimmer Train Stories, Tin House*, and *World Literature Today*.

COPYRIGHT NOTICES

INDEX